Teradata
Enterprise Architecture

*An Authorized
Teradata Certified
Professional Program
Study Guide*

Exam TE0-126

First Edition

ISBN 978-0-9830242-5-5
Printed by Cerulium Corporation

**David Glenday
Stephen Wilmes**

Copyright

© Copyright 2012 by Cerulium Corporation – 1st printing. All rights reserved. No part of this publication may be reproduced, stored in a retrieval system, or transmitted in any form or by any means, electronic, mechanical, scanning or otherwise, except as permitted by Sections 107 and 108 of the 1976 United States Copyright Act without prior permission of the copyright owner.

Limit of liability/disclaimer of warranty: The publisher and authors make no representation or warranties with respect to the accuracy and completeness of the contents of this work and specifically disclaim all warranties, including without limitation warranties of fitness for a particular purpose. Neither the publisher nor the authors shall be liable for damages arising from the use of information contained herein.

Trademarks

The following names are registered names and/or trademarks, and are used throughout the book: Teradata, Teradata BYNET, Teradata Administrator, Teradata SQL Assistant, Teradata Raising Intelligence, Teradata Decision Experts, Teradata Source Experts, Raising Intelligence, Smarter.Faster.Wins., Active Enterprise Intelligence, DECISIONCAST, WEBANALYST, MYCOMMERCE, SEECHAIN, SEERISK, CLARAVIEW, GRIDSCALE, and XKOTO are registered trademarks and/or products of Teradata Corporation. Microsoft Windows and .NET are either registered trademarks or trademarks of Microsoft Corporation. Sun Java and GoldenGate are trademarks or registered trademarks of Oracle Corporation in the U.S. or other countries. In addition to these product names, all brand and product names in this manual are trademarks of their respective holders in the United States and/or other countries.

Special Acknowledgement

A special thank you to the following individuals that contributed to the Study Guide content: Walter Alexander, Barbara Christjohn, David Glenday, Susan Hahn, David Micheletto, and Larry Rex.

About the Author - Steve Wilmes

Steve Wilmes founded Cerulium Corporation in 2007. As Chief Executive Officer, his goal is to establish Cerulium as a premier data warehousing Technology Company. Cerulium's strategic growth is globally focused on six lines of business including education, consulting, BI solutions, productivity tools, application integration and assessment services. These lines of business have been highly successful by utilizing strategic data warehousing solutions provided by Teradata that spans across the consumer, and commercial markets.

Mr. Wilmes has over 20 years of experience in the computer industry and is known to be a detail oriented, results-focused leader. He is an internationally recognized expert in several aspects of data warehousing including hardware, software, SQL, operating systems, implementation, data integration, database administration, and BI solutions.

Mr. Wilmes earned a bachelor's degree in business administration and economics in 1994 from Augsburg College and he is also a Teradata Certified Master.

Mr. Wilmes resides just outside of Columbia, South Carolina, with his wife, Becky. He has been involved with numerous civic, educational, and business organizations throughout his career. Some of his more recent associations include working with the Richland County Sheriff's Department – Region 4 Community Member, and volunteer for local organizations where he shares his technical expertise.

About the Author - David Glenday

David Glenday has 10 years' Teradata consulting experience in the Entertainment, Semiconductor and Telecommunication industries, specifically in the following lines of business: Finance, Strategic Planning, Product Development, Marketing, and Sales.

Mr. Glenday leveraged his business experience, formal education and extensive Teradata knowledge to develop numerous reporting solutions. Solutions include developing and optimizing queries, creating ETL processes and reports using Microsoft Excel and BI tools. He has extensive knowledge integrating web analytic data into Teradata.

Mr. Glenday graduated with a BA in International Business in 1991 and received an MBA in 1997 from California State University Fullerton. He is a Teradata Certified Master.

Mr. Glenday is based outside of Las Vegas, Nevada. He, his wife Kristi and their two children are very active with Cub Scouts, Girl Scouts and his family finds volunteer work very rewarding. David enjoys flying. He received his commercial pilots' license in 1989 and is always looking for more time to devote to this hobby.

Contents

Chapter 1: The Teradata Certified Professional Program 1
   Enhance your knowledge and career 1
   Certification... Knowledge Building to Mastery 6
   Path to Teradata 12 Mastery 7
   Exam Registration 8
   Where to Find More Information 9
Chapter 2 – Architecture 11
   Certification Objectives 11
   Before You Begin 11
   Nodes 12
   Operating System 12
   Dual Systems 13
   Cliques 16
   Hot-standby Node 17
   Space Allocation 17
   Databases 20
   Tables 22
   Fallback 24
   Indexes 25
   Practice Questions 26
Chapter 3 - Client Environment 29
   Certification Objectives 29
   Before You Begin 29
   TTU 30
   Connectivity Protocols 30
   Connectivity Options 32
   Practice Questions 35
Chapter 4 - LDM/PDM 37
   Certification Objectives 37
   Before You Begin 37
   3NF LDM to PDM 38
   Data Volatility 42
   Semantic Layer 43

PDM Changes to LDM...44
Practice Questions 45
Chapter 5 – Security...49
Certification Objectives..49
Before You Begin 49
Logons...50
Users..50
Passwords 53
Account Strings 54
Profiles...56
Lightweight Directory Access Protocol (LDAP) 59
Access Rights..62
Roles..66
Encryption...68
Stored Procedures 70
Personally Identifiable Information (PII) 74
Network Security...79
Access Monitoring..80
Views...82
Practice Questions 86
Chapter 6 - Workload Management..91
Certification Objectives..91
Before You Begin 91
Teradata Dynamic Workload Manager.....................................92
Priority Scheduler 96
Resource Partitions and Performance Groups 99
Schmon Utility 105
Teradata Workload Analyzer 106
Teradata Query Scheduler 108
Teradata Query Director 110
Teradata Manager.. 112
Practice Questions 115
Chapter 7 - Application Deployment... 119
Certification Objectives... 119
Before You Begin 119

vii

Test Environments 120
Capturing Authoritative Data 122
Estimating Space Requirements... 125
Production System Impact 131
Measuring Changes... 135
Practice Questions 140
Chapter 8 – System Planning and Space Management 143
Certification Objectives.. 143
Before You Begin 143
Transient Journal.. 144
Dictionary Tables 145
CRASHDUMP 148
PDE DUMP... 148
Archive and Recovery Utility (ARC).. 149
Archive Strategies 177
Minimizing User Impact... 177
Determining Space Shortages.. 178
PACKDISK... 179
Shared Resources.. 182
Ingesting Data – Planning for growth... 187
Practice Questions 189
Chapter 9 - Data Integration 193
Certification Objectives.. 193
Before You Begin 193
FastLoad... 194
MultiLoad 199
FastExport.. 203
TPump 207
BTEQ... 209
Teradata Parallel Transporter 211
SQL Merge 221
NUPI.. 222
Partitioned DML.. 223
Recursive Views.. 225
Metadata Management... 226

Practice Questions 231
Chapter 10 - Data Migration 235
   Certification Objectives.. 235
   Before You Begin 235
   Data Marts... 236
   Strategies... 238
   BTEQ.. 238
   TPT... 241
   ARC.. 241
   Dual System Architecture 242
   Costs.. 245
   Security 246
   Privacy 247
   Data Governance... 250
   Master Data Management (MDM).. 252
   Change Control Management 254
   Practice Questions 256
Chapter 11 - Measuring Performance 259
   Certification Objectives... 259
   Before You Begin 259
   SLA Statistics... 260
   Index Choices 262
   DBQL 267
   PMON 267
   ResUsage... 269
   Specifying ResUsage Tables and Logging Rates 270
   Full Table Scans 271
   AmpUsage 273
   Explain... 274
   Joins 275
   Analytical Processing Choices 276
   Practice Questions 287
Chapter 12 - Improving Performance 291
   Certification Objectives... 291
   Before You Begin 291

    Teradata Index Wizard 292
    Teradata Statistics Wizard... 298
    Teradata Visual Explain 300
    Teradata System Emulation Tool (TSET) 302
    System Resources.. 309
    Dictionary Objects... 314
    ELT vs. ETL 315
    Compression 315
    Surrogate Keys 316
    Changing Indexes 316
    Queries and Joins.. 318
    Summary Data 319
    Practice Questions 322
Chapter 13 - Maintaining Performance 325
    Before You Begin 325
    Ad hoc Environment 326
    Tactical and Workload Consistency 327
    Practice Questions 331
APPENDIX 333
INDEX... 335

Chapter 1: The Teradata Certified Professional Program

Enhance your knowledge and career

The Teradata Certified Professional Program (TCPP), launched in 1999, develops and manages Teradata's premier, and only, certification testing program. Teradata authorized training and proctored exams, available globally to customers, partners, and associates are instrumental in establishing an industry-standard measure of technical competence for IT professionals using Teradata technology. Recognized and valued by major global companies using Teradata, more than 51,000 Teradata Certifications have been awarded.

The new Teradata 12 Certification Track consists of seven exams that combine for achievement of six certifications and provides a logical progression for specific job roles. Starting with the core Teradata 12 Certified Professional credential, individuals have an opportunity to demonstrate knowledge by achieving Certification as a Technical Specialist, Database Administrator, Solutions Developer, Enterprise Architect, and the most prestigious Teradata Certification – Teradata 12 Certified Master.

The purpose of this Certification Exam Study Guide is to assist you in your goal of becoming Teradata Certified. The Guide will provide focused content areas, high level explanations around the key areas of focus, and help you to determine areas of further study prior to sitting for the Teradata Certification examination.

The Exam Study Guide will assist you in your Exam preparation, but you must be knowledgeable of the subject areas in order to pass the exam. This Guide is intended for individuals who have completed the recommended training and have the recommended amount of

Teradata 12 Enterprise Architecture

Teradata experience. We do not guarantee that you will pass the exam simply by reading the Exam Study Guide. Only hard work, hands-on experience, and a positive attitude will help you to achieve exam success. We wish you the very best of luck!

> "The certification process promoted a systematic learning opportunity on a broad spectrum of topics. This enabled me to apply changes at work that never would have been done otherwise."
> – Teradata Certified Master, Blue Cross Blue Shield of NC

The flowchart and matrix below are designed to help you define a path to the knowledge, skills, and experience needed to achieve Teradata 12 Certifications.

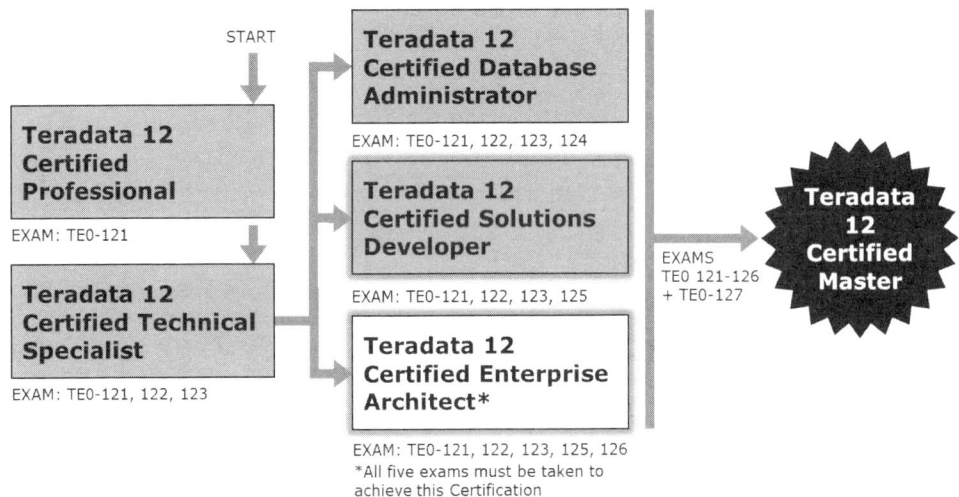

THE TERADATA CERTIFIED PROFESSIONAL PROGRAM

Teradata 12 Certifications

Teradata 12 Certified Professional

Exams Required:

- TE0-121 – Teradata 12 Basics

Must be passed before continuing on certification path

Recommended Teradata Experience:

6-12 months

Recommended Preparation Courses:

- Introduction to the Teradata Database

Teradata 12 Certified Technical Specialist

Exams Required:

- TE0-121 – Teradata 12 Basics
- TE0-122 – Teradata 12 SQL
- TE0-123 – Teradata 12 Physical Design and Implementation

3 Exams to be passed in sequential order

Recommended Teradata Experience:

1-2 years

Recommended Preparation Courses:

- Introduction to the Teradata Database
- Teradata SQL
- Advanced Teradata SQL
- Physical Database Design
- Physical Database Tuning

Teradata 12 Enterprise Architecture

Teradata 12 Certified Database Administrator

Exams Required:

- TE0-121 – Teradata 12 Basics
- TE0-122 – Teradata 12 SQL
- TE0-123 – Teradata 12 Physical Design and Implementation
- TE0-124 – Teradata 12 Database Administration

4 Exams to be passed in sequential order

Recommended Teradata Experience:

2-3 years

Recommended Preparation Courses:

- Introduction to the Teradata Database
- Teradata SQL
- Advanced Teradata SQL
- Physical Database Design
- Physical Database Tuning
- Teradata Application Utilities
- Teradata Warehouse Management
- Teradata Warehouse Administration

Teradata 12 Certified Solutions Developer

Exams Required:

- TE0-121 – Teradata 12 Basics
- TE0-122 – Teradata 12 SQL
- TE0-123 – Teradata 12 Physical Design and Implementation
- TE0-125 – Teradata 12 Solutions Development

4 Exams to be passed in sequential order

Recommended Teradata Experience:

2-3 years

Recommended Preparation Courses:

- Introduction to the Teradata Database
- Teradata SQL
- Advanced Teradata SQL
- Physical Database Design
- Physical Database Tuning
- Teradata Application Utilities
- Teradata Application Design and Development

THE TERADATA CERTIFIED PROFESSIONAL PROGRAM

Teradata 12 Certified Enterprise Architect

Exams Required:	Recommended Teradata Experience:
• TE0-121 – Teradata 12 Basics • TE0-122 – Teradata 12 SQL • TE0-123 – Teradata 12 Physical Design and Implementation • TE0-125 – Teradata 12 Solutions Development • TE0-126 – Teradata 12 Enterprise Architecture 5 Exams to be passed in sequential order	2-3 years Recommended Preparation Courses: • Introduction to the Teradata Database • Teradata SQL • Advanced Teradata SQL • Physical Database Design • Physical Database Tuning • Teradata Application Utilities • Teradata Warehouse Management • Teradata Warehouse Administration • Teradata Application Design and Development

Teradata 12 Certified Master*

Exams Required:	Recommended Teradata Experience:
• TE0-121 - TE0-126: Successful completion of all exams and certifications **PLUS**: • TE0-127 – Teradata 12 Comprehensive Mastery 7 Exams to be passed in sequential order ***Path for V2R5 Certified Masters (only)** • TE0-12Q: Teradata 12 Qualifying Exam for V2R5 **PLUS:** • TE0-127 – Teradata 12 Comprehensive Mastery	A minimum 5 years practical hands-on experience is highly recommended Recommended Preparation Courses: Taking all courses recommended for the Teradata 12 job role certifications: • Introduction to the Teradata Database • Teradata SQL • Advanced Teradata SQL • Physical Database Design • Physical Database Tuning • Teradata Application Utilities • Teradata Warehouse Management • Teradata Warehouse Administration • Teradata Application Design and Development

Teradata 12 Enterprise Architecture

Certification... Knowledge Building to Mastery

In today's economy, many companies are investing in the training and validation of employees' expertise and knowledge. Teradata's Certification process helps meet these discerning demands in the global market. Teradata has developed a new generation of certification exams and requirements that bring premium value to Teradata 12 Certification credentials.

Top 10 "What's new about the Teradata 12 Certification Track?"

1. Seven exams with all new content based on Teradata Database 12.0.
2. More rigorous certification criteria including a combination of training, study, and practical, hands-on experience.
3. Six new certifications require passing a combination of exams in sequential order starting with the Teradata 12 Basics exam.
4. Five Teradata 12 Certifications must first be achieved to gain eligibility for Teradata 12 Certified Master status.
5. A new Teradata 12 Comprehensive Mastery Exam, among other requirements, has been added to create a more rigorous Teradata 12 Master Certification track.
6. New IP security measures are in place to protect the integrity of exams and certifications.
7. Independent exam scoring procedure provides electronic Results Reports outside of the testing center.
8. Freshly designed certificates and logos available electronically.
9. New state of the art Certification Tracking System manages certification records, fulfillment, transcripts, and credentials validation.
10. The Teradata Certified Professional Program is well established with an experienced team available to support your successful Teradata Certification journey.

THE TERADATA CERTIFIED PROFESSIONAL PROGRAM

Path to Teradata 12 Mastery

A Teradata Certified Master enjoys a distinct advantage in the global marketplace. Employers seek Teradata Certified staff with verifiable knowledge and skills that support their business-critical Teradata systems. The TCPP Certification process helps those individuals who want to deepen their knowledge and build their skills to the highest level.

The path to achieve Teradata 12 Certified Master status is summarized in the matrix below.

If You Are...	Exams Required for Teradata 12 Master Certification
Starting on the Teradata 12 Certification Track	• TE0-121 – TE0-127 All 7 Exams required
Certified V2R5 Master	• TE0-12Q: Teradata 12 Qualifying Exam for V2R5 Masters • TE0-127: Teradata 12 Comprehensive Mastery Exam Both Exams required

The six core Teradata V2R5 exams were retired on March 31, 2010. Teradata V2R5 Certifications will not expire. However, individual V2R5 exams completed in the V2R5 Certification Track are not transferable to the new Teradata 12 Certification Track.

Exam Registration

All Teradata Certification exams are administered and proctored by authorized Prometric Testing Centers. Schedule exams at any authorized Prometric Testing Center by phone or online. In the US and Canada, you may call 1-877-887-6868. Also, a listing of Prometric telephone numbers is available at: www.prometric.com/Teradata. Some countries do not offer online registration.

Where to Find More Information

Information on all authorized Teradata Certification levels, exams, curriculum maps and recommended training, is supplied by a convenient matrix and links located on the TCPP website: www.Teradata.com/Certification.

Teradata Corporation's official certification exams and credentials are developed, copyrighted, and managed solely by the Teradata Certified Professional Program team. There are no other Teradata authorized exams, certifications, or legitimate credentials in the IT industry. To achieve your training and certification goals, pursue only authorized processes and approved courses of study as outlined on the official TCPP website.

Chapter 2 - Architecture

Certification Objectives

- ✓ Determine the operational aspects needed to be considered in implementing a data warehouse architecture.
- ✓ Given a scenario, determine the appropriate system hardware configuration.
- ✓ Describe options and considerations for single system availability.

Before You Begin

You should be familiar with the following terms and concepts.

Terms	Key Concepts
Node	A rack mounted processing unit
Clique	A grouping of nodes
Space Allocation	Perm, Spool, Temp space
Database	A repository for tables, view, macros, etc.
User	Someone who can logon to the system
Table	Used to store data
Index	Used to facilitate table access
Cluster	A "logical" grouping of AMPs

Teradata 12 Enterprise Architecture

Nodes

A node is a hardware unit that is configured to run the Teradata RDBMS software. It contains Parsing Engines (PE), Access Module Processors (AMP) and "the" BYNET.

The PEs connect to other systems using LANs and channels. This is the way users logon to Teradata, and data is passed back and forth. The PEs provide session control.

The AMPs connect to Disk Arrays where data is stored. The AMPs are responsible for file maintenance, and all logical and physical I/O.

The BYNET software on each node connects the PEs and AMPs together and has a copy of the Hash Maps. If there are multiple nodes in a system, they are connected to each other through the BYNET Interface using fiber-optic cables.

Operating System

The nodes of a Teradata system must all have the same operating system, which may be UNIX MP-RAS, Windows, or Linux.

Linux is a 64-bit operating system, whereas UNIX and Windows are both 32-bit operating systems.

Many existing customers are switching to Linux for the expanded capabilities and improved performance it provides. Teradata does have a conversion group to help.

Dual Systems

Dual-Active Systems are two or more active database systems that operate in tandem to provide a highly available production environment with rapid disaster recovery. Though a system can sustain multiple failures and keep running with cliques, the response times may fall outside your SLAs. A dual-active solution virtually eliminates all down-time and provides seamless disaster recovery protection for critical users and applications.

Dual-system architecture, also known as Dual-Active Solutions, is provided by Teradata Replication Services.

Teradata Replication Services allows users to capture changes made to a specific set of tables in one database and have those changes applied to corresponding tables in another database in near real-time. Replication of tables can serve several purposes:

- Replication can provide a backup of specified table data in the event of problems with your source database. This is another form of an archive.
- If your site has Teradata Dual-Active Solutions, and one system becomes unavailable, the remaining system will automatically take over database operations. The data on the systems is automatically synchronized via replication. There are various database replication tools and methodologies available for use with Teradata Dual-Active Solutions. GoldenGate Software® is one such tool.
- When implemented between a Teradata Database and databases from other vendors, you can migrate data from one system to the other, making data accessible across the different environments. This capability can support data acquisition, and updating-dependent data marts.

Teradata 12 Enterprise Architecture

Teradata Replication Services are made up of Teradata Database and GoldenGate.

Figure 2.1 illustrates the various ways Replication Solutions can be used.

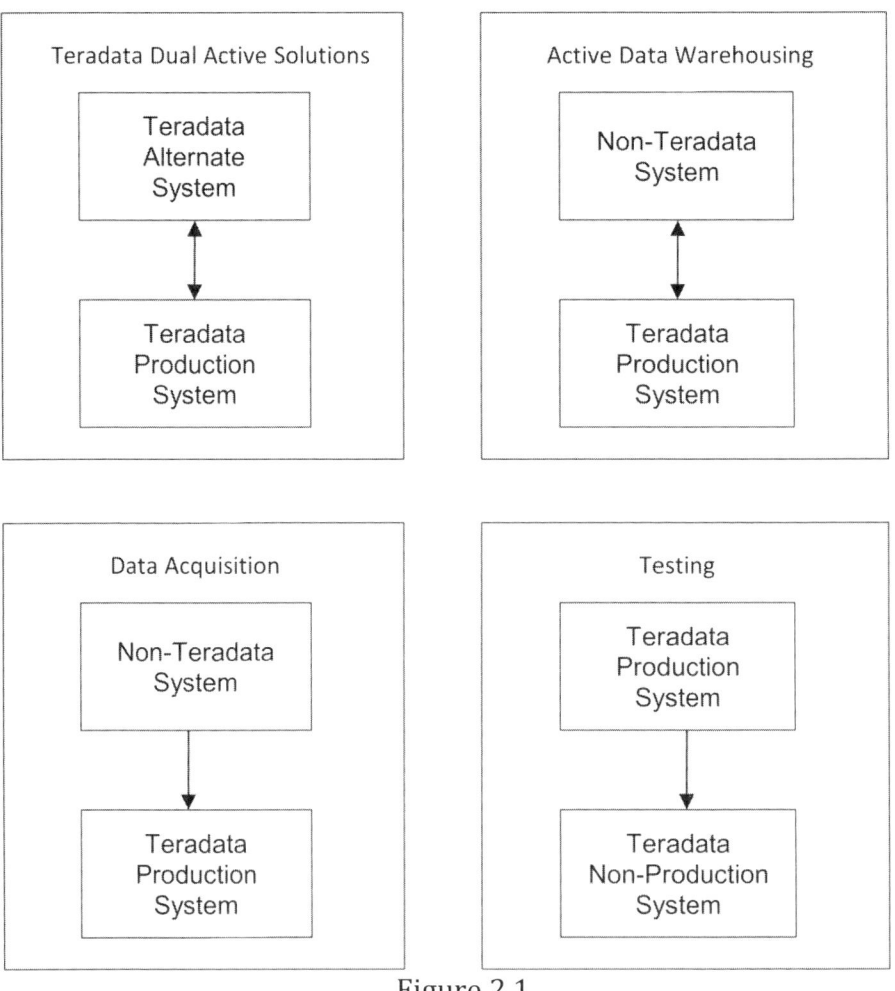

Figure 2.1

A Dual-Active solution is a set of components or technologies that allow another Teradata Database to act as a standby for a primary

ARCHITECTURE

instance of Teradata Database. Such a solution addresses a number of business continuity needs:

- Allows business operations to continue if an outage (planned or unplanned) occurs.
- Provides quick restoration of access to system resources.
- Enables businesses to enjoy consistent levels of service from their systems.

Replication support is a key capability of a Dual-Active solution. When implemented as part of Teradata Dual-Active Solutions, Teradata Replication Services captures and synchronizes data between two instances of a database, where one is a production system and the other is a backup. As a result, the backup system will take over if the production system fails and will maintain data availability and integrity.

Figure 2.2 illustrates the architecture of a Dual-Active solution.

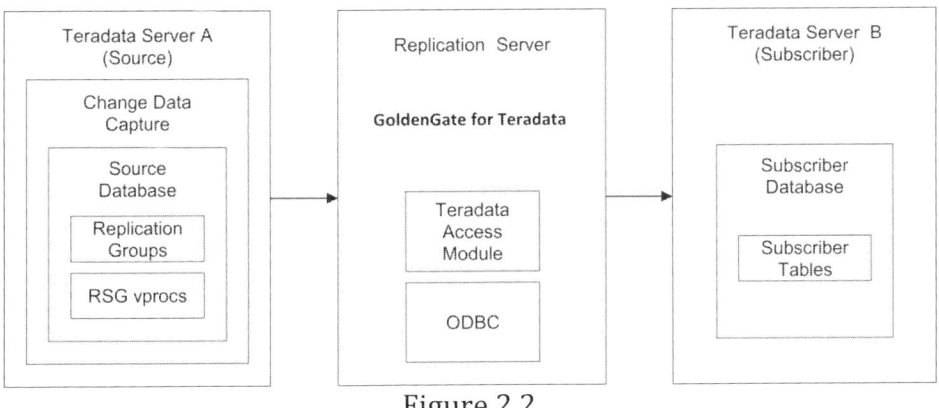

Figure 2.2

Teradata Replication Services can capture data from other types of databases and apply it to a Teradata Database. This data acquisition capability **is not** a replacement for a high-volume ETL (extract, transform, load) capability that requires significant transformation capabilities, but it is designed to be used where:

- Real-time capture and apply is required
- There is a need to eliminate batch windows
- The volume of data that changes regularly is relatively moderate
- The customer wants to pull data from a non-Teradata database, minimizing the overhead to the source system

Note: Teradata Replication Services ***does not*** replace bulk data loading utilities, such as FastLoad and MultiLoad.

Cliques

A clique is a collection of nodes with shared access to the same disk arrays. Each multi-node system has at least one clique.

Nodes are interconnected via the BYNET. Nodes and disks are interconnected via shared buses and thus can communicate directly.

While the shared access is defined to the configuration, it is not actively used when the system is up and running.

The shared access allows the system to continue operating during a node failure. The Virtual Processors (vprocs) remain operational and can access stored data.

If a node fails and then resets:

1. Teradata Database restarts across all the nodes.
2. Teradata Database recovers and the BYNET redistributes the vprocs of the node to the other nodes within the clique.
3. Processing continues while the node is being repaired.

Hot-standby Node

You can greatly improve performance continuity by allowing the database to automatically switch between standby nodes and failed nodes of a production system. During the restart period caused by the failed node, vprocs can migrate from a failed node to the available nodes in the clique, including the newly joined hot-standby node.

When the failed node is repaired or recovered it becomes the new hot-standby node.

Use the PUT utility to designate a node within a clique as the "hot spare." Once a node is assigned as the hot-standby node, PUT will not assign any vprocs to that node.

Assigning a hot-standby node:

- Helps with planned or unplanned restarts.
- Eliminates the need for restarts to bring a failed node back into service. This eliminates the downtime and transaction aborts associated with a restart.

With a hot-standby node as part of the configuration, the system always has a node available since it can use the spare node in place of the down node to maintain the same performance as before. SLAs will not be impacted.

Space Allocation

PERM SPACE
Perm space is allocated at the database/user level, not at the individual table level. It represents the total number of bytes (including table headers) currently allocated for data tables, index

Teradata 12 Enterprise Architecture

tables and subtables, stored procedures, triggers, and permanent journals residing in a particular database/user.

The allocated space is divided equally among all of the AMPs. If any AMP attempts to use more than its allocated amount, the database/user is considered "full", and an error message is returned to the requestor.

PERMANENT SPACE TERMINOLOGY

CurrentPerm

The total number of bytes (including table headers) currently allocated to existing data tables, index tables and subtable, stored procedures, triggers, and permanent journals residing in a particular database/user.

PeakPerm

The largest number of bytes ever used to store data in a user or database since the last reset of this value to zero.

Note: To reset the PeakPerm value to zero, use the DBC.ClearPeakDisk macro.

MaxPerm

The maximum number of bytes available for storage of all (current and future) data tables, index tables and subtables, stored procedures, triggers, and permanent journals owned by a particular database/user. It's the allocated PERM amount from the CREATE statement divided by the number of AMPs.

The following figure shows the relationship between these three definitions.

ARCHITECTURE

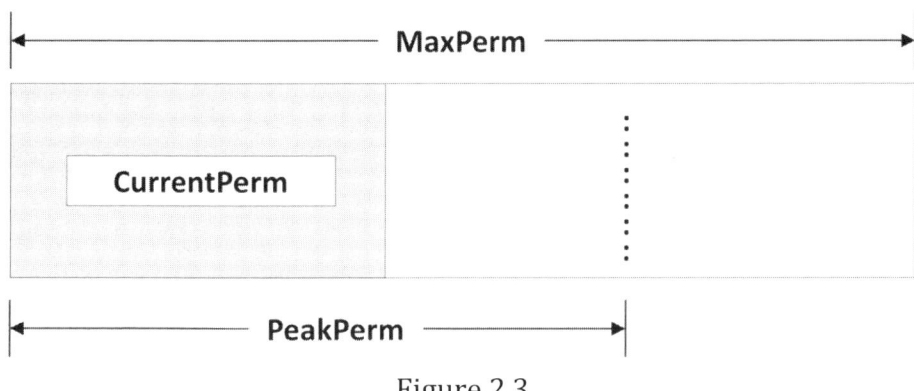

Figure 2.3

SPOOL SPACE

Spool space is work space used by the system to perform SQL requests. Only users consume spool space, databases do not. The spool limit assigned to a user cannot exceed the spool limit of the immediate parent. The spool limit is divided evenly across all of the AMPs, and represents a threshold that no AMP can exceed.

The DBA specifies the spool limit of each user; taking into consideration the tables they access, to reduce the impact of "runaway" transactions, such as accidental Cartesian product joins.

TEMP SPACE

Temp space specifies the limit of space available for global temporary tables. This limit is divided equally among all of the AMPs.

The value may not exceed the limit of:

- The creator or owner of the profile, when setting TEMPORARY in a profile.
- The immediate owner of the user being created if a profile does not apply.

Teradata 12 Enterprise Architecture

Databases

In the Teradata system, a User is a database that also represents a logon point into the system. It is through the CREATE USER and CREATE DATABASE commands that the hierarchical structure is built. In looking at the following database structure, all of the following are databases and depending on the access rights you have been granted, you can access their contents. Some users may not be given any Perm space and only use Perm space given to other databases.

In Figure 2.4 below, all of these are databases, unless they have a password and you know what it is. That is why "DBC" is usually referred to as "database DBC", since only a select few know its password.

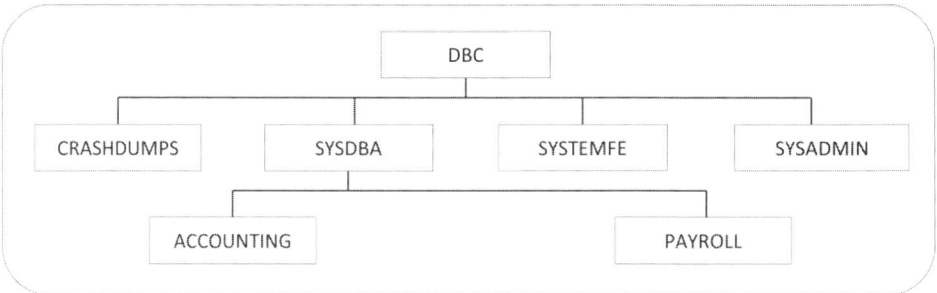

Figure 2.4

In an initial Teradata Database, DBC owns all the space in the system. Teradata recommends that you create an administrative user from User DBC, move the majority space available to that user and log on as that user to perform normal daily administrative tasks. The example above uses the name SYSDBA.

Creating an administrative user from User DBC is standard practice and allows you to protect sensitive data and system objects owned by User DBC. It enables you to manage all the users and databases you subsequently create.

ARCHITECTURE

Teradata also recommends creating a separate security administrator to perform security-related tasks.

Teradata recommends that you set up users and databases similar to the following hierarchy.

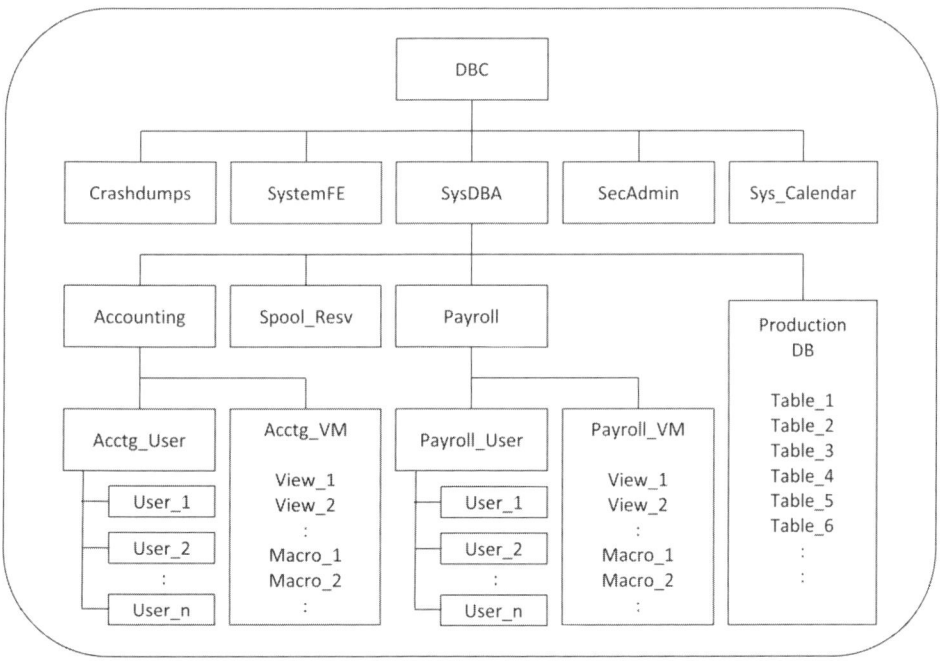

Figure 2.5

This hierarchy helps protect data and ensures users do not inadvertently make changes to the actual data in the base tables. For example, users in the Accounting department depicted in figure 2.5 do not have direct access to any of the production tables. Instead, they are assigned to a role called "Acctg_User" created for accessing accounting information through views and macros in the Acctg_VM database. Furthermore, they do not have to be given any Perm space.

The same is true for users in the Payroll department.

As a general guideline, only the load utilities (FastLoad, MultiLoad, TPump) should have direct access to the base tables. All other access (BTEQ, SQLA, etc.) should be through views.

If you have multiple people acting as database or security administrators, consider creating separate roles for DBAs, security administrators, and shared administration duties. Roles will be covered in a Chapter 5 Security.

Tables

Teradata tables may be permanent or temporary. Permanent tables consume Perm space. Global Temporary tables consume Temp space. Volatile and derived temporary tables consume Spool.

A table may be a normal data table, or it may be a Queue table.

Tables may prohibit duplicate rows (SET), or allow them (MULTISET).

Permanent tables may be accessed by multiple sessions, and their data rows remain until a DELETE removes them.

VOLATILE temporary tables are created, loaded, used, and dropped within a session. Data cannot be shared with other sessions.

ARCHITECTURE

GLOBAL TEMPORARY tables have a permanent definition. Global Temporary tables are materialized, loaded, used, and dropped within a session. Data cannot be shared with other sessions.

COMPARISON:

VOLATILE TABLE	GLOBAL TEMPORARY TABLE
Logon; Create volatile table; Load private data into the volatile table; Use the data; Logoff;	Logon; Create global temporary table definition; Logoff; Now, authorized users can: Logon; Load private data into their materialization of the global temporary table; Use their data; Logoff;

Figure 2.6

The following summarizes the space used by the various table types:

Table Type	Space Used	Exists
Permanent	PERMANENT	Until dropped
Derived	SPOOL	Until the end of the query
Volatile	SPOOL	Only for the duration of the user's session
Global Temporary	TEMPORARY	Definition is permanent, but data exists only for the duration of the user's session

Figure 2.7

Fallback

Fallback is an optional data protection feature accomplished by grouping AMPs within a clique into clusters. The clusters are spread across the nodes in the clique so that no cluster has more than one AMP on any node.

Within a cluster, a fallback copy of each data row is distributed to a different AMP from the one containing the primary row.

Should two disk drives of the same rank fail, the associated AMP goes down.

Should a node in a clique go down, it will be seen as a single-AMP failure in the clusters of that clique.

If the primary AMP fails, the system can still access data on the fallback AMP. This ensures that one copy of a row is available if one or more hardware or software failures occur within one rank, an entire array, or an entire node.

Fallback consumes twice the disk space and twice the I/Os for Insert/Update/Delete operations.

For 7x24 systems, having hot stand-by nodes, along with the fallback option on important tables are recommended for maintaining SLAs and minimizing the risks of system downtime. Dual-Active systems should also be considered.

Indexes

Teradata Database supports the following types of indexes:

- Primary
    - Unique and non-unique, non-partitioned (UPI and NUPI)
    - Unique and non-unique, partitioned (PPI)
    - Identity Column used as a PI
- Unique and non-unique Secondary (USI and NUSI)
- Join (JI)
- Hash (HI)

Primary indexes serve to distribute the rows of a table for storage and to enable direct-path access. Unique primary and unique secondary indexes also enforce row uniqueness.

Any combination of secondary, join, and hash indexes can be defined on one table. You can define up to a maximum of 32 indexes per table. However:

- Some load utilities cannot insert rows into a table that has been defined with an identity column, trigger, or secondary, join, or hash index.
- An identity column cannot be defined as part of a join index, hash index, partitioned primary index, or value-ordered index.
- An ordered non-unique secondary index counts as two indexes against the 32 maximum.
- A Large Object (LOB) column cannot be a component of any index.

Performance advantages can far outweigh the maintenance and resource costs of properly chosen indexes.

Teradata 12 Enterprise Architecture

Practice Questions

1. Of the three operating systems available for Teradata nodes, which is becoming the most popular?
    a. Linux
    b. UNIX MP-RAS
    c. Windows

2. Which two statements apply to Dual-Active Solutions? (Choose 2)
    a. Only allows data transfer between Teradata systems.
    b. Uses a replication server to control data transfers.
    c. Can be used as a replacement for FastLoad and MultiLoad.
    d. Can be used to eliminate batch windows.

3. Which three statements apply to Cliques and Hot-standby Nodes? (Choose 2)
    a. A grouping of AMPs providing Fallback protection.
    b. A grouping of nodes providing node failure protection.
    c. Available on single node and multi-node systems.
    d. One clique contains all of the hot-standby nodes.
    e. Hot-standby nodes help maintain SLAs when a node fails.

ARCHITECTURE

Match the following table types to the space they use.

4. ___ Permanent	a. TEMP
5. ___ Volatile	b. SPOOL
6. ___ Global Temporary	c. PERM
7. ___ Derived	

8. What is the maximum number of secondary, join, and hash indexes that can be defined on one table?
    a. 8
    b. 16
    c. 32
    d. 64
    e. 128

Chapter Notes

Utilize this space for notes, key points to remember, diagrams, areas of further study, etc.

Chapter 3 - Client Environment

Certification Objectives

- ✓ Describe hardware connectivity options supported by the Teradata environment.
- ✓ Describe the TTU client operating environments supported by the Teradata environment.
- ✓ Describe client connectivity protocols supported by the Teradata environment.

Before You Begin

You should be familiar with the following terms and concepts.

Terms	Key Concepts
CLI	Call Level Interface
MOSI	Micro Operating System Interface
MTDP	Micro Teradata Director Program
PDE	Parallel Database Extensions
TDP	Teradata Director Program

TTU

Teradata Tools and Utilities (TTU) can be installed / run on the following:

- Microsoft Windows
- IBM VM
- IBM z/OS
- Linux
- UNIX

Connectivity Protocols

ODBC (Open Database Connectivity)

ODBC defines a standard C API for accessing a relational DBMS. It was developed by the SQL Access Group in 1992 to standardize the use of a DBMS by an application. ODBC provides a universal middleware layer between the application and DBMS, allowing the application developer to use a single interface. If changes are made to the DBMS specification, only the driver needs updating. An ODBC driver can be thought of as analogous to a printer or other driver, providing a standard set of functions for the application to use, and implementing DBMS-specific functionality.

An application that can use ODBC is referred to as "ODBC-compliant". Any ODBC-compliant application can access any DBMS for which a driver is installed. Drivers exist for all major DBMSs and even for text or CSV files.

JDBC (Java Database Connectivity)

JDBC is an API for the Java programming language that defines how a client may access a database. It provides methods for querying and updating data in a database. JDBC is oriented towards relational databases. A JDBC-to-ODBC bridge enables connections to any ODBC-accessible data source in the JVM host environment.

Bus and Tag

Control units are connected to the channels with gray "bus and tag" cable pairs. The bus cables carry address and data information and the tag cables identify what data is on the bus. The general configuration of a channel is to connect the devices in a chain like this: Mainframe—Control Unit X—Control Unit Y—Control Unit Z.

ESCON

ESCON (Enterprise Systems Connection) is a data connection created by IBM and is commonly used to connect their mainframe computers to peripheral devices such as disk storage and tape drives. ESCON is an optical fiber, half-duplex, serial interface. It originally operated at a rate of 10 MB/s, which was later increased to 17 MB/s. The current maximum distance is 43 kilometers.

ESCON was introduced by IBM in the early 1990s. It replaced the older, slower (4.5 MB/s), copper-based, parallel, Bus & Tag channel technology of the 1960-1990 era mainframes. Optical fiber is smaller in diameter and weight, and hence could save installation costs. Space and labor could also be reduced when fewer physical links became required - due to ESCON's switching features. ESCON is being supplanted by the substantially faster FICON, which runs over Fiber Channels.

Connectivity Options

Connecting to Teradata: Local Area Network

To make a successful connection between Teradata and a client PC on the Local Area Network (LAN), hardware and software components are required.

Hardware (both Teradata and client PC):

- Ethernet card: The network interface card that allows a computer to connect to a high-speed network. Often, two Ethernet cards are used for redundancy.

Client Software:

- CLI - The CLI (Call Level Interface) issues commands directly to Teradata and handles blocking/unblocking requests.
- MOSI - The MOSI (Micro Operating System Interface) is a library of routines that provides the networking interface.
- MTDP - The MTDP (Micro Teradata Director Program) is a library of session management routines and it provides Teradata with information about the client so that it knows how to properly format the result set for the client.
- The following drivers allow tools, such as Teradata SQL Assistant to communicate to the MTDP:
    - ODBC
    - JDBC
    - OLE DB (Object Linking and Embedding, Database)
    - .NET Data Provider

Teradata Software:

- Gateway: The Gateway controls access between all of the LAN computers and Teradata. The Gateway controls user logons and can enable or disable user access.
- AMP, PE, and PDE (Parallel Database Extensions): Software on the node that handles the data request and retrieval.

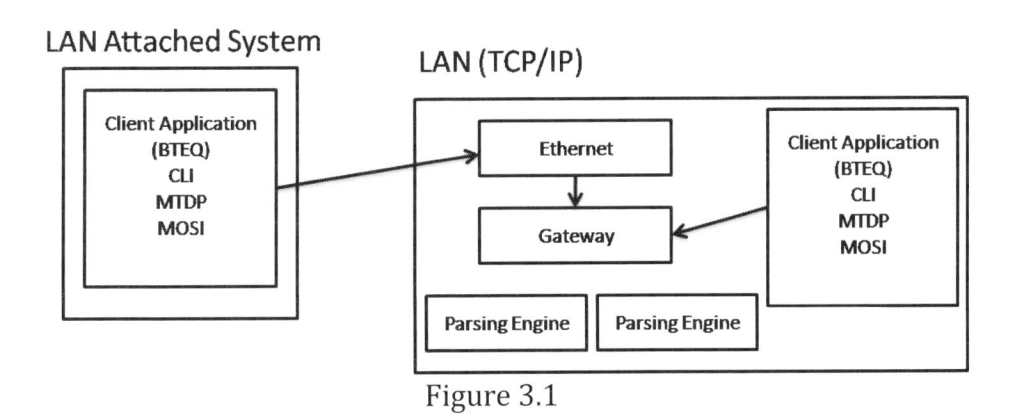

Figure 3.1

CONNECTING TO TERADATA: MAINFRAME

Mainframe connections work differently than LAN connections.

Hardware

To connect to Teradata from a mainframe, a physical connection is required. A mainframe can either connect directly using an ESCON connection or using BUS/TAG cables, and then to a Host Channel Adapter. Finally, the Host Channel Adapter connects to a dedicated Parsing Engine (PE).

Teradata 12 Enterprise Architecture

Software

The mainframe connects (via utilities, such as BTEQ, or other applications) to the CLI and the Teradata Director Program (TDP). The CLI issues commands directly to Teradata, and is responsible for request and response control, parcel creation and blocking / unblocking, buffer allocation and initialization. The TDP provides Teradata with information about the client so that it knows how to properly format the result set for the client and it handles session balancing and failure notification.

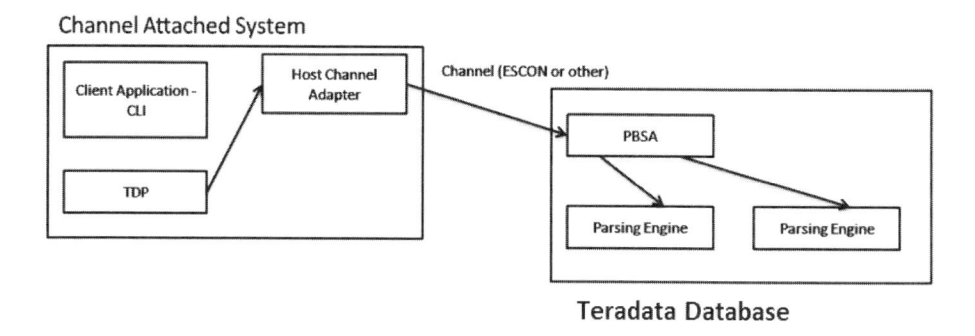

Figure 3.2

Call Level Interface (CLI)

The Teradata **Call Level Interface (CLI)** is a collection of routines that speak natively to Teradata and can be invoked by outside applications. Because the CLI speaks directly to Teradata, it is an extremely efficient mode of communication.

The CLI is an Application Programming Interface (API) that operates with LAN and mainframe attached systems. It is composed of multiple callable service routines that can be referenced by third party applications. These routines allow the application developer to communicate with Teradata directly, rather than using ODBC, OLE DB, or other protocols.

CLIENT ENVIRONMENT

Practice Questions

Match the following labels to their definition.

1. ___ CLI		a.	A programming API
2. ___ JDBC		b.	An operating system
3. ___ MOSI		c.	Issues commands directly to Teradata
4. ___ MTDP		d.	Library of session management routines
5. ___ ODBC		e.	Networking interface library of routines
6. ___ z/OS		f.	Universal middleware layer

Chapter Notes

Utilize this space for notes, key points to remember, diagrams, areas of further study, etc.

Chapter 4 - LDM/PDM

Certification Objectives

- ✓ Describe how the LDM as an input is valuable in designing an integrated data architecture.
- ✓ Determine the application characteristics and other factors that affect table design, including using the different types of advanced indexes.
- ✓ Given a LDM, determine what needs to be added to create an Extended LDM in order to choose the appropriate indexes.
- ✓ Identify the objects in a semantic layer.

Before You Begin

You should be familiar with the following terms and concepts.

Terms	Key Concepts
Logical Data Model	Data in relational tables normalized to 3NF
Activity Transaction Modeling	Modeling known data access requirements
Extended LDM	Accessed columns, access type, rows per value, data volatility
Physical Data Model	Table names, column names, data types, data attributes, indexes
Semantic Layer	Constraints. Business-specific views. Business rules
Joins	Combining rows from multiple tables to produce a result
Join Index Aggregate Join Index	Used to improve join processing by reducing the redistribution of rows prior to doing a join

3NF LDM to PDM

The success of the data warehouse depends on keeping the data in 3NF. Any denormalization should be reserved for dependent data marts. This means there is only one version of the truth, while supporting multiple views of that single version. It is only by maintaining a single version of the truth that people can rely on the information.

The steps involved in implementing a 3NF database are:

- Requirements Analysis
- Logical Database Design
- Activity Transaction Modeling
- Physical Database Design

Requirements Analysis

Any design process must begin with the knowledge of what is to be designed. This includes not only the proposed structure of the tables, but also the systems, policies, and procedures -- the processes of the designed product.

This fundamental knowledge is derived through a process of accumulating facts about what the eventual users of the product require to do their work in support of the enterprise. The process includes, at minimum, the following tasks:

- Interviewing notable employees, both management and support staff for information such as the following:
    - What information do they need?
    - What is the source of that information?
    - What are the tasks involved with creating and reporting the information?
    - How is the information used?

- Gathering all input screens and reports generated by the legacy system and interviewing management and support staff about what is right and wrong about these components as well as determining what sorts of new or different input and report items should be added to the new system.
- Compiling and circulating the cumulative research information you have gathered to obtain affirmation of its accuracy from all involved parties.
- Writing a requirements specification from the approved research information and making it available to the designer of the logical database.

Logical Database Design

The requirements analysis phase of the design process reveals the real world objects and their attributes that the database must represent as well as the relationships among them.

The logical database design phase formalizes the objects, or entities, and their relationships.

Another primary task of logical design is to ensure that the modeled entities are modified by attributes that uniquely pertain to them. No attribute should appear in an entity unless it describes the entire primary key. This is referred to as normalization.

Activity Transaction Modeling

Once a fully normalized logical data model has been realized, the next step is to enter the transaction modeling phase. In this phase, which Teradata refers to as Activity Transaction Modeling, you translate the entities, attributes, and relationships into a set of worksheets that feed into the physical database design process.

Teradata 12 Enterprise Architecture

The Activity Transaction Modeling (ATM) process extends the logical data model by beginning to assign attributes to it. In doing so, the ATM process undertakes the following activities:

- Identifies the business rules of the enterprise that apply to the information to be stored in the data warehouse
- Initiates the process of identifying and defining attribute domains and constraints for physical columns
- Identifies and models database applications
- Identifies and models application transactions
- Summarizes table and join accesses by column across transactions
- Compiles a preliminary set of data demographics by computing table row counts, value distributions, and attaching change ratings to columns. This information is compiled and used as input to the physical design process.

You use the early ATM process forms as input to more complex forms later in the process. The final ATM process forms are used when you create the physical objects in your database, ensuring that the universe of domains, constraints, table accesses, reports and queries are understood well in advance of the process of creating the physical database objects that derive from those constructs.

The ATM process is the first step in the transition from your logical data model to the implementation of your physical database.

LDM/PDM

The second and final step in that transition is to collect or prototype data demographics. The following table indicates the activities of this process and the forms required to complete each activity.

Step	Action	Form Used
1	Define all domains in the system.	Domains
2	Define all constraints for the system.	Constraints
3	Identify all applications in the system.	System
4	Model application processing activities including their transactions and run frequencies.	Application
5	Model each transaction using the following information. • Identify tables used. • Identify columns required for value and join access. • Estimate qualifying cardinalities.	Report/Query Analysis
6	Summarize value and join access information across all transactions.	
7	Transfer access information	Table
8	Add data demographics to the Table Access Summary by Columns report. • Table cardinalities • Column value distributions (histograms) • Column change ratings	
9	Identify column change rating.	

Figure 4.1

Teradata 12 Enterprise Architecture

Physical Database Design

Physical database design is the commitment of all the previous design stages to a physical reality.

In previous phases of the design process, entities, attributes, and relationships were identified and normalized.

All attributes were assigned to domains, while some were identified as primary and secondary index candidates.

The physical design phase identifies and creates the actual databases, base tables, indexes, views, macros, stored procedures, triggers, and other objects that define the physical database that drives your data warehouse.

Data Volatility

Part of the ATM process involves determining how frequently column values change. This affects choices of Secondary and Join indexes, since any change to the base table requires change to the indexes as well.

Primary indexes should be defined on columns that rarely, if ever, change. Changing the value of a primary index almost certainly means that affected rows must be redistributed to different AMPs, which results in excessive I/O traffic on the BYNET and disk subsystems. If the primary index equals the Primary Key, changing it also invalidates all the PK value's history.

Figure 4.2 reviews the Change Rating code values and their meanings.

Code	Description
0	Data for this column never changes. Examples include primary key columns and columns that contain historical information.
1	Data for this column rarely changes.
2 – 8	User-determined. These codes cover anything not covered by codes 0, 1, and 9.
9	Data for this column frequently changes.

Figure 4.2

Teradata Index Wizard uses column change ratings as a parameter in determining the candidacy of columns for use as indexes.

Semantic Layer

The semantic layer consists of the views, Join Indexes, and Aggregate Join Indexes which provide and control access to the base tables. It is through these structures that the same fact can be viewed in different ways.

Typical categories are:

- Analytical views
- Administrative views
- Summary views

Leveraging the Teradata aggregate join index feature will optimize ROLAP performance. Relational online analytical processing (ROLAP) is a form of online analytical processing (OLAP) that performs dynamic multidimensional business intelligence analysis of data stored in a Teradata Database.

PDM Changes to LDM

The logical data model, including the semantic layer objects should always agree with the implemented objects. These data structure descriptions should always be available to anyone writing SQL against the database.

Examples of changing data structures would be:

- Adding/dropping/altering tables
- Adding/dropping/altering columns
- Adding/dropping/altering views
- Adding/dropping/altering join indexes
- Adding/dropping/altering aggregate join indexes

Without up-to-date documentation, users cannot function optimally. It is the responsibility of the DBAs to keep their users properly informed about the data structures available to them.

In summary, the heart of the data warehouse is your data modeled in such a way that it matches your business. Just as the warehouse is used as a tool to change the business, so it must change over time if it is to continue to be a critical tool for supporting the enterprise. A true data warehouse sows the seeds that force its own change. The only static warehouse is the warehouse with little or no value to the business.

Practice Questions

1. Indicate the proper sequence (1 – 4) of the following steps.

    a. _____ Activity Transaction Modeling
    b. _____ Logical Database Design
    c. _____ Physical Database Design
    d. _____ Requirements Analysis

2. The _____ consists of the views, Join Indexes, and Aggregate Join Indexes which provide and control access to the base tables.
    a. Logical Data Model
    b. Semantic layer
    c. Activity Transaction Model
    d. Physical data model

3. Which two are part of the ATM process? (Choose 2)
    a. Defining entities and their relationships
    b. Identifying column change ratings
    c. Documenting and creating physical objects
    d. Interviewing notable employees
    e. Defining all domains
    f. Defining views, join indexes, and aggregate join indexes
    g. Normalization

Teradata 12 Enterprise Architecture

4. Which two are part of Logical Data Modeling? (Choose 2)
    a. Defining entities and their relationships
    b. Identifying column change ratings
    c. Documenting and creating physical objects
    d. Interviewing notable employees
    e. Defining all domains
    f. Defining views, join indexes, and aggregate join indexes
    g. Normalization

5. Which one is part of Physical Data Modeling?
    a. Defining entities and their relationships
    b. Identifying column change ratings
    c. Documenting and creating physical objects
    d. Interviewing notable employees
    e. Defining all domains
    f. Defining views, join indexes, and aggregate join indexes
    g. Normalization

Chapter Notes

Utilize this space for notes, key points to remember, diagrams, areas of further study, etc.

Chapter 5 - Security

Certification Objectives

- ✓ Describe the options to secure access to the database.
- ✓ Describe the methods available to meet privacy requirements within an application that contains personally identifiable information.
- ✓ Given a scenario, determine the security objects and requirements needed to organize the database user environment.
- ✓ Identify the available methods to meet user access auditing requirements.
- ✓ Given a scenario, determine the effects of embedded (nested) views.

Before You Begin

You should be familiar with the following terms and concepts.

Terms	Key Concepts
Nested Views	A view of a view (of a view . . .)
Profiles	Management of user settings
Roles	Management of user privileges.
Access Rights	Rights, access rights, permissions, or privileges
Access Logging	Tracking system entry and object use

Logons

To access the database, users must submit their username, password, and other related information as part of a logon request. Each username is associated with a default storage area and an array of access rights that define the privileges the user has within the system. Upon successful logon, Teradata Database associates the username with a unique session number under which the session runs until the user logs off.

Logon strings must include some or all of the following elements, depending on system configuration and security policy:

- Security mechanism
- Username
- Domain or Realm
- Password
- Tdpid (see figure 5.3)
- Account string

Upon receipt of the logon string, the selected security mechanism authenticates the user and establishes a session based on the user's rights and privileges.

Note: The size of these logon string items cannot exceed a total of 128 bytes.

Users

Each database user should be created by the Security Administrator using the Teradata SQL CREATE USER statement. You can retrieve information on Teradata Database usernames from DBC.DBase by querying the system view DBC.Databases.

CREATE USER requires that you define:

- A unique username
- A password
- A permanent space allocation in which the user can create other database objects

You can also optionally use the CREATE USER statement to specify other security-related user attributes, such as:

- Default database
- A profile and/or role of which the user is a member
- Account string

Teradata 12 Enterprise Architecture

Here is the syntax diagram (Figure 5.1) of the CREATE USER statement.

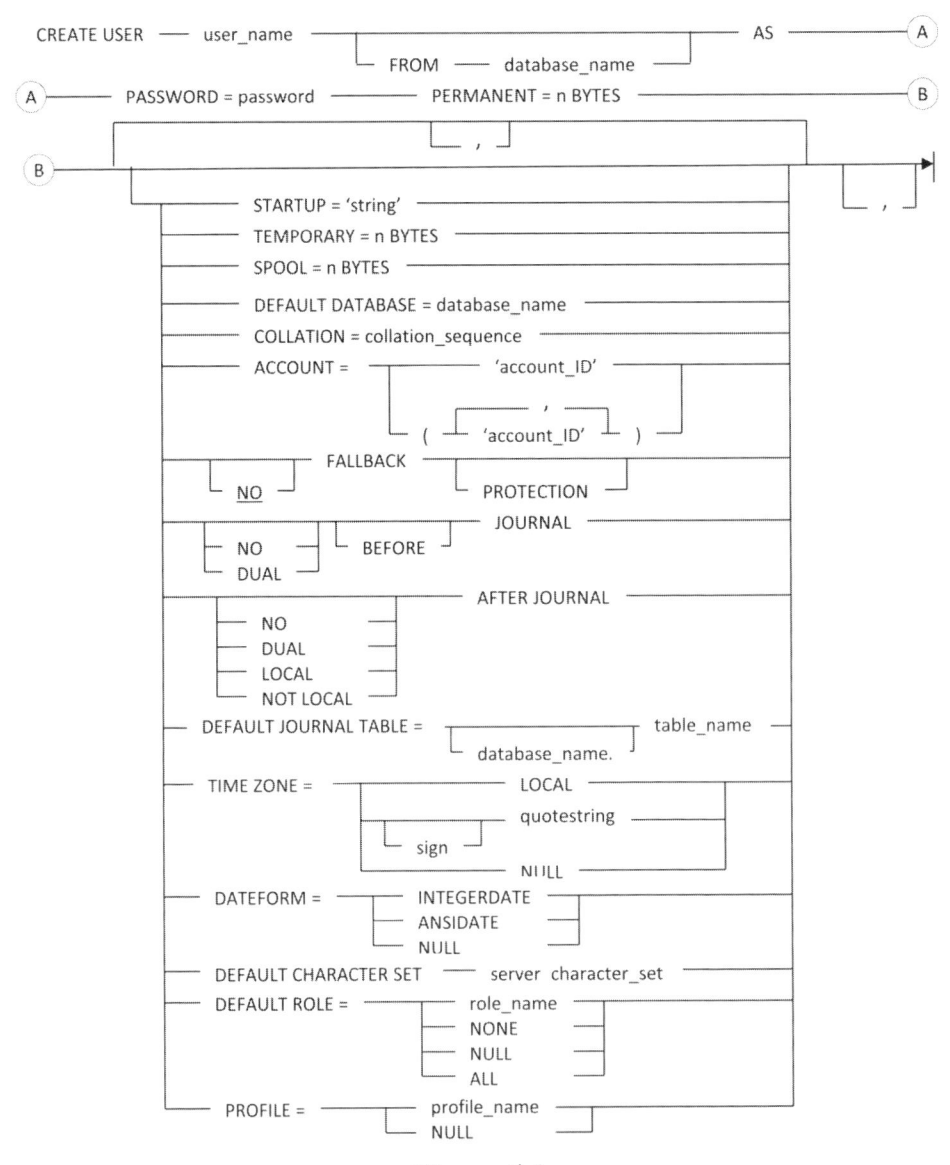

```
CREATE USER ── user_name ─────────────────────── AS ──── (A)
               └─ FROM ── database_name ─┘

(A) ── PASSWORD = password ──── PERMANENT = n BYTES ─────── (B)
                              └─────── , ───────┘

(B) ──┬─ STARTUP = 'string' ─┐
      ├─ TEMPORARY = n BYTES ─┤
      ├─ SPOOL = n BYTES ─────┤
      ├─ DEFAULT DATABASE = database_name ─┤
      ├─ COLLATION = collation_sequence ───┤
      ├─ ACCOUNT = ┬─ 'account_ID' ─────┐  ┤
      │            └─ ( ┬─ 'account_ID' ┬─ ) ┘
      │                 └──── , ───────┘
      ├─ ┬── ──┬── FALLBACK ──┬─────────────┬─
      │  └─NO─┘               └─ PROTECTION ┘
      ├─ ┬── ──┬─ ┬── ──────┬─ JOURNAL
      │  ├─NO─┤  └─ BEFORE ─┘
      │  └DUAL┘
      ├─ ┬── ──┬─ AFTER JOURNAL
      │  ├─NO──┤
      │  ├─DUAL┤
      │  ├─LOCAL┤
      │  └NOT LOCAL┘
      ├─ DEFAULT JOURNAL TABLE = ┬─ table_name ─
      │                          └─ database_name. ─┘
      ├─ TIME ZONE = ┬─ LOCAL ──────────┐
      │              ├─ sign ─ quotestring ┤
      │              └─ NULL ────────────┘
      ├─ DATEFORM = ┬─ INTEGERDATE ─┐
      │             ├─ ANSIDATE ────┤
      │             └─ NULL ────────┘
      ├─ DEFAULT CHARACTER SET ── server character_set
      ├─ DEFAULT ROLE = ┬─ role_name ─┐
      │                 ├─ NONE ──────┤
      │                 ├─ NULL ──────┤
      │                 └─ ALL ───────┘
      └─ PROFILE = ┬─ profile_name ─┐
                   └─ NULL ─────────┘
```

Figure 5.1

Passwords

Teradata Database offers several options for controlling password format and usage requirements to help administrators customize password security to meet individual needs.

Teradata Database 12.0 and up automatically converts all passwords to Unicode prior to applying password controls. Therefore, all character sets are subject to password controls.

The DBC.SysSecDefaults dictionary table contains a set of global controls that restrict the usage and content of passwords for all users, as shown in the following table:

Field Name	Description
ExpirePassword	The number of days that must elapse before a password expires.
MaxLogonAttempts	The number of erroneous logons allowed before the user is locked out.
LockedUserExpire	The number of minutes to elapse before a locked user is unlocked.
PasswordReuse	The number of days that must elapse before a password can be reused.
PasswordMinChar	Sets the minimum number of characters required in a password.
PasswordMaxChar	Sets the maximum number of characters allowed in a password.
PasswordDigits	Determines whether ASCII digits are: • *allowed* in a password • *not allowed* in a password • *required* in a password
PasswordSpecChar	Indicates whether or not ASCII special characters are: • *allowed* in a password • *not allowed* in a password

Field Name	Description
	• *required* in a password You can place tight restrictions on passwords to require that: • passwords must contain at least one ASCII alpha character • passwords must contain a mixture of ASCII upper/lower case letters • no password can contain a database username
PasswordRestrictedWords	Determines whether or not passwords are rejected if they contain words in the Restricted Words list.

Figure 5.2

The global control options for a user can be set/reset using an UPDATE statement.

For those users assigned to a profile, you can use a CREATE or MODIFY PROFILE statement to override global password control parameters defined in SysSecDefaults.

Account Strings

System resource accounting requires the use of an account string to identify which account is to be charged for the resources used by the user. The account name appears in the following system views:

- AccessLog
- AccountInfo
- AllSpace
- AMPUsage
- Databases

SECURITY

- DiskSpace
- LogOnOff
- SecurityLog
- SessionInfo
- TableSize

Users can specify an account string at logon. If the logon does not include an account string, the system assigns a default value.

You can assign account strings to users as part of the CREATE/MODIFY USER statement. Each username may have one or more associated account strings. The first account string assigned becomes the default.

The account string may also be set up to include a priority-level Performance Group prefix code, which establishes the session priority. Priorities are useful when interactive users are competing for system resources with long-running batch applications.

The elements of a LOGON are shown in the following table:

Syntax element...	Specifies...
tdpid/	the identifier associated with a particular Teradata server. (Optional)
userid	a user identifier. (Required)
password	the password associated with the userid. The password cannot include the semicolon character. (Required)
acctid	the account identifier associated with the userid. (Optional)

Figure 5.3

A logged-on user can switch to a different assigned account using the SET SESSION ACCOUNT for an individual request, or for the session.

Controlling Access to Data

After users are authenticated and authorized, there is still several ways security and access can be restricted. Use any combination of the following to limit access to the data:

- **Privileges** control user access to data by granting privileges only to specific users for certain database objects.
- **Views** limit user access to table columns or rows that may contain sensitive information.
- **Macros** limit the types of actions a user can perform on the columns and rows. Also, you can define which users are granted the EXECUTE privilege on a macro.
- **Triggers** can automate, and limit the types of actions a user can perform on tables. Also, you can define which users are granted the privilege on a trigger along with providing an audit trail.
- **Stored Procedures,** as with macros, limit the types of actions a user can perform on the columns and rows. Grant the EXECUTE privilege on stored procedure only to those who should be authorized.

Profiles

Profiles simplify the management of user settings such as accounts, default database, spool space, temporary space, and password attributes for a group of users. Assign specific settings to a profile, and then assign a profile to a user in the CREATE USER or MODIFY USER statement. This way, rather than managing settings for users on an individual basis, you can modify the settings for a profile to immediately apply the changes to all users that use the profile. With profiles, you can manage the following attributes:

- Password settings, including:
- Account strings (i.e. ASE codes and Performance Groups)

SECURITY

- Default database assignments
- Spool and temporary space limits

In a profile, the SPOOL and TEMPORARY limits may not exceed the current space limits of the profile owner.

All members inherit changed profile parameters. The impact is immediate, or in response to a SET SESSION statement, or upon next logon, depending on the parameter:

Profile Parameter	Activation
SPOOL space	Immediately
TEMPORARY space	Immediately
Password Attributes	Next logon
Account ID	Next logon
	SET SESSION ACCOUNT statement. The specified account ID must agree with the profile definition.
Default database	Next logon
	SET SESSION DATABASE statement. The specified databasename must agree with the profile definition.

Figure 5.4

Profile definitions apply to every assigned user, overriding specifications at the system or user level. The value in each SysSecDefaults column applies to all users.

Warning: If you set MaxLogonAttempts and LockedUserExpire at the system level, user DBC could potentially be locked out. Remember, only DBC can submit a MODIFY USER DBC statement to change the DBC password.

Teradata 12 Enterprise Architecture

Here is the syntax diagram (Figure 5.5) for the CREATE PROFILE statement:

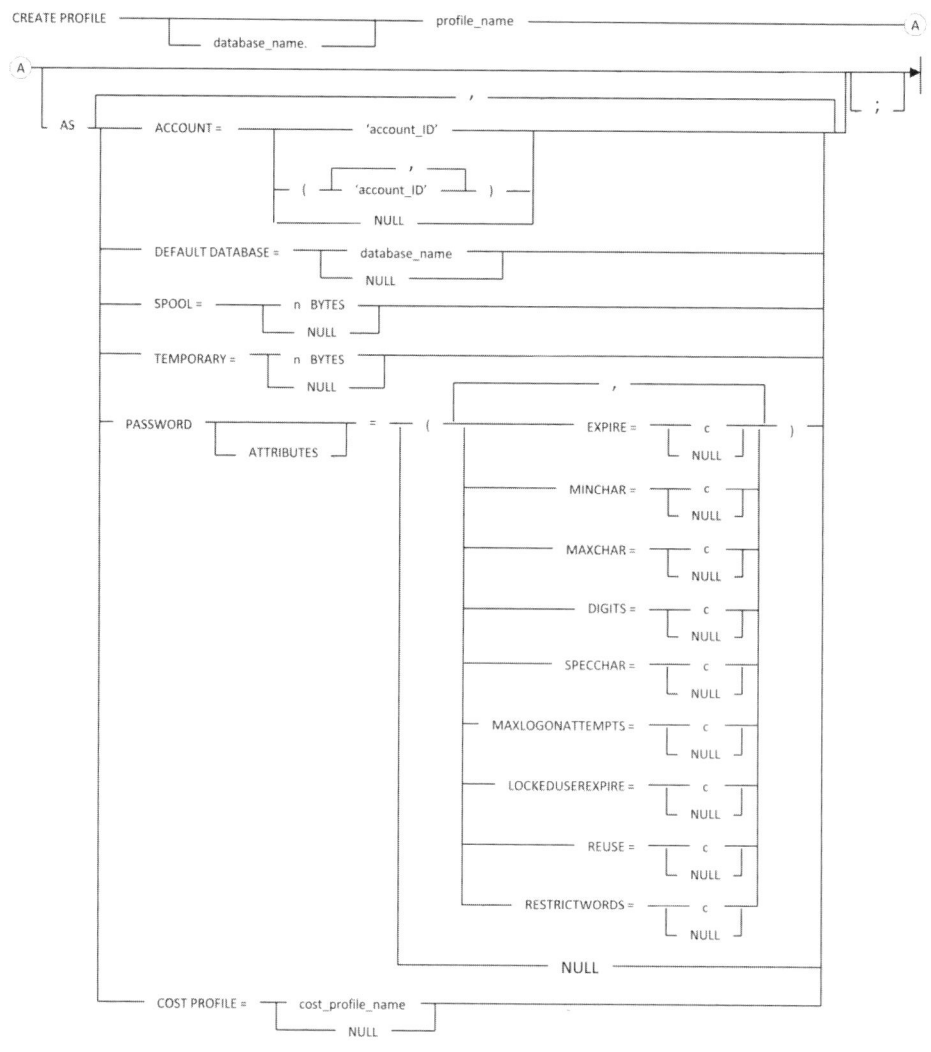

Figure 5.5

You can assign a user to a different profile any time using the MODIFY USER statement.

Lightweight Directory Access Protocol (LDAP)

The LDAP mechanism is used to support external authentication and authorization of users defined in a supported, LDAP-compliant directory.

An LDAP directory user is defined on a directory server rather than on the Teradata Database itself. Setting up directory user access to Teradata Database involves mapping the user in the directory entry to either a permanent user in Teradata Database or to a Teradata supplied generic user called EXTUSER (EXTernal USER).

Directory users log on using the LDAP mechanism and their directory user names and passwords. Directory users must observe the following rules when executing an LDAP logon:

- If a directory *is not* configured to map directory users to Teradata Database objects, the directory username must match a database username and the LDAP AuthorizationSupported property must be set to **no** on the client from which the directory user is logging on.
- If the directory *is* configured to map directory users to Teradata Database objects, directory users must log on with their directory user names, not their database usernames.

The actual creation of a directory server entry must be coordinated between the DBA and the directory server administrator.

LDAP Logon Formats

The LDAP mechanism supports two logon formats:

- Authcid logons
- UPN logons

Use LDAP logon *authcid* form with all TDGSS-supported directories.

```
.logmech ldap
.logdata authcid=robert password=password realm=domain
.logon cs4400s3/,,"account"
```

Figure 5.6

In addition to the logon string shown in the previous example, you can also use this variation of the LDAP authcid logon form on Active Directory and on other directories if they are specially configured to accept it.

```
.logmech ldap
.logdata authcid=diruser@dirrealm password=dirpassword
.logon cs4400s3/,,"account"
```

Figure 5.7

Use the following logon string example for LDAP UPN logons through Active Directory and on other supported directories if they are specially configured to accept it.

```
.logmech ldap
.logdata diruser@dirrealm@@dirpassword realm=domain
profile=profilename
.logon cs4400s3/,,"account"
```

Figure 5.8

SECURITY

Note: The UPN logon for LDAP is limited to use with compatible LDAP directories.

The LDAP mechanism appears in the TDGSS Library Configuration file as follows:

```xml
</Mechanism>
<!-- LDAP -->

    <Mechanism Name="ldap"
        ObjectId="1.3.6.1.4.1.191.1.1012.1.20"
        LibraryName="gssp2ldap"
        Prefix="ldapv3"
        InterfaceType="custom">

        <MechanismProperties
            AuthenticationSupported="yes"
            AuthorizationSupported="yes"
            SingleSignOnSupported="no"
            DefaultMechanism="no"

            GetCredentialsFromLogon="no"
            MechanismEnabled="yes"
            MechanismRank="70"

            DelegateCredentials="no"
            MutualAuthentication="yes"
            ReplayDetection="yes"
            OutOfSequenceDetection="yes"
            ConfidentialityDesired="yes"
            IntegrityDesired="yes"
            AnonymousAuthentication="no"
            DesiredContextTime=""
            DesiredCredentialTime=""
            CredentialUsage="0"
            LdapServerName=""
            LdapServerPort="389"
            LdapServerRealm=""
            LdapSystemFQDN=""
            LdapBaseFQDN=""
```

Teradata 12 Enterprise Architecture

```
                LdapGroupBaseFQDN
                LdapUserBaseFQDN
                LdapClientReferrals
                LdapClientDeref
                LdapClientDebug
                LdapClientRebindAuth

                VerifyDHKey="no"

DHKeyP="E4BE0A78F54C4A0B17E7E9249A78BCC08868C17281D8463C880
937853E73DDC787E41580A8AFE2594D984C9E0814C590790354ECCD1BE8
EA85961E5E0974B32EFE178335F061E80189B4BDAA20F67B47"
DHKeyG="050000000000000000000000000000000000000000000000000
000000000000000000000000000000000000000000000000000000000000
0000000000000000000000000000000000000000000000000"
                />
        <MechQop Value="0"> GLOBAL_QOP_0 </MechQop>
</Mechanism>
```

Figure 5.9

Access Rights

Sometimes referred to as rights, access rights, or permissions, a privilege is the right to access or manipulate another object within the Teradata Database. Privileges control user activities such as creating, executing, viewing, deleting, or tracking objects. Privileges also include the ability to grant privileges to other users in the database.

SECURITY

There are two types of privileges -- Explicit and Implicit.

Privilege Type	Description
EXPLICIT PRIVILEGE	- A privilege that you explicitly grant with the GRANT statement. - A privilege that is automatically granted by the system as though a GRANT statement was issued. - An Inherited Privilege is an explicit privilege that is assigned by means of a role.
IMPLICIT PRIVILEGE	A privilege for a user who directly or indirectly owns an object.

Figure 5.10

The user who submitted the CREATE statement is the creator of an object. Every object has one and only one creator.

Any database or user above the object in the database hierarchy is an owner of that object. The database space in which the new object resides is the immediate owner of a new object.

The default database is the created user's database, but can be a different database if you precede the object name with the database name and a period separator, such as databasename.objectname, in the CREATE statement.

Teradata 12 Enterprise Architecture

Figures 5.11 and 5.12 illustrate creators and owners.

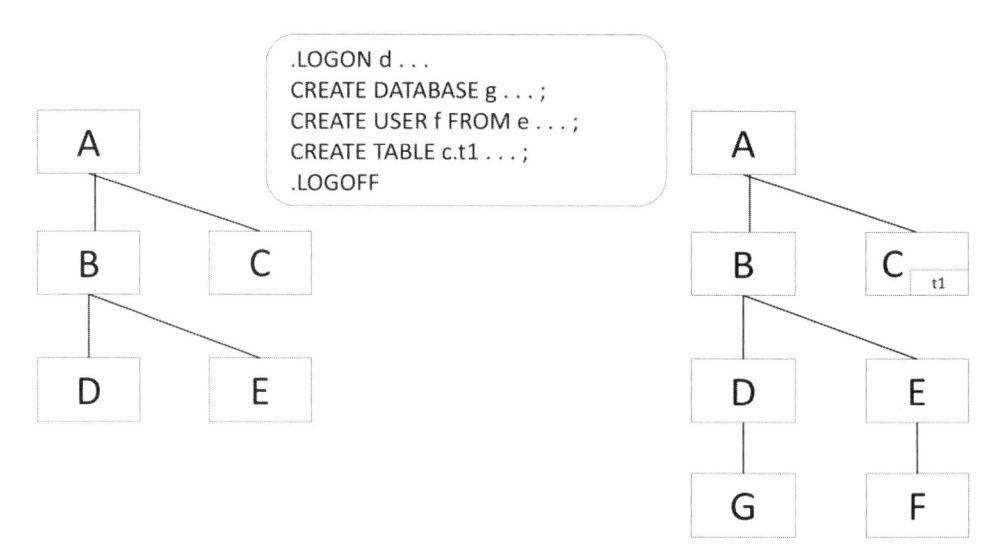

```
.LOGON d . . .
CREATE DATABASE g . . . ;
CREATE USER f FROM e . . . ;
CREATE TABLE c.t1 . . . ;
.LOGOFF
```

Figure 5.11

OBJECT	CREATOR	IMMEDIATE OWNER	ALL OWNERS
F	D	E	E B A
G	D	D	D B A
t1	D	C	C A

Figure 5.12

SECURITY

The following table lists the privileges. The term *column_list* indicates a parenthetically enclosed list of comma-separated column names the specified privilege applies to.

ALTER FUNCTION	DROP TABLE
ALTER EXTERNAL PROCEDURE	DROP TRIGGER
ALTER PROCEDURE	DROP USER
AUTHORIZATION	DROP VIEW
CHECKPOINT	DUMP
CREATE AUTHORIZATION	EXECUTE
CREATE DATABASE	EXECUTE FUNCTION
CREATE EXTERNAL PROCEDURE	EXECUTE PROCEDURE
CREATE FUNCTION	INDEX
CREATE MACRO	INSERT
CREATE PROCEDURE	REFERENCES *column_list*
CREATE TABLE	REFERENCES ALL BUT ... *column_list*
CREATE TRIGGER	
CREATE USER	RESTORE
CREATE VIEW	SELECT
DELETE	UDTMETHOD
DROP AUTHORIZATION	UDTTYPE
DROP DATABASE	UDTUSAGE
DROP FUNCTION	UPDATE column_list
DROP MACRO	UPDATE ALL BUT ... *column_list*
DROP PROCEDURE	

Figure 5.13

Teradata 12 Enterprise Architecture

Two extensions to the GRANT are [ALL] *user_name* and PUBLIC. If you specify ALL *user_name*, then the object privileges are granted to the named database or user and to every database or user owned by that database or user now and in the future. If you specify PUBLIC, the privileges are inherited by all existing and future Teradata Database users and databases.

```
GRANT privilege_list
ON object_name
TO {ALL user_name | PUBLIC}
[WITH GRANT OPTION]
```

Figure 5.14

Roles

Roles simplify the management of privileges for users. Roles help improve performance by reducing the number of rows added to and deleted from DBC.AccessRights. To use roles, assign privileges to a specific role and then grant the role to users. The users can then access all the objects for which their assigned role and nested roles have privileges.

Roles work best when based on job functions or responsibilities. Some users may belong to more than one role. By creating roles and granting them the necessary privileges, the DBA only has to grant or revoke roles to/from users as personnel and needs change. As the business changes, the DBA can grant or revoke privileges to the roles, and those changes will immediately affect all users of the modified role.

In the example illustrated in figure 5-15, *pa_001, pa_002, pa_003* have the same rights that the role *pa_user* has, and any new users added to the role *pa_user* will also have the same rights. Also, *acc_001, acc_002,*

SECURITY

acc_003 will have all of the rights that the role *acc_user* has, and any new users added to the role *acc_user* will also have the same rights.

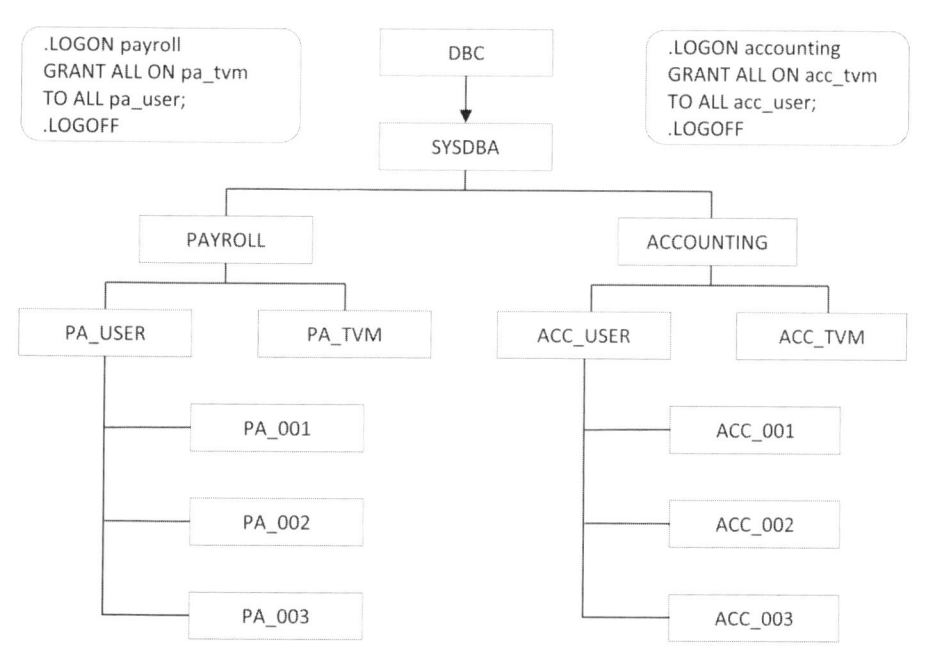

Figure 5.15

When a user, who is defined in the Teradata Database, logs on to the system, the assigned default role is the initial current role for the session. This current role is used to authorize privileges after all checks against individually granted privileges have failed. Once the session is active, the user can submit a SET ROLE statement to change or nullify the current role. For example: if a user is assigned to RoleA and RoleB, but logs in as RoleA, then the system only checks against RoleA and all nested roles for privileges. The user cannot use the privileges of Role B in this example. To use privileges of both RoleA and Role B, the user must activate all roles with the SET ROLE ALL statement.

If you are logging on as a directory-based user, and the proper set-up has been made on the directory server; you can have all directory-assigned roles enabled within a session. The initial current roles for the session are any external roles mapped to the directory user. If there are no mapped external roles, then the directory user will use Teradata user mappings.

If a directory user, who is mapped to a permanent database user, logs on with external roles assigned, the external roles override the default role of the permanent user as the initial current role for the session. The initial set of enabled roles does not include database-assigned roles. If, however, no external role is assigned, then the default role of the permanent user and its nested roles are the initial set of enabled roles. If neither external nor database-assigned roles are assigned to the user, then the initial current role is NULL.

Encryption

All standard Teradata Database security mechanisms are factory preset to support encryption of data transmitted during a session for which they have been selected. However, because there are significant resource costs associated with encrypting a session, *encryption is disabled by default for all applications and must be explicitly enabled from within the application if needed.* The method for enabling and disabling encryption also varies with the application used.

Logon Encryption

Teradata Database encrypts logon strings to ensure the confidentiality of passwords transmitted between client applications and the Teradata Gateway. Client applications cannot enable or disable encryption of the logon string. The Teradata Gateway determines whether or not logon encryption is enabled.

SECURITY

Password Encryption

Teradata Database uses encryption type SHA-256, which is a 256-bit encryption level. This is used automatically for all passwords created or changed after upgrade to Release 12.0 or greater.

Logons from Channel-Attached Systems

Channel-attached systems do not support network security features such as security mechanisms, encryption, or directory integration. Unless you have made modifications using the security functions in the Teradata Director Program (TDP), logons from a channel attached clients use only the .logon command.

Logons from Teradata Database Nodes

In some cases, administrators may need to log on to Teradata Database from a database node, such as when using a utility to do internal system maintenance. Although communication among Teradata Database nodes is done across a network using TCP/IP, you will probably not need to exercise network security functions.

Replication Logons

Some Teradata Databases may use the Replication feature, which ensures that changes to data on one database system are automatically captured and sent through an intermediary server (that directs the replication process) to another database system. By means of such automatic updates, replication maintains data equivalency between two separately addressable databases.

Each transfer of data requires that the intermediary server logon to both the initiator (source) system and the target (destination) system. The logon process is automatic for properly configured systems,

Encryption of Replication Sessions

You can choose whether or not to encrypt both control message transmissions and data transmissions when using the replication feature. Because many of the replication transmissions are automatic, choosing to encrypt replication transmissions cannot be done at logon, but must be done as part of the replication setup process using the tam.ini file.

Stored Procedures

A stored procedure is a combination of SQL statements and control and condition handling statements that provide an interface to the Teradata Database. The term *stored procedure* refers to a stored procedure you write with SQL statements. The term *external stored procedure* refers to a stored procedure you write in C, C++, or Java.

A stored procedure is a database object executed on the Teradata Database. Typically, a stored procedure consists of a procedure name, input and output parameters, and a procedure body.

For each stored procedure, the database includes a stored procedure table that contains the stored procedure body you write and the corresponding compiled stored procedure object code. Data dictionary tables contain stored procedure parameters and attributes.

A stored procedure provides control and condition handling statements. It also provides multiple input and output parameters and local variables. These features make SQL a computationally complete programming language.

Applications based on stored procedures provide the following benefits over equivalent embedded SQL applications:

SECURITY

- Better performance because of greatly reduced network traffic between the client and server.
- Better application maintenance because business rules are encapsulated and enforced on the server.
- Better transaction control.
- Better application security by restricting user access to procedures rather than requiring them to access data tables directly.
- Better application execution because all SQL language statements are embedded in a stored procedure to be executed on the server through one CALL statement.

Nested CALL statements extend stored procedure capabilities by combining all transactions and complex queries in the nested procedures into one transaction, and by handling errors internally in the nested procedures.

Stored Procedures allow the combination of both SPL (Stored Procedures Language) and SQL control statements to manage the delivery and execution of the procedure.

Triggers

A trigger contains one or more stored SQL statements that are executed, or fired, when some other event, called a triggering event, occurs. Triggers must be associated with an event and cannot be executed independently.

A trigger is associated with a subject table, and is stored as a named database object. Triggers exist in enabled or disabled states; when disabled, triggers remain as inactive database objects.

Typically, triggers execute when an INSERT, UPDATE, or DELETE modifies one or more specified columns in the subject table. The stored statements then perform operations such as INSERT, UPDATE, or DELETE on indicated tables, which may include the subject table.

UDFs

SQL provides a set of useful functions, but they might not satisfy all of the particular requirements you have to process your data.

User-defined functions (UDFs) allow you to extend SQL by writing your own functions in the C/C++ or Java programming language, installing them on the database, and then using them like standard SQL functions.

You can also install UDF objects or packages from third party vendors without providing the source code.

Teradata Database supports four types of UDFs:

Function Type	Programming Language
Scalar	C/C++, Java
Aggregate	C/C++, Java
Window Aggregate	C/C++
Table	C/C++, Java

Figure 5.16

SCALAR FUNCTIONS

Scalar functions take input arguments and return a single value result. Some examples of standard SQL scalar functions are POSITION, CHARACTER_LENGTH, and SUBSTRING.

You can use a scalar function in place of a column name in an expression. When Teradata Database evaluates the expression, it invokes the scalar function. No context is retained after the function completes.

You can also use a scalar function to implement user-defined type (UDT) functionality such as cast, transform, or ordering.

AGGREGATE FUNCTIONS

Aggregate functions produce summary results. They differ from scalar functions in that they take grouped sets of relational data, make a pass over each group, and return one result for the group. Some examples of standard SQL aggregate functions are AVG, SUM, MAX, and MIN.

Teradata Database invokes an aggregate function once for each item in the group, passing the detail values of a group through the input arguments. To accumulate summary information, an aggregate function must retain context each time it is called.

You do not need to understand or worry about how to create a group, or how to code an aggregate UDF to deal with groups. Teradata Database automatically takes care of all of those difficult aspects. You only need to write the basic algorithm of combining the data passed in to produce the desired result.

WINDOW AGGREGATE FUNCTIONS (C/C++ only)

You can apply the ordered analytical window feature to a user-defined aggregate function.

Ordered analytical functions provide support for common operations in analytical processing that require an ordered set of rows or use the values from multiple rows in computing a new value.

The window feature provides a way to dynamically define a subset of data, or window, and allows the aggregate function to operate on that window of rows. Without a window specification, aggregate functions return one value for all qualified rows examined, but window aggregate functions return a new value for each of the qualifying rows participating in the query.

TABLE FUNCTIONS

A table function is invoked in the FROM clause of an SQL SELECT statement and returns a table one row at a time in a loop to the SELECT statement. The function can produce the rows of a table from the input arguments passed to it or by reading an external file or message queue.

The number of columns returned by a table function can be specified dynamically at runtime in the SELECT statement that invokes the table function.

Personally Identifiable Information (PII)

The escalation of security breaches involving personally identifiable information (PII) has contributed to the loss of millions of records over the past few years. Breaches involving PII are hazardous to both individuals and organizations. Individual harms may include identity theft, embarrassment, or blackmail. Organizational harms may include a loss of public trust, legal liability, or remediation costs. To appropriately protect the confidentiality of PII, organizations should use a risk-based approach.

Although the concept of PII is ancient, it has become much more important as information technology and the Internet have made it easier to collect PII, leading to a profitable market in collecting and reselling PII. PII can also be exploited by criminals to stalk or steal the

SECURITY

identity of a person, or to plan a person's murder or robbery, among other crimes. As a response to these threats, many website privacy policies specifically address the collection of PII, and lawmakers have enacted a series of legislation to limit the distribution and accessibility of PII.

(The preceding information is from "Guide to Protecting the Confidentiality of Personally Identifiable Information (PII)", published by the National Institute of Standards and Technology (NIST) of the U.S. Department of Commerce, and from Wikipedia, both of which are available on the web.)

Organizations should identify all PII residing in their environment.

An organization cannot properly protect PII it does not know about. The first step is to identify as many potential sources of PII as possible (e.g., databases, shared network drives, backup tapes, contractor sites). PII is —any information about an individual maintained by an agency, including:

1. any information that can be used to distinguish or trace an individual's identity, such as name, social security number, date and place of birth, mother's maiden name, or biometric records; and
2. any other information that is linked or linkable to an individual, such as medical, educational, financial, and employment information.

Examples of PII include, but are not limited to:

- Name, such as full name, maiden name, mother's maiden name, or alias
- Personal identification number, such as social security number (SSN), passport number, driver's license number,

taxpayer identification number, or financial account or credit card number
- Address information, such as street address or email address
- Personal characteristics, including photographic image (especially of face or other identifying characteristic), fingerprints, handwriting, or other biometric data (e.g., retina scan, voice signature, facial geometry)
- Information about an individual that is linked or linkable to one of the above (e.g., date of birth, place of birth, race, religion, weight, activities, geographical indicators, employment information, medical information, education information, financial information).

Organizations should minimize the use, collection, and retention of PII to what is strictly necessary to accomplish their business purpose and mission.

The likelihood of harm caused by a breach involving PII is greatly reduced if an organization minimizes the amount of PII it uses, collects, and stores. For example, an organization should only request PII in a new form if the PII is absolutely necessary. Also, an organization should regularly review its holdings of previously collected PII to determine whether the PII is still relevant and necessary for meeting the organization's business purpose and mission. For example, organizations could have an annual PII purging awareness day.

Organizations should categorize their PII by the PII confidentiality impact level.

All PII is not created equal. PII should be evaluated to determine its PII confidentiality impact level. This is different than the Federal Information Processing Standard (FIPS) Publication 1999 confidentiality impact level. Organizations should apply appropriate

SECURITY

safeguards to the PII. The PII confidentiality impact level—*low, moderate, or high*—indicates the potential harm that could result to the subject individuals and/or the organization if PII were inappropriately accessed, used, or disclosed. The FIPS Publication provides a list of factors an organization should consider when determining the PII confidentiality impact level. Each organization should decide which factors it will use for determining impact levels and then create and implement the appropriate policy, procedures, and controls.

Organizations should apply the appropriate safeguards for PII based on the PII confidentiality impact level.

Not all PII should be protected in the same way. Organizations should apply appropriate safeguards to protect the confidentiality of PII based on the PII confidentiality impact level. Some PII does not need to have its confidentiality protected, such as information that the organization has permission or authority to release publicly (e.g., an organization's public phone directory). NIST recommends using operational safeguards, privacy-specific safeguards, and security controls.

- **Creating Policies and Procedures.** Organizations should develop comprehensive policies and procedures for protecting the confidentiality of PII.
- **Conducting Training.** Organizations should reduce the possibility that PII will be accessed, used, or disclosed inappropriately by requiring that all individuals receive appropriate training before being granted access to systems containing PII.
- **De-Identifying PII.** Organizations can de-identify records by removing enough PII such that the remaining information does not identify an individual and there is no reasonable basis to believe that the information can be used to identify an individual. De-identified records can be used when full records

are not necessary, such as for examinations of correlations and trends.
- **Using Access Enforcement.** Organizations can control access to PII through access control policies and access enforcement mechanisms (e.g., access control lists).
- **Implementing Access Control for Mobile Devices.** Organizations can prohibit or strictly limit access to PII from portable and mobile devices, such as laptops, cell phones, and personal digital assistants (PDA), which are generally higher-risk than non-portable devices (e.g., desktop computers at the organization's facilities).
- **Providing Transmission Confidentiality.** Organizations can protect the confidentiality of transmitted PII. This is most often accomplished by encrypting the communications or by encrypting the information before it is transmitted.
- **Auditing Events.** Organizations can monitor events that affect the confidentiality of PII, such as inappropriate access to PII.

Organizations should develop an incident response plan to handle breaches involving PII.

Breaches involving PII are hazardous to both individuals and organizations. Harm to individuals and organizations can be contained and minimized through the development of effective incident response plans for breaches involving PII. Organizations should develop plans that include elements such as determining when and how individuals should be notified, how a breach should be reported, and whether to provide remedial services, such as credit monitoring, to affected individuals.

SECURITY

Organizations should encourage close coordination among their chief privacy officers, senior agency officials for privacy, chief information officers, chief information security officers, and legal counsel when addressing issues related to PII.

Protecting the confidentiality of PII requires knowledge of information systems, information security, privacy, and legal requirements. Decisions regarding the applicability of a particular law, regulation, or other mandate should be made in consultation with an organization's legal counsel and privacy officer because relevant laws, regulations, and other mandates are often complex and change over time. Additionally, new policies often require the implementation of technical security controls to enforce the policies. Close coordination of the relevant experts helps to prevent incidents that could result in the compromise and misuse of PII by ensuring proper interpretation and implementation of requirements.

Network Security

In addition to logon and password encryption mentioned earlier, users have the option of encrypting data transmitted between client and server. Although security provided by the encryption of transmitted data is desirable, you should not use this feature indiscriminately. Depending on the application you use and the type of session being run, encrypting data may significantly reduce system performance. Users should not encrypt a session unless the value of the security outweighs the potential performance losses. The security administrator should provide a clear policy statement to all database uses about when network encryption should or should not be used.

Access Monitoring

The session-related system views are available to monitor database access include:

- DBC.LogOnOff
- DBC.LogonRules
- DBC.QryLog
- DBC.SessionInfo
- DBC.Software_Event_Log

DBC.LogOnOff View

The DBC.LogOnOff view provides information about the success and duration of user sessions, in addition to Logon Source information. This view is helpful when you need to know about failed attempts to log on.

DBC.LogonRules View

Security administrators who have EXECUTE privilege on the DBC.LogonRule macro must specifically authorize a user to logon without a password. This is done with the SQL GRANT LOGON... WITH NULL PASSWORD statement.

The result of each successfully processed GRANT LOGON statement is stored as a row in DBC.LogonRuleTbl.

DBC.QryLog View

The Database Query Log (DBQL) is an optional feature that you can employ to log query processing activity for later analysis. Query counts and response times can be charted and SQL text and processing steps can be compared to fine-tune your applications for optimum performance.

SECURITY

Logging can be resource intensive and use up database space quickly. If you intend to regularly log queries, you must clean up the DBQL data on a regular basis. This means you will usually examine and send only the analyzed information to a user-defined table. Moving the data off DBC and storing it in a different database will help keep DBC from running out of space.

Note: Do *not* off-load data during peak busy times as this may block ongoing queries.

Enable Teradata Database access logging or query logging to provide an audit trail of database events that can be used to detect security violations.

Enabling access logging can help track necessary actions and changes for rollback or reassignment of privileges.

While access logging tells you when a user tried to access data objects, DBQL can log the actual SQL executed by a user. In addition, query logging provides better performance than access logging.

DBC.SessionInfo View

This view provides information about users who are currently logged on, including the session source (host connection, logon name, and application), query band, the current partition, collation, role, password status, type of transaction such as 2PC, LDAP status, and audit trail ID.

If you use a multi-tier client architecture, the LogonSource field of this view can provide distinct source identification as it originated from the server tier, including the user ID and application name.

Teradata 12 Enterprise Architecture

DBC.Software_Event_Log

This view contains system error messages for Teradata Database Field Engineers. Rows are inserted by the system in response to software error conditions.

The messages can also contain information about Teradata Database feature software. For example, execution of the Performance Monitor commands SET RESOURCE, SET SESSION, and ABORT SESSION are considered major system events and thus are logged to DBC.Software_Event_Log.

Query Bands

A query band is a set of name-value pairs assigned to a session or transaction that you can use to identify the originating source of a query. This is particularly useful for identifying specific users submitting queries from a middle-tier tool or application since these often use pooling mechanisms that hide the identity of the users when each connection in the pool logs in to the database using the same user account.

When you enable query logging, query band information is stored in the DBC.DBQLogTbl table. Use the DBC.QryLog view to access this table.

Views

ACCESS RIGHTS AND VIEWS

In order to create a view, the creator must have the CREATE VIEW privilege. In addition, the creator must have the appropriate privileges (such as SELECT, INSERT, UPDATE, DELETE, . . .) on the objects being accessed by the view.

SECURITY

To allow someone else to retrieve data through a view, that user must be granted SELECT on the view.

To allow someone else to update (INSERT, UPDATE, DELETE) through a view, grant that user UPDATE on the view. Be certain to include the WITH CHECK OPTION if the view contains a WHERE clause that should be enforced.

Using Nested Views

Views that reference other views are called nested views. Access to the underlying objects is as follows:

- Nested views are fully expanded (database and all underlying tables resolved) at creation time.
- Teradata Database validates the nested view privileges of the creator at creation time.
- Teradata Database validates nested view privileges of the immediate owner of the view at execution time.

Nested views are useful for protecting the data in the underlying base table. You can define the WHERE clause to restrict what data a user can view or access. The query must pass each restriction on each view in order to successfully execute.

Example of Nested View Privilege Checking

Figure 5.17 illustrates how privileges are checked when using nested views.

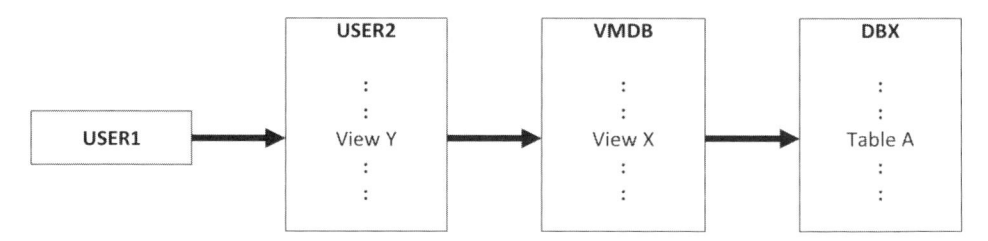

```
USER1  →  USER2     →  VMDB      →  DBX
          View Y       View X       Table A
```

Figure 5.17

- User 1 accesses View Y.
- User 2 is the immediate owner of View Y.
- Database VMDB owns View X.
- Database DBX is the immediate owner of Table A.

Privileges checked are:

- User 1 privileges on View Y.
- User 2 privileges on View X WITH GRANT OPTION. If User 2 is the same as User1, then the WITH GRANT OPTION is not needed.
- Database VMDB privileges on Table A WITH GRANT OPTION.

If you REVOKE an explicit privilege from any user in the chain, the system issues the following message:

```
3523 An owner referenced by the user does not have
[privilege] access to [databasename.tablename].
```

Dropping a column from a table invalidates all views that reference that column. A column added to a table will not be seen by any existing views. Dropping a view will invalidate any views which reference it.

Teradata 12 Enterprise Architecture

Practice Questions

If the following profile parameters are changed, identify when the change becomes active. There may be more than one correct match.

1. ____ Account ID	a. Immediately
2. ____ Default database	b. Next logon
3. ____ Password Attributes	c. SET SESSION
4. ____ SPOOL space	
5. ____ TEMPORARY space	

6. Which two password controls should not be set at the system level? (Choose 2)

    a. ExpirePassword
    b. LockedUserExpire
    c. MaxLogonAttempts
    d. PasswordDigits
    e. PasswordMaxChar
    f. PasswordMinChar
    g. PasswordRestrictedWords
    h. PasswordReuse
    i. PasswordSpecChar

SECURITY

7. Which of the following LOGON elements are <u>O</u>ptional and which are <u>R</u>equired?
   a. ___ tdpid/
   b. ___ userid
   c. ___ password
   d. ___ acctid

Match the following session-related views to their definition.

8. ___ DBC.Software_Event_Log	a. Database Query Log
9. ___ DBC.SessionInfo	b. EXEC privilege required to issue the SQL GRANT LOGON... WITH NULL PASSWORD statement
10. ___ DBC.QryLog	c. Information about the success and duration of user sessions
11. ___ DBC.LogonRules	d. Information about users who are currently logged on
12. ___ DBC.LogOnOff	e. System error messages for Teradata Database Field Engineers

Teradata 12 Enterprise Architecture

13. Which of the following UDF function types can be written using the Java programming language? (Choose 3)

    a. Aggregate
    b. Scalar
    c. Table
    d. Window Aggregate

SECURITY

Chapter Notes

Utilize this space for notes, key points to remember, diagrams, areas of further study, etc.

Chapter 6 - Workload Management

Certification Objectives

- ✓ Given a scenario, discuss how to use Teradata workload management to satisfy service level agreements.
- ✓ Given a scenario with a heavily loaded system, describe the process of balancing and reserving system resources.
- ✓ Given a scenario, identify the potential system and application availability characteristics including active data warehousing that can affect a database architecture.
- ✓ Given a scenario, determine the inputs necessary to establish a query management and workload policy.
- ✓ Determine options that are available to ensure that business critical reporting requirements are met.

Before You Begin

You should be familiar with the following terms and concepts.

Terms	Key Concepts
Workload	A class of queries
AWT	Amp Worker Task
Session	Established through a successful logon

Teradata Dynamic Workload Manager

Teradata DWM allows you to manage workloads through filtering, throttling, and prioritizing queries against rules you define, so that you can adjust behaviors under different system conditions and operational environments.

Teradata DWM can help avoid unusual situations that would otherwise require manual intervention. For example, you can employ certain rules and actions to take place when specific events occur or make the system dynamically adjust behaviors in the case of a specific event. You can create rules that allow high priority work to run while you throttle lower priority work to be delayed until the system can optimally manage it.

Teradata DWM can help you:

- Filter out queries based on restrictions such as resource limits or statement type. Queries that do not pass the rules can be rejected or can be executed with a warning.
- Control the flow of queries or utility sessions for concurrency and delay them if necessary.
- Classify queries into "workload definitions" where you specify classification criteria along with behaviors such as query limits, exceptions, and priority settings.
- Create global exceptions.
- Manage system conditions or operational environments. Define combinations of events that trigger a system condition. For example, you can define a normal, a degraded, and a problem system condition. The combination of current operational environment and a just-triggered system condition can result in a state change that changes workload management behaviors.

WORKLOAD MANAGEMENT

Teradata DWM Rule Categories

There are three categories of Teradata DWM rules. These rules are stored in the TDWM database. To make a rule effective, enable the rule and activate its corresponding Rule Sets category. The types of rules you can set are described in the following table.

Category Type	Description
Filter Rules	Restrict access to the system based on: • **Object Access**: Limit access to or from specific database objects. For example, set a rule to limit access to a certain table or from a certain user. • **Query Resource**: Permit or deny access to database resources based on things such as estimated row counts, processing time, joins, whether it causes a full table scan, and so on. Session and query requests that reference restricted objects are immediately rejected. For example, you can create a rule to ban UserA and UserB from issuing any requests. Or you could create a rule that prevents any DML by anyone on TableC. SQL queries from any supported Teradata Database interface (including, but not limited to, BTEQ, CLIv2, ODBC, JDBC) are validated against these user-defined rules stored in tables in the DBC.TDWM database. Queries that are rejected are logged in the TDWMExceptionLog table and DBQLogTbl if DBQL is enabled for that user. You can make filter rules global or just have them warn but not actually limit access. **Note:** Unless otherwise specified, Teradata DWM checks every query of every session. However,

Teradata 12 Enterprise Architecture

Category Type	Description
	users "DBC" and "TDWM" are always bypassed. You can set up other users to also bypass TDWM checking.
Throttle Rules	Throttle incoming work based on: • **Object Throttle**: Manage how many sessions and/or queries can concurrently run for specific database objects. • **Utilities Throttle**: Define how many utilities can run, either individually per type of utility or collectively for total number of utility jobs for the entire system. You can control if queries or **sessions are rejec**ted or delayed. **Note:** Values set in throttle rules for load utility concurrency override the DBS Control MaxLoadTasks value. Setting a rate through Teradata DWM rather than the DBS Control utility allows you to avoid having to change the DBS Control setting. You can specify limits for a mix of utilities. For example, you can define rules to allow only up to 3 FastLoad jobs, 2 ARC jobs, and 6 load jobs in total for the entire system. If there are any changes to the rules with respect to throttle values, the running queries are not subject to any new delay or abort directives.
Workload Definitions	Workload rules provide more complex management of queries. Within each workload, set criteria for: • Which queries to include (classification criteria) • Query limit • Priority Scheduler mappings (Workload Definition to Allocation Group) • Run-time exceptions

Category Type	Description
	• Service Level Goals (SLGs) for reporting and analysis
	The DBS classifies a query into a Workload Definition (WD). It takes the query attributes and puts the query into the correct WD based on the classification criteria. Classification criteria includes things like estimated processing time, estimated row count, statement type, query bands, user id, account name, application name and so on.
	Each WD is associated with an Allocation Group that is assigned to a Performance Group within a Resource Partition (Priority Scheduler groups). Throttle values and exception handling directives can also be placed on WDs. Exception handling directives allow a running query to be monitored and acted upon if conditions are met.
	You can define up to 36 different workload class definitions. Teradata provides four standard definitions (R, H, M, & L) plus a Default WD for query requests that do not fall into any of the other WDs.
	You can also create global exceptions that apply to multiple or all WDs or you can create multiple local exceptions that apply to only one WD. Exception directives allow a running query to be monitored and acted upon if conditions are met. Exception criteria includes things like CPU consumption thresholds, CPU to I/O ratio, skew, and so on.

Figure 6.1

Priority Scheduler

With Priority Scheduler, you can:

- Balance resource usage across different applications and utilities
- Authorize users for access to prioritized levels of service based on the PG, carried in the user account string
- Dynamically alter the PG of a user or (with profiles) user group
- Regulate access to AMP worker tasks (AWTs)
- Dynamically modify parameters that define your scheduling strategy, plus:
  - Record these parameters as profiles
  - Automatically change the profiles at scheduled times
- Set CPU usage limits at a variety of levels

The parameters available for defining your scheduling strategy include:

- A prioritized weighting system
- Methods for dynamically adjusting your strategy based on resource use or calendar schedule

These capabilities allow you to control your workload flow.

WORKLOAD MANAGEMENT

Priority Scheduler Architecture

Priority Scheduler consists of Resource Partitions, Resource Groups, and Allocation Groups, as shown in figure 6.2.

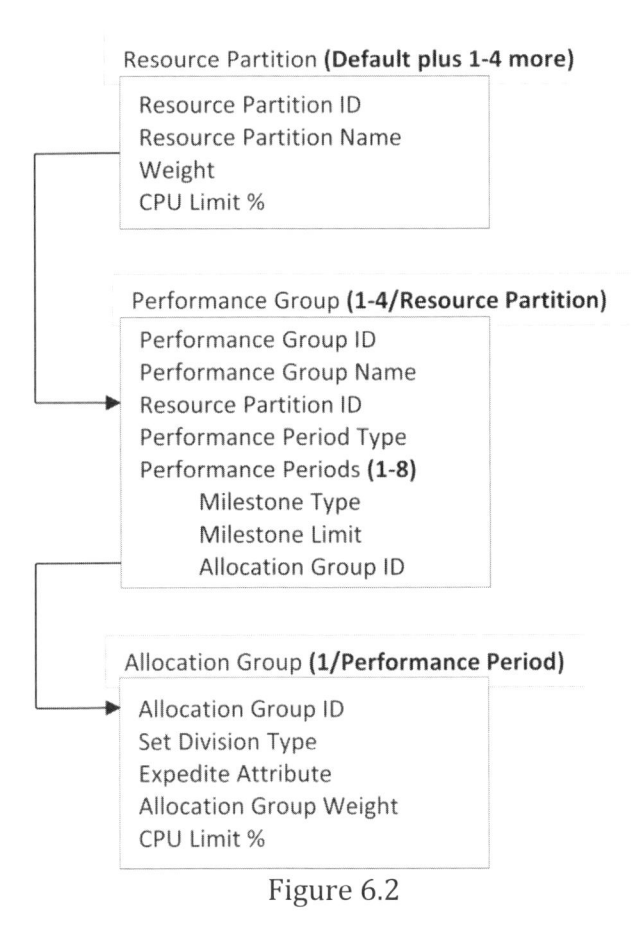

Resource Partition **(Default plus 1-4 more)**
- Resource Partition ID
- Resource Partition Name
- Weight
- CPU Limit %

Performance Group **(1-4/Resource Partition)**
- Performance Group ID
- Performance Group Name
- Resource Partition ID
- Performance Period Type
- Performance Periods **(1-8)**
    - Milestone Type
    - Milestone Limit
    - Allocation Group ID

Allocation Group **(1/Performance Period)**
- Allocation Group ID
- Set Division Type
- Expedite Attribute
- Allocation Group Weight
- CPU Limit %

Figure 6.2

Priority Scheduler with TDWM Workloads

If you have been using Priority Scheduler Administrator to manage resource utilization by database requests, Priority Definition (PD) sets are stored on your system. You can transfer these PD sets from

Teradata 12 Enterprise Architecture

Priority Scheduler Administrator and convert them to WD Sets for use with Teradata DWM.

A Workload Definition (WD) is a workload grouping and its operating rules to assist in managing queries. The requests that belong to the same workload will share the same resource priority and exception conditions. These conditions consist of the following:

- Classification Criteria: Criteria to determine which queries belong to the workload. This criteria defines characteristics which are detectable prior to query execution. This is also known as the *"who"*, *"where"*, and *"what"* criteria of a query. For example, *"who"* may be an account name, *"where"* is the database tables being accessed, and *"what"* may be the type of statement (INSERT) being executed.

- Exception Criteria: Criteria to specify "abnormal" behavior for queries in this workload. This criterion is only detectable after a query has begun execution. If an exception criterion is met, the request is subject to the specified exception action which may be to lower the priority or abort the query.

- Operating Periods: A description of hours of the day and/or days of the week (or month). Directives may be specified for exception handling and Priority Scheduler settings can be changed for each operating period.

The maximum workloads are 40, with 5 system workloads, leaving 35 available for user defined workloads, each with its own criteria for:

- Queries to include (classify)
- Throttle (concurrency) limit to use
- Priority Scheduler priority to use
- Run-time exception directives
- Service Level Goals (SLGs)

Resource Partitions and Performance Groups

WHAT IS A WEIGHT?

Every Teradata Database logon session is assigned to a Performance Group. Performance Groups control the prioritization of jobs started by sessions under their control. When a Performance Group is defined, it is assigned to a Resource Partition.

Weights are assigned at the Resource Partition level and to Allocation Groups within a Resource Partition. Weights are used at these levels to determine the relative proportion of resources to allocate to the user. Basically, weights are:

- A numeric value used at the Resource Partition Level to compute a relative weight (compared to other Resource Partitions) to determine the proportion of resources the processes of the entire Resource Partition are to receive.

- A numeric value used at the Allocation Group Level to compute a relative weight (within the Resource Partition) to determine the proportion of resources the processes of the Allocation Group is to receive.

Allocation Groups are also associated with Performance Groups. Like Resource Partitions, Allocation Groups have weights that determine the proportion of resources allocated relative to the other Allocation Groups that are active within the same Resource Partition.

EXAMPLE OF PRIORITY WEIGHTS

Let's assume there are four defined Resource Partitions, with individual weight assignments of R1 = 10, R2 = 20, R3 = 40, and R4 = 80. These weights mean nothing to Priority Scheduler unless more than one Resource Partition is active. If there are multiple active

Teradata 12 Enterprise Architecture

Resource Partitions, the weights are used to determine how much of the system's resources a given partition will receive compared to the other active partitions. The formula is very straight forward: Divide the weight of the active partition being measured by the sum of the weights of all of the active partitions. As an example, if R1 and R2 are active, their combined weights add up to 30. The means the R1 will receive 10/30 (.33, or 33%) of the system's resources, and R2 will receive 20/30 (.66 or 66%) of the system's resources. If partitions R2, R3, and R4 are active, the sum of their weights is 140. That means that the system's resource will be distributed across the three active partitions as R2 = 14% (20/140), R3 = 28% (40/140), and R4 = 57% (80/140). If only one Resource Partition is active, it gets 100% of the system's resources.

This same process is used to determine the percentage of resources Allocation Groups within a Resource Group can use. Let's assume the three Allocation Groups under R4, have assigned weights of U1 = 30, U2 = 60, and U3 = 90. If all of them are active, the amount of resources available to R4 will be distributed as U1 = 16% (30/180), U2 = 33% (60/180), and U3 = 50% (90/180).

WORKLOAD MANAGEMENT

When a user logs on, a PG's can be specified in the Account String during logon time, but it is not required. PGs do not link RPs and AGs. Queries will be assigned to a PG, either through specifying it in the account string, the default PG or the Milestone. The AG of the query step will be assigned to is based on the Performance Period(s) defined.

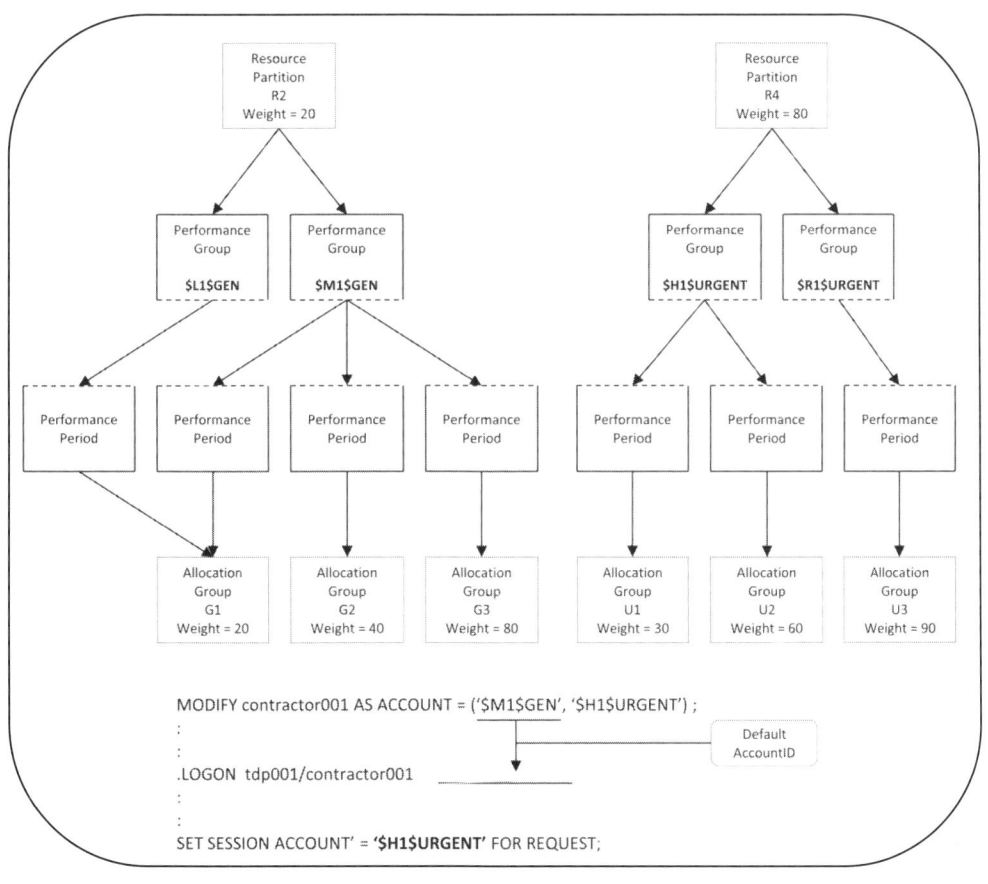

Figure 6.3

Referring to the example illustrated in Figure 6.3, only Resource Partitions R2 and R4 are active at the moment, and the Allocation Groups shown are active. When *contractor001* logged on, the default

Teradata 12 Enterprise Architecture

AccountID put the user in Performance group $M1$GEN. Presently, R2 can use 20% of the system's resources, and R4 can use 80%. Since all three Allocation Groups are active, G1 can use 14% of R2's 20%, G2 and use 28%, and G3 can use 57%. To determine the relative weight of a Performance Group (what percentage of the total system's resources a Performance Group can use), the system simply has to multiply the Resource Partition's active weight against the Allocation Group' active weight. The rules defined for the individual Performance Groups will determine which Allocation Group will service *contractor001*'s requests. Based upon parameters, like time-of-day, contractor001's requests may dynamically switch Allocation Groups. Assuming that all three Allocation Groups remain active, here are the relative Performance Group weights for $M1$GEN depending upon which Allocation Group is used.

G1 = 20/(20+80) * 20/(20+40+80) = .2 * .14 = 2%
G2 = 20/(20+80) * 40/(20+40+80) = .2 * .28 = 5%
G3 = 20/(20+80) * 80/(20+40+80) = .2 * .57 = 11%

When *contractor001* switches AccountIDs, the next request will be processed by U1 or U2. At the present time, if all three Allocation Groups under R4 are active, the relative Performance Group weight for $H1$URGENT can vary across the two Allocation groups.

U1 = 80/(20+80) * 30/(30+60+90) = .8 * .16 = 12%
U2 = 80/(20+80) * 60/(30+60+90) = .8 * .33 = 26%

PERFORMANCE PERIODS

As shown earlier, each Performance Period defines a Milestone and an Allocation Group. A Milestone is made up of a Milestone Type and a Milestone Limit. Figure 6.4 Illustrates their content.

Component	Definition
Milestone Type	The type of threshold used to define each Performance Period for a Performance Group. You can express types in the following units: • Time-of-day (T) • Session resource usage (S or R) • Query resource usage (Q)
Milestone Limit	The value of the threshold used to change Performance Periods for a Performance Group. You can express this value in the following units: • A valid time-of-day, such as 0800 for 8:00 a.m. • A number of seconds of CPU usage.
Allocation Group	The number of the Allocation Group used to control sessions during this Performance Period.

Figure 6.4

All Performance Periods within a Performance Group must use the Milestone Type.

When the threshold for the Performance Period is exceeded, the session is transferred to the next Performance Period, and the processes belonging to that session are placed under the control of a different Allocation Group. Typically, the change is to a lower-priority

Allocation Group. Consequently, access to resources will be progressively reduced for longer-running sessions. This is expressed in seconds to hundredths of a second, representing an amount of session CPU resource consumption per node.

Note: The compare and adjust concept monitors resource consumption and will modify queries that exceed threshold and that have been established by the workload parameters.

Time-of-day Performance Periods monitor the clock time, and optionally the day of the week. This is expressed in military time, representing time periods during a 24-hour day. For example, 0800 is 8:00 A.M. These types of Performance Periods are used to dynamically switch the Allocation Group of a session based on changes in business priority of different work at different times of day. For example, a session can be switched to a higher-priority Allocation Group after business hours or on weekends, when competition for database resources is not high.

CPU USAGE LIMITS WITH PRIORITY SCHEDULER

Priority Scheduler uses Milestones and CPU limits to manage CPU usage.

Milestones (either Query or Session) monitors CPU consumption for each query step and moves the query to another AG once the threshold is met. Milestones are time-based, you can limit a Resource Partition to a specified percentage of CPU resource usage.

CPU limits restrict CPU consumption on the system. This limit has no effect on the scheduling strategy defined by other Priority Scheduler parameters. The relative weights of Allocation Groups and Resource Partitions are observed. The normal distribution of resources prevails within the specified amount of CPU usage.

Note: You can also limit the percentage of total CPU usage by sessions controlled by an Allocation Group. The Milestone Limit of CPU usage is defined in seconds or fractions of seconds.

Schmon Utility

The schmon utility provides a command line interface that allows you to display and alter Priority Scheduler parameters.

Schmon runs on the following platforms and interfaces:

Platform	Interface
MP-RAS	Command line Database Window **Note:** On MP-RAS, Priority Scheduler includes an X11-based graphical user interface, xschmon.
Windows	Command line ("Teradata Command Prompt") Database Window
Linux	Command line Database Window

Figure 6.5

If Workload Definitions have been activated using Teradata Dynamic Workload Manager, schmon and xschmon cannot be used to make changes to Priority Scheduler.

The Teradata Priority Scheduler Administrator (Teradata PSA) is a resource management tool that provides an easy-to-use graphical

Teradata 12 Enterprise Architecture

interface to define Priority Definition Sets and generate schmon scripts to implement these sets. PSA is part of Teradata Manager.

Teradata Workload Analyzer

The workload analysis process consists of the following steps:

1. The user may optionally migrate existing priority scheduler definitions (PDSets created in PSA), to automatically create workload definitions with the same priority scheduler settings as currently exist. If users choose not to migrate existing settings, they can instead choose to be guided to define workload definitions from scratch. In doing so, users first collect query log information for the existing workload mix. Then they specify the dimensions to analyze and group queries against to form candidate workloads (account-based, application-based, and existing PDSets) and the date and time range to analyze for analysis of the previously collected query log data.
2. Using this input, Teradata WA recommends candidate workload definitions based on analysis of Priority Scheduler Facility settings and/or Database Query Log data.
3. With the DBQL analysis path, the user can further refine the candidate workload definition and the queries in which it contains by either merging with another candidate workload or splitting the candidate workload into two or more separate candidate workloads to aid with accounting granularity or workload control. (For example, tactical queries need higher priority and therefore should be split out from the "parent" candidate workload.) Next, users creating workload definitions from scratch (not for users migrating from existing PSF settings) are guided through mapping workload definitions to PSF allocation groups and allocation group weights. Those settings are guided to minimize necessary DBA involvement, though the DBA has the "advanced" option to refine those settings according to the administrator's preference.

4. After the user has satisfactorily fine-tuned the candidate workload definition, the user sets service-level goals, optionally guided by Teradata WA. For example, the user might request recommendations based on actual response times achieved at a particular service-level percent, or other factors.

Teradata WA performs analysis using three fundamental criteria, with each representing a greater level of granularity:

- "Who" is requesting the work?
- "What" are the request's performance characteristics?
- "Where" is the request targeted?

"Who" is the account or application that initiated the queries, "what" are performance related characteristics of the queries, and "where" is the database against which the queries run. Based on these criteria, some obvious associations can be made between similar queries in order to assign them to the same workloads for the sake of efficiency. However, for best results, look next at the query components and characteristics at finer levels of detail, to ensure they are appropriately for greatest optimization.

The data Teradata WA uses to tune workloads for management according to criteria and granularity level is described in the following table.

Granularity Level	Type of Criteria	Includes
Low	Who	- Account - Account String - Application - Client IP Address - Client ID for logon - Profile - Username

Granularity Level	Type of Criteria	Includes
Medium	Who, What	The Who criteria plus: • Type of statement (SELECT, DDL, or DML), individually or in combination • Load utilities in use if any (FastExport, FastLoad, or MultiLoad) • AMP usage (one or a few at most) • Minimum and maximum estimated row counts, including final row counts • Minimum and maximum estimated CPU time
High	Who, What, Where	The Who and What criteria plus: • Databases • Tables • Views • Macros • Stored Procedures

Figure 6.6

Teradata Query Scheduler

Teradata QS consists of client and server system components, and a separate database within your Teradata Database called **tdwm**.

Teradata QS provides a database request scheduling service. Queries can be scheduled through client applications such as the Scheduled Request Viewer and Teradata SQL Assistant. The Teradata QS Server is a back end process that accepts new requests, executes scheduled requests at specified times, and returns request information and status to the clients.

Scheduled requests are SQL queries submitted to a Teradata Database that become scheduled for off-line execution. You can schedule requests in two ways:

- Using the **Teradata Query Scheduler Submit Request** dialog box
- Using Teradata SQL Assistant

When you know of existing database rules that will prevent your SQL request from running or if you suspect that your queries will overload your database, you can proactively schedule your request using the **Teradata Query Scheduler Submit Request** dialog box.

When you schedule a request, you provide information that defines preferences for when it is executed. You can schedule a request to run periodically or only once during a specified time period without an active user connection to the Teradata Database.

However, scheduling a request does not guarantee that it is executed at the date and time you specify. Your scheduled requests are subject to the same Teradata Database workload management rule checking as are interactive requests.

In addition, an execution time frame must be available during the time you specified to execute the request.

Note: The **tdwm** database is shared by Teradata DWM (Teradata Dynamic Workload Manager). However, Teradata QS maintains its own tables within the **tdwm** database.

Teradata Query Director

Teradata Query Director (Teradata QD) is a session-routing tool that allows administrators to make full use of primary and standby systems by routing sessions between two or more systems while maintaining full backup status.

Teradata QD sits between the client application and two or more Teradata Database systems and routes sessions using rules set by the administrator. The routing methods are used to spread workloads evenly among systems and to failover from one system to another if a database goes down. Teradata QD also performs a failover on user-defined Teradata Database errors.

Teradata QD is a command line application (or can be run as a Windows service) that is configured at start up. Teradata QD uses command line parameters (or the parameter file if running as a service), routing configuration file, and error code files to make routing decisions.

WORKLOAD MANAGEMENT

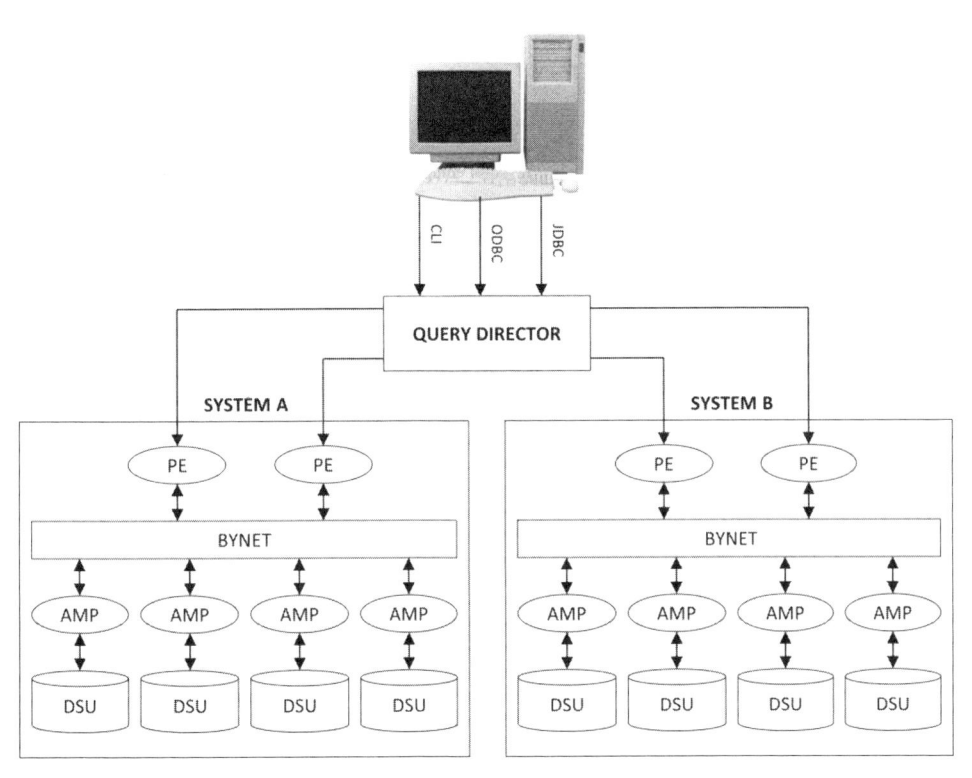

Figure 6.7 shows an overview of Teradata QD.

Figure 6.7

Teradata QD sits between the client and the Teradata Database systems and listens for sessions to be started. When a session is initiated, Teradata QD uses a routing algorithm and a routing configuration file to decide which system the session should be routed to. The process is transparent to the client.

Sessions are routed using the startup parameters and an optional routing file. The routing file, created by an administrator, links specific *userid* and account strings to specific system(s).

The parameters give Teradata QD a set of routing algorithms that help balance session loads.

The routing algorithms are designed to give the administrator the ability to take advantage of the type of systems and client applications and maximize the efficiency of all the equipment.

Teradata QD also performs a failover from one system to another system using routing rules and the error codes files. These files are created by the administrator before starting Teradata QD.

Teradata Manager

Teradata Manager collects, analyzes, and displays database performance and utilization information in either report or graphic format, displaying it all on a Windows PC.

The client-server feature in Teradata Manager replicates performance data on the server for access by any number of clients. Because data is collected once, workload on the database remains constant while the number of client applications varies.

Teradata Manager allows the DBA to do the following:

- Set up an SNMP (Simple Network Management Protocol) agent that allows third party management applications to monitor Teradata system performance and to be notified of exceptions using SNMP traps.
- Monitor overall system utilization in real time.
- Monitor jobs that are in the delay queue.
- Monitor real-time and historical workload statistics.
- Analyze workload usage through time.
- Get a historical view of how your system is being utilized.
- Monitor space usage and move space from place to place.
- Analyze the maximum and average usage for Logical Devices (LDVs), AMP vprocs, nodes, and PE vprocs on your system.
- Check the results of privilege checks.

WORKLOAD MANAGEMENT

- Schedule system priorities.
- Set up alert actions to generate notifications of, and actively respond to, Teradata Database events.
- Investigate the various system administration options available with your Teradata Manager software.
- Schedule activities on your system.
- Set up an ActiveX (COM) object that exposes methods to allow retrieval of PMPC data.
- Use the various Teradata Manager applications.

The various applications provided by Teradata Manager are:

- Alert Policy Editor
- Alert Viewer
- BTEQ Window
- Configuration Check
- Error Log Analyzer
- Locking Logger
- LogOnOff Usage
- Database Setup
- Priority Scheduler Administrator
- Remote Console
- Session Information
- Statistics Collection
- Teradata Performance Monitor

The Teradata Manager Dashboard provides a single tabbed page view of current performance and workload information, as well as recent trends. This is accomplished by showing real-time gauges and graphs displaying:

- Virtual and physical CPU utilization
- Requests-per-minute
- I/O-per-request

- Response time
- Sessions (idle, active, blocked, responding, Parsing, aborting, details, and prolonged idles)
- Recent history graphs showing trends and providing analytic data
- Workload snapshots and history

All this enables rapid problem resolution to drill down quickly to the most useful detailed information.

Practice Questions

Match the facility with its definition.

1. ___ Dynamic Workload Manager	a. Balance resource usage across different applications and utilities
2. ___ Priority Scheduler	b. Collects, analyzes, and displays database performance and utilization information
3. ___ Query Director	c. Manage workloads through filtering, throttling, and prioritizing queries
4. ___ Query Scheduler	d. Provides a database request scheduling service
5. ___ Teradata Manager	e. Recommends candidate workload definitions
6. ___ Workload Analyzer	f. Session routing

Teradata 12 Enterprise Architecture

7. Which of the following criteria does Workload Analyzer consider a LOW granularity level?

    a. Tables
    b. CPU time
    c. Load utilities in use
    d. Account string
    e. Row counts

Use the following information to answer questions 8, 9, and 10.

GIVEN: Four Resource Partitions with individual weight assignments of R1 = 10, R2 = 20, R3 = 40, R4= 80, and four Allocation Groups under R3 with individual weight assignments of U1 = 10, U2 = 20, U3 = 40, U4 = 80.

8. If R3 and U1 are currently active, U1 will get ____ of the system's resources.
    a. 25%
    b. 35%
    c. 50%
    d. 100%

9. If R1 and R3 are currently active, and U1 and U3 are currently active, U3 is getting _____ of R3's resources.
    a. 10%
    b. 20%
    c. 40%
    d. 80%

Teradata 12 Certification Study Guide

WORKLOAD MANAGEMENT

10. If R2 and R3 are currently active, and U3 and U4 are currently active, U4 is getting _____ of the system's resources.
    a. 12%
    b. 21%
    c. 37%
    d. 54%

11. The maximum number of Performance Periods within a Performance Group is _____.
    a. 2
    b. 4
    c. 6
    d. 8
    e. 16

12. What is the maximum number of workload class definitions you can define?
    a. 2
    b. 4
    c. 8
    d. 16
    e. 32
    f. 64

Chapter Notes

Utilize this space for notes, key points to remember, diagrams, areas of further study, etc.

Chapter 7 - Application Deployment

Certification Objectives

- Given a scenario, determine how to create a test environment.
- Given a scenario, determine which capacity factors to consider prior to promoting an application into production.
- Given a data integration scenario, determine which application requirements are needed to configure an overall database architecture.

Before You Begin

You should be familiar with the following terms and concepts.

Terms	Key Concepts
Perm, Spool, Temp	Space allocation limits.
Cylinders, Blocks	Disk allocation units
Transient Journal	Before-change images
Heartbeat Queries	Measuring response times

Test Environments

The Target Level Emulation facility permits you to emulate a target (production environment) system by capturing system-level environmental cost information, table-level random AMP sample statistics, and Optimizer-relevant DBSControl information from that environment and storing it in the relational tables:

SystemFE.Opt_Cost_Table,
SystemFE.Opt_RAS_Table, and
SystemFE.Opt_DBSCtl_Table.

You can then use the information from these tables together with appropriate column and index statistics to make the Optimizer on the test system generate query plans as if it were operating in the target environment rather than the test environment.

This feature produces a query plan for the emulated target system: it does *not* emulate the performance of that system.

This feature offers the following benefits to a DBA:

- Models the impact of various environmental changes and DBSControl parameter settings on SQL request performance.
- Provides an environment for determining the source of various Optimizer-based production database query problems using environmental cost data and random AMP sample-based statistical data.

There are two forms of target level emulation: cost-based and random AMP sample-based. The two forms can be changed independently, but are definitely *not* mutually exclusive: they are meant to be used together as a tool for the precise analysis of production system query generated on much smaller test systems.

Environmental cost parameters are constant across a system configuration because there is only one set of environmental cost values per system. Table statistics, on the other hand, are different for each base table and do not vary as a function of system configuration. For example, the cardinality of a given table is the same whether that table is on a two AMP system or a 100 AMP system; however, environmental costs vary considerably as a function of system configuration.

These differences account for the sometimes dissimilar syntax of analogous SQL DIAGNOSTIC statements for handling cost and random AMP statistical information.

Cost-based target level emulation has two possible forms: static and dynamic.

- Static emulation refers to setting environmental cost parameters at the SYSTEM level. Once set, the cost parameters persist across system restarts and reboots.
- Dynamic emulation refers to setting environmental cost parameters at the IFP, REQUEST, or SESSION levels.

When you first set cost parameters, they are read dynamically from *SystemFE.Opt_Cost_Table* and copied to a memory-resident data structure. The Optimizer then initializes its cost parameters from this memory-resident structure dynamically.

The advantage of dynamic target level emulation is that multiple users in multiple sessions can simultaneously emulate environmental cost parameters from multiple target systems on the same test system.

Random AMP sample-based target level emulation permits you to generate random AMP statistical samples on a production system and then export the captured data to a test system for detailed query analysis.

Teradata 12 Enterprise Architecture

The target level emulation feature is closely related to other Teradata Database support tools, particularly those detailed in the following list:

- CHECK STATISTICS option of the INSERT EXPLAIN and DUMP EXPLAIN statements.
- Query Capture Facility.
- Statistics Collection tool (Teradata Manager).
- Teradata Index Wizard.
- Teradata Statistics Wizard.
- Teradata System Emulation Tool (TSET).
- Visual Explain Tool.

Capturing Authoritative Data

TERADATA PARALLEL TRANSPORTER (TPT)

Teradata Parallel Transporter is a new client software product that uses a single script language to accomplish tasks that were done using the traditional ('standalone') utilities of FastLoad, MultiLoad, FastExport, and TPump. Jobs are run using 'producer' operators and 'consumer' operators which define the type of task (load or unload) to be performed.

Though source data may come from a variety of inputs, including any ODBC database, data files or devices, the target for the load operators must always be the Teradata database.

TPT can be invoked via a script, or it can be activated by an API (Application Program Interface). There is also a GUI-based TPT Wizard which can be used for script generation.

APPLICATION DEPLOYMENT

Utility Limits

The setting of two control fields, *MaxLoadTasks* and *MaxLoadAWT*, affect how many utilities can run concurrently.

The MaxLoadTasks field specifies the combined number of FastLoad, MultiLoad, and FastExport tasks (jobs), and their TPT counterparts, that are allowed to run concurrently on a Teradata system.

Throttle rules for load utility concurrency set by Teradata Dynamic Workload Manager override the MaxLoadTasks setting.

AMP Worker Tasks (AWTs) are processes (threads on some platforms) dedicated to servicing the Teradata Database work requests. A fixed number of AWTs are pre-allocated during Teradata Database system initialization for each AMP vproc. Each AWT looks for a work request to arrive in the Teradata Database system, services the request, and then looks for another. An AWT can process requests of any work type.

The number of AWTs required by FastLoad and MultiLoad will change as their jobs run. More AWTs are required in the early phases of the jobs than in the later phases. Teradata Database dynamically calculates the total AWTs required by active jobs, and allows more jobs to start as AWTs become available.

Figure 7.1 shows the different number of required AWTs at different phases of execution for FastLoad and MultiLoad.

Load Utility Phase	Number of AWTs Required
FastLoad: Loading	3
FastLoad: End Loading	1
MultiLoad: Acquisition	2
MultiLoad: Application	1 per target table

Figure 7.1

Teradata 12 Enterprise Architecture

If MaxLoadAWT is greater than zero, new FastLoad and MultiLoad jobs are rejected when the MaxLoadAWT limit is reached, regardless of the MaxLoadTasks setting. Therefore, FastLoad and MultiLoad jobs may be rejected before MaxLoadTasks limit is reached.

Here is how the MaxLoadTasks field works together with the MaxLoadAWT field.

If MaxLoadAWT is zero (the default):

- MaxLoadTasks can be an integer from zero through 15.
- The MaxLoadTasks field specifies the maximum number of combined FastLoad, MultiLoad, and FastExport jobs that can run concurrently.
- The system does not consider the number of available AWTs when limiting the number of load utilities that can run concurrently.

If MaxLoadAWT is greater than zero:

- MaxLoadTasks is an integer from zero through 30.
- The MaxLoadTasks field sets the maximum number of combined FastLoad and MultiLoad jobs that can run concurrently. MaxLoadTasks does not directly limit the number of FastExport jobs that can run.
- The number of combined FastLoad and MultiLoad jobs that can run concurrently is limited by the values of both the MaxLoadTasks field and the MaxLoadAWT field. When either limit is met, no further FastLoad or MultiLoad jobs are allowed to start until the limiting factor is reduced.
- The maximum number of load utility jobs of any type—FastLoad, MultiLoad, or FastExport—that can run concurrently is 60. Consequently, the number of FastExport jobs allowed to run at any time is 60 minus the number of combined FastLoad and MultiLoad jobs that are running.

- If MaxLoadAWT is set to anything greater than zero, it can only be reset to zero if MaxLoadTasks is 15 or less.

Estimating Space Requirements

If the tables and indexes required by the application exist, then estimating Spool usage and/or Transient Journal usage are the only things remaining to estimate (see the following Production System Impact section).

If a table used by the application doesn't exist, then the following steps need to be taken:

1. Calculate the physical row size by using the 32-bit or 64-bit Row Size Calculation Form. Using the estimated row count from the Table form, calculate the number of base table data blocks using the following formulas.

    Maximum block size = 64 KB (127 sectors) = 127 * 512 = 65,024

    Typical block size = MAX/2 + 512

    32-bit systems
    Rows per block (rounded down) = (Typical block size – 38)/Row size

    64-bit systems
    Rows per block (rounded down) = (Typical block size – 66)/Row size

    Number of blocks (rounded up) = Row count/Rows per block

2. Use the next formula to allow space for a table header row on every AMP.
Number of header bytes = (Number of AMPs)*(Header row size))

3. The next formula will yield the estimated space for the base table.

Number of base table bytes (without fallback) = (Number of blocks * Typical block size) + Number of header bytes

Number of base table bytes (with fallback) = 2 * (Number of base table bytes (without fallback)) - Number of header bytes

4. Use the next formula to calculate the amount space for any USI. The formula is the same for 32-bit and 64-bit systems.

NPPI USI subtable size = ((Row Count) × (Index Value Size + 29))
PPI USI subtable size = ((Row Count) × (Index Value Size + 31))

If fallback is defined for the base table, then double the calculated result.

The system implicitly creates a unique secondary index on any column set specified as PRIMARY KEY or UNIQUE, so you must take these indexes into consideration for your capacity planning as well.

5. The next formula applies to any NUSIs the table has.

APPLICATION DEPLOYMENT

The number of AMPs in the configuration is an important factor in estimating the total size of any NUSIs defined on a base table, as summarized in the following table.

IF the number of AMPs is...	THEN at least...	AND the result is that...
less than the number of rows per value	one row from each NUSI value is probably distributed to each AMP.	• Every AMP has every value. • Every AMP has a subtable row for every value.
greater than the number of rows per value	some AMPs are missing some NUSI values.	• Not every AMP has every value. • Not every AMP has a subtable row for every value.

Figure 7.2

The following parameter definitions are used with this equation:

Parameter	Definition
Cardinality * 8 Cardinality * 10	Each base table RowID is stored in a NUSI subtable. {| FOR this type of base table..	THEN RowID is this long... | |---|---| | NPPI | 8 bytes | | PPI | 10 bytes |} This means that you must use the Cardinality * 8 factor for NUSI subtable for NPPI base tables and the Cardinality * 10 factor for NUSI subtable for PPI base tables.
NumDistinct	The value is an estimate of the number of distinct NUSI subtable values and is based on each NUSI

Teradata 12 Enterprise Architecture

Parameter	Definition
	subtable having at least one index row per AMP for each distinct index value of a base table row stored on that AMP.
IndexValueSize	The number of index data bytes.
NUSI Block Overhead	Sum of the following factors. • Block headers and trailers • Row headers and trailers • NUSI row RowID • Spare byte • Presence octets = 21 bytes
MIN(NumAmps Row per value)	The lesser of the two parameters.

Figure 7.3

If fallback is defined for the base table, then double the calculated result.

NUSI Sizing Equation for NPPI Base Table

NUSI subtable size = 8(Cardinality) + ((NumDistinct) * (IndexValueSize + 21)) * MIN(NumAMPs | Rows per value)))

NUSI Sizing Equation for PPI Base Table

NUSI subtable size = 10(Cardinality) + ((NumDistinct) * (IndexValueSize + 21)) * MIN(NumAMPs | Rows per value)))

6. You must also allow space for Reference indexes.

A Reference Index is an internal structure that the system creates whenever a referential integrity constraint is defined between tables using a PRIMARY KEY or UNIQUE constraint on the parent

APPLICATION DEPLOYMENT

table in the relationship and a REFERENCES constraint on a foreign key in the child table.

The index subtable row contains a count of the number of references in the child, or foreign key, table to the PRIMARY KEY or UNIQUE constraint in the parent table.

A maximum of 64 referential constraints can be defined for a table.

Similarly, a maximum of 64 *other* tables can reference a *single* table. Therefore, there is a maximum of 128 Reference Indexes that can be stored *in the table header* per table.

The limit on Reference Indexes in the table header includes both references to and from the table and is derived from 64 references to other tables plus 64 references from other tables to the current table = 128 Reference Index descriptors.

However, the maximum number of Reference Indexes stored in the Reference Index subtable for a table is limited to 64, defining only the relationships between the tables as a parent with its child tables.

Reference Index Sizing Equation

The following parameter definitions are used with this equation:

Parameter	Definition
Row count * 4	A count of the number of foreign key row references is stored in a Reference Index subtable. Each foreign key row count is 4 bytes long.
FKLength	The length of a fixed length foreign key value in bytes. Use one of these parameters depending on the

Parameter	Definition
	Reference Index in question: <table><tr><th>IF the FK field value is...</th><th>THEN use this parameter...</th></tr><tr><td>fixed</td><td>length of the value</td></tr><tr><td>variable</td><td>average length of the variable length Foreign Key values</td></tr></table>
NumDistinct	The value is an estimate of the number of distinct foreign key subtable values. Exclude null foreign keys from this estimate.
Presence Overhead	Use the following equation to calculate this parameter: Overhead = (1 + Number nullable FK fields)/8 If there are no variable length foreign keys, then the value for this parameter is 0.
RI Block Overhead	Sum of the following factors. • Row length • RI row RowID • Spare byte • Presence octets • Offsets • Valid flag • Foreign key count • Reference array = 25 bytes

Figure 7.4

RI Subtable Size = (NumDistinct) × (FKLength + PresenceOverhead + VarLengthOverhead+ 25)

Note: If fallback is defined for the child table in the relationship, then double the calculated result.

Production System Impact

There are three areas of space use that also need to be considered in launching new applications, Spool, Transient Journal, and Temporary space.

ESTIMATING SPOOL SPACE REQUIREMENTS

Spool, or temporary space, is frequently overlooked in capacity planning, yet it is critical to the operations of the database. Spool space needs vary from table to table, application to application, and with frequency of use. Very large systems use even more spool than smaller systems.

Spool falls into three categories:

- Intermediate
- Output
- Volatile

Intermediate Spool Space

Intermediate spool results are retained until no longer needed. You can determine when intermediate spool is flushed by examining the output of an EXPLAIN. The first step performed after intermediate spool has been flushed is designated "Last Use."

Output Spool Space

Output spool results are the final information returned for a query or the rows updated within, inserted into, or deleted from a base table. The length of time output spool is retained depends on the subsystem and various system conditions, as described in the following table:

Subsystem/Condition	When Output Spool Is Released
BTEQ	Last spool response
Embedded SQL	The open cursor is closed
CLIv2	• ERQ received • Function terminated
Session terminates asynchronously due to any number of conditions, including the following. • Job abort • Timeout • Logoff	At the time the termination occurs.
System restart	At the time the restart occurs.

Figure 7.5

Volatile Spool Space

The system uses volatile spool space for volatile tables. This is necessary because volatile tables do not have a persistent stored definition. Volatile spool space is released with either a drop table statement or the end of the session.

Sources of Spool Space

Spool space is taken only from disk cylinders that are not being used for data. Data blocks and spool blocks cannot coexist on the same cylinder. When spool is released, the file system returns the cylinders it was using to the free cylinder list.

Spool Limits

The amount of spool space allocated to each user and database is assigned at CREATE USER or CREATE DATABASE time. Only users consume spool space, but their spool limit cannot exceed the limit of their immediate owner which may be a database or another user.

If you find that queries do not run because they run out of spool space, then investigate the reasons the query ran out of spool. First try to eliminate the issue through optimization techniques. If nothing else works, increase the spool assignment for the user or database having the problem using the MODIFY USER or MODIFY DATABASE statements.

Guidelines for Setting Spool Space Limits

Unless you reserve a pool of spool space, available space tends to disappear quickly. When applications consume all the spool space allocated for a system, processing will halt.

Here is a guideline for setting spool space limits:

1. Create a special database to act as a spool space reservoir. Allocate a percentage, variable depending on system size, of the total space in the system for this database.
2. Set each users upper limit to ensure that they receive at least as much space as the size of the largest tables they access concurrently.

ESTIMATING TRANSIENT JOURNAL SPACE REQUIREMENTS

The Teradata Database creates and manages a transient journal to store the before-change image of every data row involved in every SQL transaction.

The transient journal is used to recover data tables when transactions are aborted. As transactions are processed, the transient journal grows and shrinks. While transactions are in progress, the transient journal grows according to the total number of data rows being updated or deleted.

Teradata 12 Enterprise Architecture

The applicable journal rows are purged at intervals (but not before the transaction is completed or, if it was aborted, not before the affected rows are recovered).

Space for the transient journal is acquired from the current PERM space of user *DBC*. Therefore, it is important that you leave enough PERM space in *DBC* to accommodate the growth of the largest foreseeable transient journal.

To estimate the maximum size of the transient journal, follow this procedure:

1. Determine the length of the longest row in your production database. Use this figure as your maximum row length.
2. Multiply the maximum row length by the total number of rows in your application programs, batch jobs, and ad-hoc queries that users are likely to update and delete in *concurrent* transactions.

Transient Journal Data Block Size

When you know the maximum row length, double the value to calculate the size of your multirow data block definition in the JournalDBSize field of the DBSControl Record. For example, the JournalDBSize should be greater or equal to two times the maximum row length.

Note: The file system allocates any row that exceeds the current size of a multirow data block to a transient journal data block of its own.

USER TEMP SPACE REQUIREMENTS

The TEMPORARY clause in the CREATE DATABASE statement permits you to allocate default space for creating global temporary tables by users within this database. Note that Teradata Database always reserves temporary space *prior* to spool space for any user defined

APPLICATION DEPLOYMENT

with this attribute. Disk usage for a materialized global temporary table is charged against the temporary space allocation of the user who referenced the table.

If no default temporary space is defined for a database, then the space allocated for any global temporary tables created in that database is set to the maximum temporary space allocated for its immediate owner.

Note: Subtract the TEMP amount allocated to this database.

Measuring Changes

Views for Space Allocation Reporting

The following views will provide information of space utilization. You should be tracking space usage over time.

DBC.TableSize[X]

Vproc	AccountName	CurrentPerm
DatabaseName	TableName	PeakPerm

Figure 7.6

DBC.AllSpace[X]

Vproc	MaxSpool	PeakPerm
DatabaseName	MaxTemp	PeakSpool
AccountName	CurrentPerm	PeakTemp
TableName	CurrentSpool	MaxProfileSpool
MaxPerm	CurrentTemp	MaxProfileTemp

Figure 7.7

DBC.DiskSpace [V] [X]

Vproc	MaxTemp	PeakSpool
DatabaseName	CurrentPerm	PeakTemp
AccountName	CurrentSpool	MaxProfileSpool
MaxPerm	CurrentTemp	MaxProfileTemp
MaxSpool	PeakPerm	

Figure 7.8

DIFFERENT VIEWS — DIFFERENT RESULTS

The DBC.AllSpace view provides space usage information at the object level (table, join index, permanent journal, or stored procedures) *and* the database/user level. However, Teradata recommends using the DBC.DiskSpace and DBC.TableSize views instead since DBC.AllSpace can return misleading results.

CPU AND I/O UTILIZATION

The DBC.AMPUsage view provides information about the usage of each AMP for each user and account. It also tracks the activities of any console utilities. By user, account, or console utility session, DBC.AMPUsage stores information about:

- CPU time consumed
- Number of read/write (I/O) operations generated

AMPUsage reports logical I/Os explicitly requested by the database software, even if the requested segment is in cache and no physical I/O is performed. Use the information provided by DBC.AMPUsage to do the following:

- Bill an account for system resource use.
- Derive capacity needs to plan for expansion.
- Determine if one or more tables has skewed row distribution across AMPs.

APPLICATION DEPLOYMENT

- Determine what resources were used, by user and account string, after hours as well as during the day.
- Determine which session caused reduced performance.
- Summarize and archive the information, then zero it out on a per shift, per day, or per week basis.

DBC.AMPUsage [V] [X]

AccountName	DiskIO	VprocType
UserName	CPUTimeNorm	Model
CPUTime	Vproc	

Figure 7.9

MEASURING RESPONSE TIMES WITH HEARTBEAT QUERIES

System heartbeat queries, used to check for overall system/database hangs, should be written to take some kind of action when response times reach certain thresholds, or when stalled, such as send alert and/or capture system level information.

More than just a heartbeat check, a system heartbeat query should execute diagnostics that capture the state of the system if performance stalls.

System heartbeat queries are intended specifically to focus on the core system of Teradata Database. They should be short-running (one second), low impact queries on tables that are normally not write locked.

System heartbeat queries are most useful when run frequently. For example, some sites run them every 3 to 5 minutes; other sites find every 5 to 10 minutes adequate.

They should be run on a system node. This will eliminate other factors, such as middle tiers, network connections.

Teradata 12 Enterprise Architecture

Depending on their makeup, heartbeat queries can add to contention for resources. Use them selectively, where needed, with shorter queries preferable.

The simplest heartbeat query is the following:

```
select * from dbc.dbcinfo;
```

Figure 7.10

As the query runs, Teradata Manager can monitor the query, logging start and end times. If the query runs longer than the indicated threshold, an alert and possibly a diagnostic script(s) are automatically executed, as defined by the DBA using the Teradata Manager Data collection functionality.

PRODUCTION HEARTBEAT QUERIES

Production heartbeat queries may be used to:

- Take response time samplings, storing them for tracking purposes, or
- Monitor the expected response times of specific groups of queries, such as short-running tactical queries running in high priority.

Response times are an indicator of system demand. When system demand is high, heartbeat response is high. You can expect all other queries running in the same Performance Group to display similar elongations in response time.

From a user perspective, a sudden deviation in response times would have an immediate impact, since users of consistently short running queries would be the first to notice performance degradation.

APPLICATION DEPLOYMENT

Production heartbeat queries have wider uses than system heartbeat queries and can be used in a variety of ways. For example, they:

- Are run less frequently than system heartbeats, usually once every 20 to 60 minutes.
- Can be more complex and similar in nature to a particular type of production query, running in the same Priority Scheduler Performance Group.
- Can be run on production user tables.
- Could be run from other endpoints in the system architecture, such as a network client PC or MVS client to expand scope of monitoring.
- Monitor overall response.
- Monitor specific area of the job mix.

In using a production query from a non-TPA node location, other things, such as network and middle-tier monitoring, are also covered, but when it stalls, you need to investigate further to determine where the bottleneck is located.

Once the response time for a heartbeat query is stored in a table, it can be summarized for use in tracking trends.

Because production heartbeat queries will use up production resources, the frequency and scope of use should be balanced against the value gained from the results being analyzed. If you've got more heartbeat queries than you have time to evaluate, cut back.

Teradata 12 Enterprise Architecture

Practice Questions

1. What is the default setting for MaxLoadAWT?
    a. 0
    b. 8
    c. 15
    d. 32

2. What is the default setting for MaxLoadTasks?
    a. 0
    b. 8
    c. 15
    d. 32

3. What is the maximum number of load utility jobs (FastLoad, MultiLoad, FastExport) that can run concurrently?
    a. 15
    b. 30
    c. 45
    d. 60

4. Where does the disk space for the Transient Journal come from?
    a. Spool space of the user
    b. Perm space of the user
    c. Temporary space of the user
    d. Temporary space of DBC
    e. Perm space of DBC
    f. Spool space of DBC

APPLICATION DEPLOYMENT

5. The JournalDBSize field of the DBSControl Record should be set to:
    a. 2*(Average Row Length)
    b. 3*(Average Row Length)
    c. 4*(Average Row Length)
    d. 2*(Maximum Row Length)
    e. 3*(Maximum Row Length)
    f. 4*(Maximum Row Length)

6. Which of the following statements apply to production heartbeat queries? (Choose 3)
    a. Can be run from other end points
    b. Should be run frequently
    c. Can be run on production tables
    d. Should be short-running
    e. Can be similar to other queries running in the same PS Performance Group

7. The view DBC.AMPUsage reports _____.
    a. CPU time and physical I/O
    b. CPU time and logical I/O
    c. System time and physical I/O
    d. System time and logical I/O

8. Which view should be used for space usage information?
    a. DBC.AllSpace
    b. DBC.DiskSpace

Chapter Notes

Utilize this space for notes, key points to remember, diagrams, areas of further study, etc.

Chapter 8 - System Planning and Space Management

Certification Objectives

- ✓ Given a scenario to manage excessive history and/or obsolete data, determine the methods for archiving and deleting data from an application.
- ✓ Given a system planning and space management scenario, including application characteristics, configure a database architecture (e.g., space, performance, and CPU requirements).
- ✓ Given a scenario, describe the shared resource requirements and their impact on the overall database architecture and its performance.
- ✓ Given a scenario, determine the appropriate backup and recovery approach.

Before You Begin

You should be familiar with the following terms and concepts.

Terms	Key Concepts
PPI	Partitioned Primary Index
Crashdump	Used for system crash analysis
Packdisk	Disk space maintenance
Cylpack	Condensing disk cylinders
Permanent Journaling	Protecting non-Fallback tables
ASE Codes	Account String Expansion Codes

Transient Journal

It is vitally important that database DBC always has enough space to hold all the change rows generated by the total number of applications that run simultaneously during peak workload hours. The administrator should know that:

- The transient journal is maintained as a system table in database DBC.
- DBC PERM space is used to dynamically allocate space to the TJ.
- TJ data blocks are allocated as bytes of JournalDBSize. (Rows can be added to a TJ data block without a sector allocation

If processing causes CurrentPerm of DBC to be exceeded, the transaction causing the overflow is not aborted due to lack of space. Thus, you have no way of knowing when TJ space is exhausted.

It is a good idea to determine how many rows the TJ needs to store during peak workload hours when the most jobs running simultaneously are changing data. TJ entries and the statements that generate them are as follows:

- Control records for CREATE and DROP
- Before-image rows for UPDATE and DELETE
- Row IDs for INSERT
- BEGIN/END TRANSACTION images

Note: Only UPDATE and DELETE cause a full row to be inserted into the Transient Journal.

REDUCING TRANSIENT JOURNAL SPACE

Look for transactions which update or delete a large number of rows in a table.

Consider replacing those Update/Delete statements with Insert/Select statements to an empty table. If the target table is empty, only one entry is made into the Transient Journal which will cause the system to empty the table in case of a transaction failure.

Even if the update requires data from more than one input table, coding the updates as a multi-statement request will still only require one Transient Journal entry.

When the update/delete is finished, DROP the old table and RENAME the new table to the name of the old table.

Utilities can also be used to perform these statements. Fastload and Multiload do not invoke the Transient Journal.

Dictionary Tables

Managing the size of Data Dictionary tables (sometimes called logs) can help improve performance. Teradata Database does not delete system data on its own so you must manage the logs and tables yourself. Determine what you should archive and what you should delete as needed for your site.

The system does not automatically purge logs or the tables underlying views such as the AccessLog, LogOnOff, and Software_Event_Log views. You or another authorized user, such as the security administrator, should archive (as desired) and then delete information that is older than 60 to 90 days (or some interval that suits you) from the following:

- DBC.AccessRights
- DBC.AccLogTbl
- DBC.ResUsage
- DBC.SW_Event_Log

Teradata 12 Enterprise Architecture

- DBC.Logonoff
- DBC.Acctg
- All DBC TDWM tables
- DBC.Diskspace
- DBQL logs, which include all the DBQL tables, except for the tables DBC.DBQLRuleTbl and DBC.DBQLRuleCountTbl.
- QCD.DataDemographics.

Note: Entries in DataDemographics are deleted automatically when you use the INSERT EXPLAIN WITH STATISTICS AND DEMOGRAPHICS statement.

In addition to maintaining the size of system tables and logs, you can proactively reduce their size as follows:

- Using roles to reduce the size of DBC.AccessRights
- Tracking only the information you need for ResUsage, DBQL, or accounting.

For example, if you want to keep the DBC.Acctg table from growing too large, use only the ASE variables that report the level of information you need. Using &T or &I for ASE accounting will potentially make the DBC.Acctg table very large; but using &D&H or &L usually has less impact on disk space and may still provide enough level of detail.

USING TERADATA MANAGER

Use the Data Collection tab of the Administrate menu in Teradata Manager to specify the number of days you wish to keep certain the detail data (Retention Period for Detail Data).

This includes:

- AMP usage data

SYSTEM PLANNING AND SPACE MANAGEMENT

- DBQL data
- Priority Scheduler data
- Query band pairs data
- Resource usage data
- Teradata DWM data

Then schedule Teradata Manager to run the Cleanup function or reset peak spool space statistics.

Note: Do not drop these system tables. You should only delete the entries in them when the data in the tables are no longer needed. Remember, you can always archive the information in the tables if you want to review them at a later time.

You can also manually submit SQL statements to delete old data from these tables or reset values.

The DBC.AMPUsage view uses the DBC.Acctg table to provide aggregated information about CPU time and disk usage. Updates to the table are made periodically during each AMP step on each processor affected by the step. (If there are long-running steps, AMPUsage numbers show large increases periodically, instead of continuous incremental additions.) Data is collected and added to what is already in the table until you reset the counters to zero.

If you use account string expansion, ASE codes can cause the table to grow even more quickly. You may need to update DBC.Acctg on a regular basis to clear out values and reset the accumulators. However, use caution when purging rows containing accounts with ASE codes.

CRASHDUMP

When there is an unscheduled TPA reset, a crashdump is generated (PDE dump).

PDE DUMP

A PDE dump is a selective dump of system memory; including only information that might be needed to analyze a problem within PDE or TPA (the only one currently is the Teradata Database). It can also contain pages read in from swap space that are not in memory at the time of the dump. Exact contents vary depending on the cause of the dump.

PDE dumps, being selective, vary in size depending on the system configuration and the cause of the crash. PDE dumps are much smaller than memory. PDE dumps are taken in parallel on all nodes.

Allocating Crashdumps Space

During installation of a Teradata system, a user called CRASHDUMPS is created as a child of user DBC. Crashdumps is allocated 1 GB of permanent space. Teradata recommends you allocate enough space to this database to hold three crash dumps.

Dump size is approximately 150 - 250 MB per node. Dump size can vary depending on the number of vprocs running, how busy the system was at the time of the crash, and a number of other factors. The use of fallback approximately doubles the total space requirement. If a site needs additional space for the Crashdumps database, increase the MaxPerm space by submitting the MODIFY DATABASE statement.

Archive and Recovery Utility (ARC)

Teradata Database provides a number of automatic data protection features. However, these features do not cover all types of data loss. The ARC utility provides data protection for situations such as:

- Accidentally dropped tables, views, or macros
- Disaster recovery
- Failed batch processes
- Loss of an AMP for non-fallback tables
- Loss of multiple AMPs in the same cluster
- Miscellaneous user errors

Teradata ARC writes and reads sequential files on a Teradata client system to archive, restore, recover, and copy Teradata Database table data.

The difference between *copy* and *restore* is in the kind of operation being performed:

- A restore operation moves data from archived files back to the same Teradata Database from which it was archived or to a different Teradata Database *so long as the database DBC is already restored*.
- A copy operation moves data from an archived file back to a Teradata Database, not necessarily to the same system, *and* creates a new table if one does not already exist on the target database. When you copy selected partitions, the table must exist and be a table that was previously copied as a full-table copy.

Teradata ARC creates files when you archive databases, individual data tables, selected partitions of primary partition index (PPI) tables, or permanent journal tables from the Teradata Database. You provide Teradata ARC with such files when you restore databases, individual

Teradata 12 Enterprise Architecture

data tables, partitions of tables, or permanent journal tables back to the Teradata Database.

Teradata ARC also includes recovery with rollback and rollforward functions for data tables defined with a journal option. Moreover, you can checkpoint these journals with a synchronization point across all AMPs, and delete selected portions of the journals.

ARCHIVE AND RECOVERY PHASES

Archive or recovery jobs always operate in two phases: the Dictionary phase and Data phase. The steps of each phase are described below.

The archive process is intensive. You may want to create a user just for archive activities so that you can log on as the administrative user to perform other actions while archive is running.

Dictionary Phase Steps

1. Allocate an event number.
2. Issue a BEGIN TRANSACTION statement.
3. Resolve object name.
4. Check privileges.
5. Place utility locks on Data Dictionary rows and data rows.
6. Delete existing tables prior to RESTORE.
7. Issue an END TRANSACTION statement.

Data Phase Steps

1. Issue a BEGIN TRANSACTION statement.
2. Insert rows into RCEVENT and RCCONFIG.
3. Perform the operation.
4. Update RCEVENT.
5. Release locks (if user specified).
6. Issue an END TRANSACTION statement.

SYSTEM PLANNING AND SPACE MANAGEMENT

RESTORE VERSUS FASTLOAD

The FastLoad utility can restore archived information to disk. To do this, instead of archiving to tape, use the BTEQ EXPORT command or FastExport to store the information in a host file. FastLoad can quickly load large amounts of data to an empty table on a Teradata system but loads into only one table per job. To load data into more than one table, submit multiple FastLoad jobs.

The ARC utility is great for recovering a very large number of objects and can restore an entire machine with one command. Using FastLoad is an option for also quickly loading recovered data, but can only load into empty tables and load only one table per job.

SESSION CONTROL

In general, the amount of system resources (that is, memory and processing power) that are required to support the archive or recovery increases with the number of sessions. The impact on a particular system depends on the specific configuration.

Teradata ARC uses two control sessions to control archive and recovery operations. The **LOGON** statement always connects these sessions no matter what type of operation being performed.

MULTIPLE SESSIONS

Teradata ARC connects additional data sessions based on the number indicated in the SESSIONS parameter. These sessions are required for the parallel processing that occurs in archive and restore or copy operations.

If additional data sessions are required, Teradata ARC connects them at one time. Teradata ARC calculates the number of parallel sessions it can use, with maximum available being the number of sessions

Teradata 12 Enterprise Architecture

indicated with this parameter. Any connected sessions that are not actually used in the operation result in wasted system resources.

You can specify the number of archive or recover sessions with which to work, or use the default of 4. To set the number, use the SESSIONS runtime parameter.

The number of sessions to use can vary based on a number of factors.

Operation	Data Session Requirements
All-AMPS archive	No more than one session per AMP.
Cluster or specific Archive	Teradata ARC calculates the nearest multiple of online AMPs for the operation and assigns tasks evenly among the involved AMPs. For example, if you archive four AMPs with nine sessions specified, Teradata ARC actually uses eight sessions (two per AMP). The extra connected session wastes system resources since it is unused.
Restore/copy	Restore operations use all the sessions specified by the sessions parameter.

Figure 8.1

Although Teradata ARC is able to process up to 350 ARCMAIN jobs at a time, each with up to 1024 sessions, it is highly recommended that you avoid running so many jobs.

SYSTEM PLANNING AND SPACE MANAGEMENT

ARCHIVE STATEMENT

The following is the ARCHIVE statement syntax diagram (Figure 8.2).

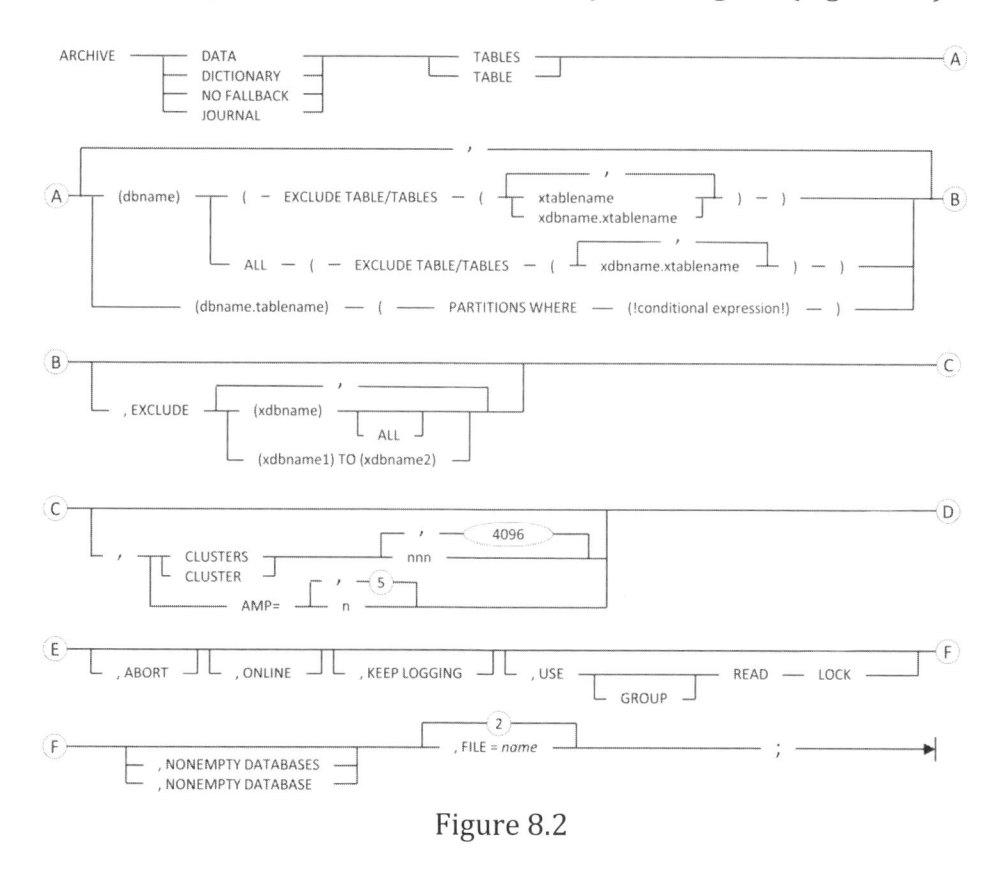

Figure 8.2

ARCHIVING SELECTED PARTITIONS OF A PPI TABLE

It is possible to perform an all-AMPs archive on one or more partitions of a table rather than performing a full-table backup and restore. This feature is limited to all-AMP archives.

Use selected partitions to archive only a subset of data and avoid archiving data that has already been backed up. (Minimizing the size of the archive can improve performance.)

RESTRICTIONS ON ARCHIVING SELECTED PARTITIONS

These restrictions apply to archiving selected partitions of a PPI table:

- Cluster, dictionary, and journal archives are not supported.
- It is recommended that tables containing large objects (BLOB and CLOB columns) not be archived with selected partitions (using PARTITIONS WHERE) because a number of manual steps are needed to restore the data. Instead of using selected partitions, use a full table archive and restore for tables that contain both PPIs and LOBs.

PARTITIONS WHERE Keyword

Use the PARTITIONS WHERE option to specify the conditional expression, which contains a definition of the rows that you want to archive. To be effective, limit this expression to the columns that determine the partitioning for the table you want to archive.

These restrictions apply to the use of PARTITIONS WHERE:

- The object is an individual table (not a database).
- The source table has a PARTITIONS BY expression defined.
- The archive is an all-AMP archive (not a dictionary, cluster, or journal archive).
- The INDEXES option is not used.
- If the table belongs to a database that is specified in the **ARCHIVE** statement, the table is excluded from the database-level object (with EXCLUDE TABLES) and is individually specified.

- Any name specified in the conditional expression is within the table being specified. (Using table aliases and references to databases, tables, or views that are not specified within the target table result in an error.) It is recommended that the only referenced columns in the PARTITIONS WHERE condition be the partitioning columns or system derived column PARTITION of the table. References to other columns do not contribute to partition elimination, and might accidently qualify more partitions than intended.

ANALYZE STATEMENT

Here is the syntax diagram (Figure 8.3) of the ANALYZE statement.

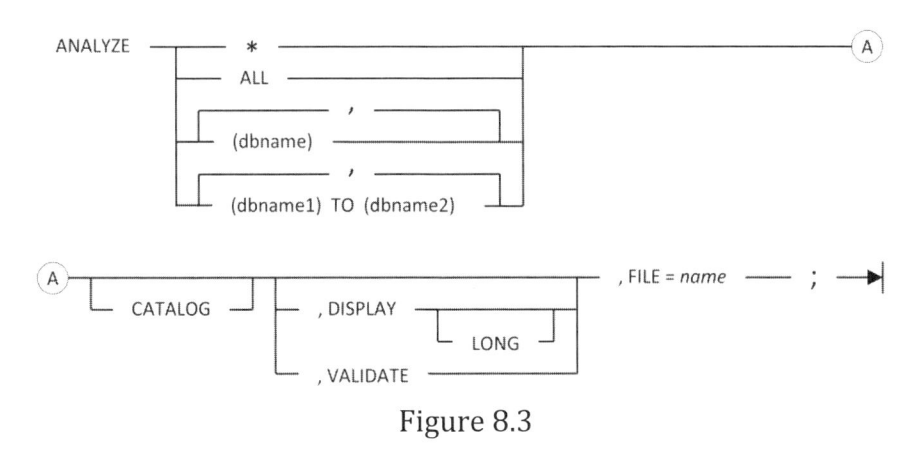

```
ANALYZE ─┬─ * ──────────────────────────────┬─(A)
         ├─ ALL ────────────────────────────┤
         │        ┌──── , ────┐             │
         ├────────┴─ (dbname) ─┴────────────┤
         │        ┌──── , ────┐             │
         └────────┴─ (dbname1) TO (dbname2) ┘

(A)─┬─────────────────────────────────────┬─, FILE = name ─ ; ─▶|
    └─ CATALOG ─┬─ , DISPLAY ─┬─ LONG ─┬──┤
                └─ , VALIDATE ─────────┘
```

Figure 8.3

The **ANALYZE** statement provides the following information about the specified databases:

- If an archive file contains a selected partition archive of a table, the bounding condition used to select the archived partitions is displayed with an indication as to whether the bounding condition is well-defined.
- Online logging information.

- The name of each database, data table, journal table, stored procedure, view and macro in each database, and the fallback status of the tables (if you specify the LONG option).
- The number of bytes and rows in each table (if you specify either the LONG or VALIDATE option).
- Time and date the archive operation occurred.
- User-Defined Method (UDM) and User-Defined Type (UDT) information.
- Whether the archive is of all AMPs, clusters of AMPs, or specific AMPs.

It is possible to specify both the DISPLAY and VALIDATE options in a single **ANALYZE** statement. The default is DISPLAY.

TYPES OF ARCHIVES

An archive operation copies database information from the Teradata Database to one or two client resident files. The archive can be from any of the following:

- All AMPs
- Specified AMPs
- Specified clusters of AMPs

In general, Teradata ARC archives have these characteristics:

- If an **ARCHIVE** statement specifies more than one database, Teradata ARC archives the databases (except for DBC and SYSUDTLIB) in alphabetical order. Within each database, all related tables, views, macros and stored procedures are archived in alphabetical order.
- If the statement specifies multiple individual tables, Teradata ARC archives the tables in alphabetical order first according to database and then by table.

SYSTEM PLANNING AND SPACE MANAGEMENT

- If an archive of database DBC is interrupted for any reason, the entire archive must be performed again. It is not possible to restart an archive operation on database DBC.
- Archives cannot contain both data tables and journal tables. A journal table archive contains only the saved portion of the table.
- Journal table archives do not delete change images from the journal table. Therefore, you can accumulate change images for several activity periods by executing a checkpoint with save after each period and then archiving the table without deleting the journal.

The following table lists the archive types.

Archive Type	Table Protection Type	Data Included
All AMP database	Fallback	- Primary data rows and Secondary Indexes (SIs) from all the tables in the database(s) - Data Dictionary rows of the tables/macros/views/ functions/stored procedures - All table/macro/view/stored procedure/triggers/UDF information - Table structure information
	No fallback	- Available data rows - Data Dictionary rows of the tables/macros/views/functions/ stored procedures/triggers/UDF - All table/macro/view/stored procedures/triggers/UDF information - Table structure information No SIs are included if an AMP is down.

157

Archive Type	Table Protection Type	Data Included
All AMP table	Fallback	<ul><li>Primary data rows</li><li>Secondary Indexes (SIs)</li><li>All dictionary information for the table</li><li>All table, column, and index definitions</li></ul>
	No fallback	<ul><li>Available data rows</li><li>All dictionary information for the table</li><li>All table, column, and index definitions</li></ul>Note that no SIs are included if an AMP is down.
Specific AMP	No fallback	<ul><li>Available data rows from the table(s) within the database(s)</li><li>Table structure information</li></ul>Note that:<ul><li>No dictionary rows are included. This information is included in the Dictionary archive.</li><li>No SIs are included.</li></ul>
Specific cluster	Fallback or no fallback	<ul><li>Available data rows from the table(s) within the database(s)</li><li>Table structure information</li></ul>Note that:<ul><li>No dictionary rows are included. This information is included in the Dictionary archive.</li><li>No SIs are included.</li></ul>
Data Dictionary		Dictionary rows for tables/macros/views/stored procedures/triggers/UDFs.

SYSTEM PLANNING AND SPACE MANAGEMENT

Archive Type	Table Protection Type	Data Included
		For tables: • DBC.TVM • DBC.TVFields • DBC.Indexes • DBC.IndexNames PJ information is not included.

Figure 8.4

ARCHIVE OPTIONS

The following table describes the ARCHIVE options.

ARCHIVE Option	Description
ABORT	Keyword to abort an all-AMPs or cluster operation for when you archive non-fallback tables or single image journal tables and an AMP goes offline during the operation.
ALL	Include/exclude the named database and its descendents.
DATA TABLES	Archives fallback, non-fallback, or both types of tables from all AMPs or from clusters of AMPs.
DICTIONARY TABLES	Archives only the dictionary rows of a table. A dictionary archive of a database includes all table, view, macro and trigger definitions, and dictionary entries for stored procedures. This option includes the table definition for the specified table in the archive only if you archive a specific table.
EXCLUDE	Keyword to prevent specific databases from being archived.

ARCHIVE Option	Description
EXCLUDE TABLES	Keyword to prevent specific tables from being archived.
FORCED	When specified, FORCED will instruct ARC to attempt to release any placed locks in the event that the ARCHIVE statement fails.
INDEXES	For all-AMP archives only, this option specifies to include secondary indexes with the archive. You will need more time and media to archive objects with their secondary indexes.
JOURNAL TABLES	Archives dictionary rows for journal table and the saved subtable of journal table.
KEEP LOGGING	Overrides the automatic termination of an online archive that was initiated with the ONLINE option.
NO FALLBACK TABLES	Archives non-fallback table from specific AMPs to complete a previous all-AMPs or cluster archive taken with processors offline.
NONEMPTY DATABASES	Instructs the ARC utility to exclude users/databases without tables, views, or macros from the archive.
PARTITIONS WHERE	Archive selected partitions of a PPI table rather than the entire table.
ONLINE	Archive rows that have update, insert, or delete operations also ongoing on those rows by using the online archive option.
RELEASE LOCK	Automatically releases utility locks when the operation completes successfully.
USE GROUP READ LOCK	Permits you to archive as transactions update locked rows. You must define after image journaling for the table during the time the archive is taking place.

Figure 8.5

SYSTEM PLANNING AND SPACE MANAGEMENT

DATABASE DBC ARCHIVE

The DBC database contains critical system tables that define the user databases in the Teradata Database.

The following are the tables archived for Database DBC.

AccessRights	AccLogRuleTbl	Accounts
CollationTbl	Dbase	Hosts
LogonRuleTbl	Next	OldPasswords
Owners	Parents	Profiles
RCConfiguration	RCEvent	RCMedia
RepGroup	RoleGrants	Roles
SysSecDefaults	Translation	UDTCast
UDTInfo	UDTTransform	

Figure 8.6

If a DBC table is not listed in the table (above), it will not be archived for database DBC. Instead, use SQL to copy the DBC table into a user-level table in another database for Teradata ARC to back up. The information cannot be copied back to the DBC user table during a restore process.

If included in an archive operation, database DBC is always archived first, regardless of alphabetical order. If included in a restore or copy operation, database DBC is always restored or copied first. Refer to the next section for specific instructions on restoring database DBC.

Teradata 12 Enterprise Architecture

UNDERSTANDING RESTORE OPERATIONS

The ARC utility provides several recovery control statements you use during restore-related operations. Each command is described in the following table.

Restore-Related Statement	Function
ANALYZE	Reads an archive tape to display information about its contents.
BUILD	Builds secondary indexes for fallback and non-fallback tables. It also builds fallback rows for fallback tables, and can build journal tables by sorting the change images.
COPY	Restores a copy of an archived file to a specified Teradata Database.
DELETE DATABASE	Deletes data tables, views, and macros from a database. Does not remove journal tables.
DELETE JOURNAL	Removes a journal subtable from the Teradata Database.
RELEASE LOCK	Releases host utility locks from specific databases or tables.
RESTORE	Restores a database or table from an archive file to specified AMPs.

Figure 8.7

A restore operation transfers database information from archive files backed up on portable storage media to all AMPs, clusters of AMPs, or specified AMPs.

You can restore archived data tables to the Teradata Database if the Data Dictionary contains a definition of the object you want to restore. For example, if the object is a database, that database must be defined in the dictionary. Or, if the object is a table, that table must be defined

SYSTEM PLANNING AND SPACE MANAGEMENT

in the dictionary. You cannot restore objects not defined in the Data Dictionary.

A dictionary table archive contains all table, view, macro and trigger definitions in the database, and dictionary entries for stored procedures and user-defined functions. A restore of a dictionary archive restores the definitions of all data tables, views, macros, triggers, and stored procedures. However, it does not restore any data.

Caution: You cannot restore a database with join indexes or a table referenced by a join index. You must first drop join indexes before restoring. If you attempt to restore with join indexes still defined, you will get an error message.

RESTORE Statement

The following is the syntax diagram (Figure 8.8) for the RESTORE statement.

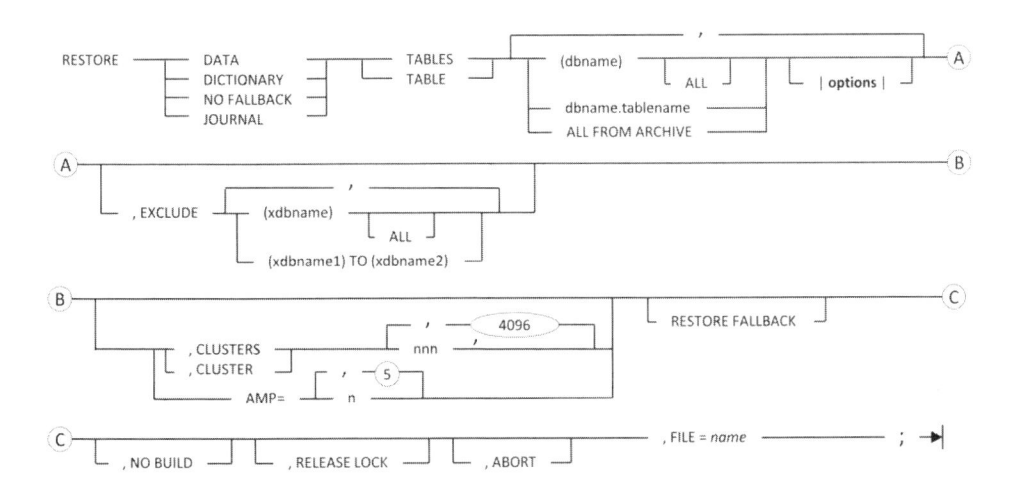

Teradata 12 Enterprise Architecture

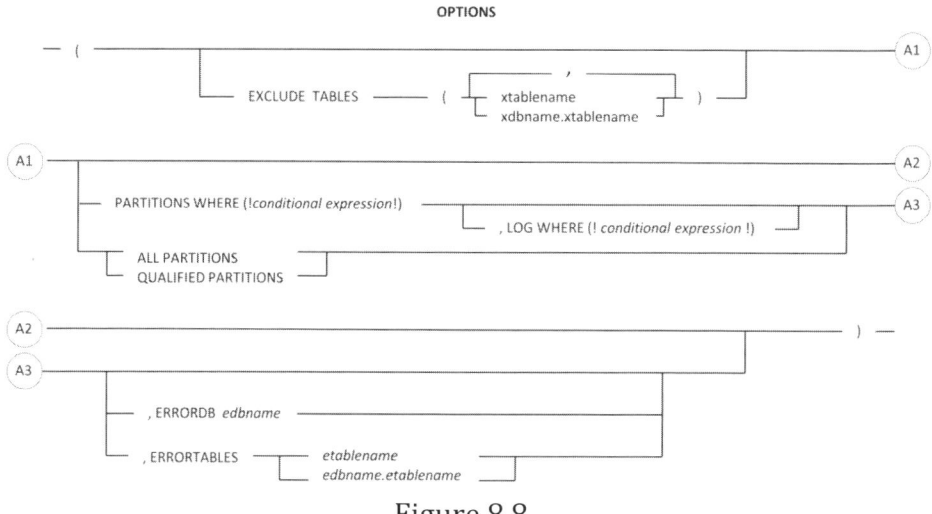

Figure 8.8

Restoring Selected Partitions of PPI Table

You can restore selected partitions of PPI tables. This allows you to archive and restore only a subset of data in a PPI table.

Restrictions on Restoring Selected Partitions

The following restrictions apply to restoring selected partitions:

- Restoring selected partitions is not allowed to a machine with a hash function that is different from the source machine, but a different configuration is allowed.

To RESTORE or COPY selected partitions, a table must already exist on the target system.

Restoring selected partitions is not allowed to a table that has undergone any of the following major DDL changes:

- Adding or changing referential integrity constraints

SYSTEM PLANNING AND SPACE MANAGEMENT

- Adding, modifying, or dropping columns.
- Certain changes during RESTORE and COPY operations.
- Changing from PPI to NPPI, or vice versa
- Changing primary index columns

COPY Statement

The following is the syntax diagram (Figure 8.9) for the COPY statement.

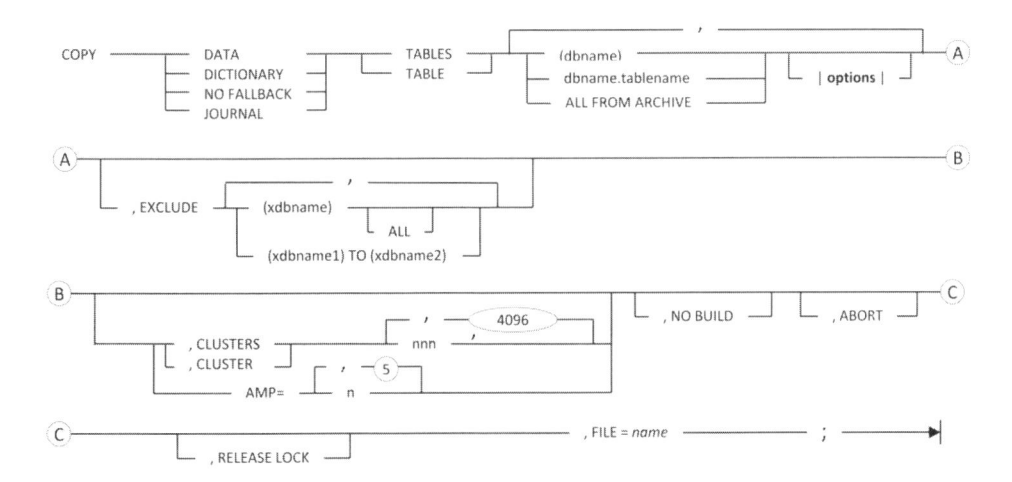

Teradata 12 Enterprise Architecture

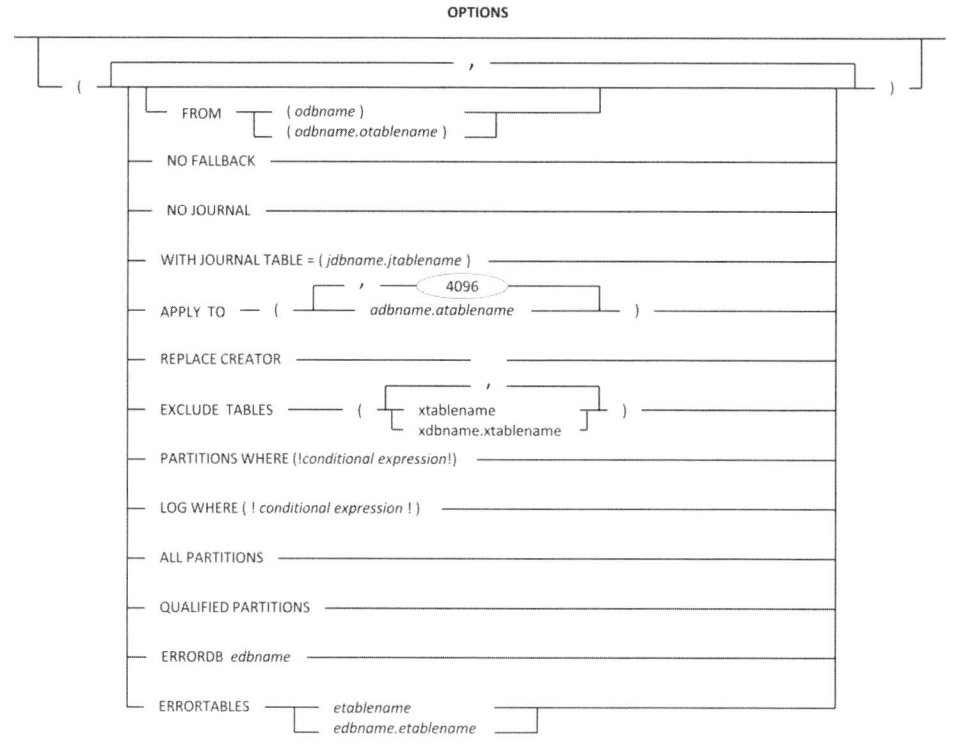

```
                                    OPTIONS
    ┌──────────────────────────────────────────────────────────────┐
    │                              ,                                │
 ──(─┬─ FROM ─┬─ ( odbname )                                ─┬─ )──
    │        └─ ( odbname.otablename ) ─┘                    │
    ├─ NO FALLBACK ──────────────────────────────────────────┤
    ├─ NO JOURNAL ───────────────────────────────────────────┤
    ├─ WITH JOURNAL TABLE = ( jdbname.jtablename ) ──────────┤
    │                      ,      4096                        │
    ├─ APPLY TO ─ ( ──┬── adbname.atablename ──┬── ) ────────┤
    ├─ REPLACE CREATOR ──────────────────────────────────────┤
    │                           ,                             │
    ├─ EXCLUDE TABLES ─── ( ─┬─ xtablename ─────┬─ ) ────────┤
    │                        └─ xdbname.xtablename ─┘         │
    ├─ PARTITIONS WHERE (!conditional expression!) ──────────┤
    ├─ LOG WHERE ( ! conditional expression ! ) ─────────────┤
    ├─ ALL PARTITIONS ───────────────────────────────────────┤
    ├─ QUALIFIED PARTITIONS ─────────────────────────────────┤
    ├─ ERRORDB edbname ──────────────────────────────────────┤
    └─ ERRORTABLES ─┬── etablename ──────────────────────────┘
                   └── edbname.etablename ─┘
```

Figure 8.9

Copying Partitioned Data

Normally, the table you want to copy does not need to exist in the target database. However, if you are going to copy selected partitions to the table, the table does need to exist in the target database. Additionally, the target table must be a full table and not just consist of selected partitions.

Copying Objects

Use different Teradata users for each archive job when running concurrent archives against the same objects. This ensures that locks placed by one job are not released by another.

SYSTEM PLANNING AND SPACE MANAGEMENT

Copying a full database archive is the same as a restore operation. Teradata ARC drops all existing tables, views, macros, stored procedures, triggers, UDFs, UDTs, and dictionary information in the receiving system. The data in the archive is then copied to the receiving database.

However, triggers cannot be copied with the **COPY** statement. Triggers must be manually recreated via SQL.

You cannot copy one or more stored procedures from one database to another using the **COPY** statement. They can only be copied as part of a full database.

If your views, stored procedures, and macros have embedded references to databases and objects that are not in the receiving environment, those views, stored procedures, and macros will not work. To make any such views, stored procedures, and macros work, recreate or copy the references to which they refer into the receiving database.

If your views, stored procedures, and macros have embedded references to databases and objects that *are* in the receiving environment, they will work correctly.

Note: Fully qualify all tables, stored procedures, and view names in a macro and all table names in a view. If you do not, you may receive an error. When you execute a **COPY** statement, partial names are fully qualified to the default database name. In some cases, this may be the name of the old database.

After an all-AMPs copy, copied tables do not have referential constraints. First, referential constraints are not copied into the dictionary definition tables, database DBC.ReferencedTbls and database DBC.ReferencingTbls, for either a referenced (parent) or referencing (child) table copied into a Teradata Database. Moreover,

Teradata 12 Enterprise Architecture

all referential index descriptors are deleted from the archived table header before it is inserted into the copied table.

UDFs & Triggers

A restore of a user database drops any new tables, views, macros, stored procedures, triggers, or UDFs created since the archive of the database.

If you restore a database from a dictionary archive created by specifying individual tables, only the dictionary rows for the specified tables are restored. The following table lists the dictionary rows that are restored by an all-AMPs data restore or a dictionary tables restore of a user database.

Table Rows	Description
Indexes	Definition of all indexed columns in the data tables and views
IndexName	Definition of named indexes on the table
TVM	Definition of all data tables, views, macros, stored procedures, triggers, and UDFs in the database
TVFields	Definition of all columns in the data tables, views, macros, stored procedure parameters, and UDFs.
TriggersTbl	Definition of all triggers in the database

Figure 8.10

SYSTEM PLANNING AND SPACE MANAGEMENT

Keyword Options with COPY

The following table describes the keyword options of the COPY statement.

Syntax Element	Description
ABORT	Aborts the copy operation if an AMP to which a non-fallback or journal table to restore is offline. This option affects only an all-AMPs copy.
ALL	Excludes the named database and all descendants.
ALL FROM ARCHIVE	Copies all databases/tables in the given archive file.
ALL PARTITIONS	Restores all archived partitions for an archived PPI object.
APPLY TO	Identifies the tables in the target system where the change images apply.
DATA TABLES	Copies data tables.
DICTIONARY TABLES	Copies dictionary tables.
ERRORDB and ERRORTABLES	Specifies the location of the error log for partition-level operations.
EXCLUDE	Prevents objects in specified databases from being copied.
EXCLUDE TABLES	Prevents individual tables in the listed database from being copied.
FILE	Copies a file.
FROM	Names the object in the archive different from the target object.
JOURNAL TABLES	Copies journal tables.
LOG WHERE	Specifies the rows that are logged to an error table for manual insertion and deletion.
NO BUILD	• Prevents the Fallback and Secondary

169

Teradata 12 Enterprise Architecture

Syntax Element	Description
	Index rows from being created. • If NO BUILD is requested when restoring database DBC, the request is ignored. • If the NO BUILD keywords are used during a **RESTORE** statement, a separate **BUILD** statement must be run for all databases and/or tables that were restored. The tables will not be accessible until a **BUILD** statement is run.
NO FALLBACK	Copies fallback tables into non-fallback tables. If the archived table is already non-fallback, this option has no effect.
NO FALLBACK TABLES	Copies non-fallback tables to specific AMPs.
NO JOURNAL	Copies all tables with journaling disabled, whether journaled in the archive or not.
PARTITIONS WHERE	Specifies the conditional expression for partition-level operations.
QUALIFIED PARTITIONS	Copies the same partitions specified in a previous selected-partition copy.
RELEASE LOCK	Releases client utility locks when the copy operation completes.
REPLACE CREATOR	Replaces the LastAlterUID, creator name, and Creator ID of the tables in the target database with the user ID and the current user name, i.e., the user name specified in the **LOGON** command.
WITH JOURNAL TABLE	Specifies that a copied database has journaling for the specified database and journal table.

Figure 8.11

SYSTEM PLANNING AND SPACE MANAGEMENT

BUILD Statement

Teradata ARC processes databases, tables, and stored procedures in alphabetical order. Because database DBC does not contain non-fallback tables and cannot be restored by clusters, Teradata ARC does not try to build indexes or fallback data for any table in database DBC. A build operation creates unique and non-unique secondary indexes for a specified table. The build operation also generates the fallback copy of fallback tables if you specify the DATA TABLES keywords.

Typically, this statement is used after one of the following:

- Cluster archive restoring
- Series of all-AMPs restores that specified the NO BUILD option (usually a restore to a changed hardware configuration)
- Specific AMP restore of non-fallback tables

Note: To speed the recovery of all AMPs, specify the NO BUILD option of the **RESTORE** statement to prevent non-fallback tables from being built after the restore is complete.

If an AMP is offline during a build operation, all unique secondary indexes of non-fallback tables are left invalidated. As a result, requests may run more slowly when secondary indexes are used for search and selection. Insert and update operations cannot occur.

You must rebuild indexes for non-fallback tables after a restore operation if any of the following situations occur:

- An AMP is offline during a dump or restore
- The archive did not include the INDEXES option
- The restore included the NO BUILD option
- The restore operation is not an all-AMP restore

Teradata 12 Enterprise Architecture

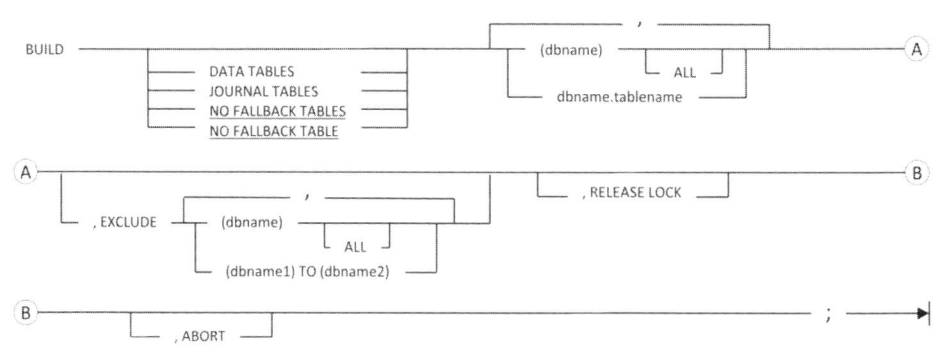

Figure 8.12

RELEASE LOCK Statement

Client utilities (BTEQ, FastExport, FastLoad, MultiLoad, Teradata Parallel Data Pump, and Teradata Parallel Transporter) use standard database locks. The Archive/Recovery (ARC) utility uses HUT Exclusive locks when restoring, copying, rolling back, rolling forward, or building a database. These locks remain active during a Teradata Database or client restart, and must be explicitly released by the **RELEASE LOCK** statement or by the **RELEASE LOCK** keywords available on the ARCHIVE, REVALIDATE REFERENCES FOR, ROLLBACK, ROLLFORWARD, RESTORE and BUILD statements. Teradata ARC issues a message to report that the release operation is complete. It releases HUT locks when the AMPs return to online operation.

SYSTEM PLANNING AND SPACE MANAGEMENT

Figure 8.13

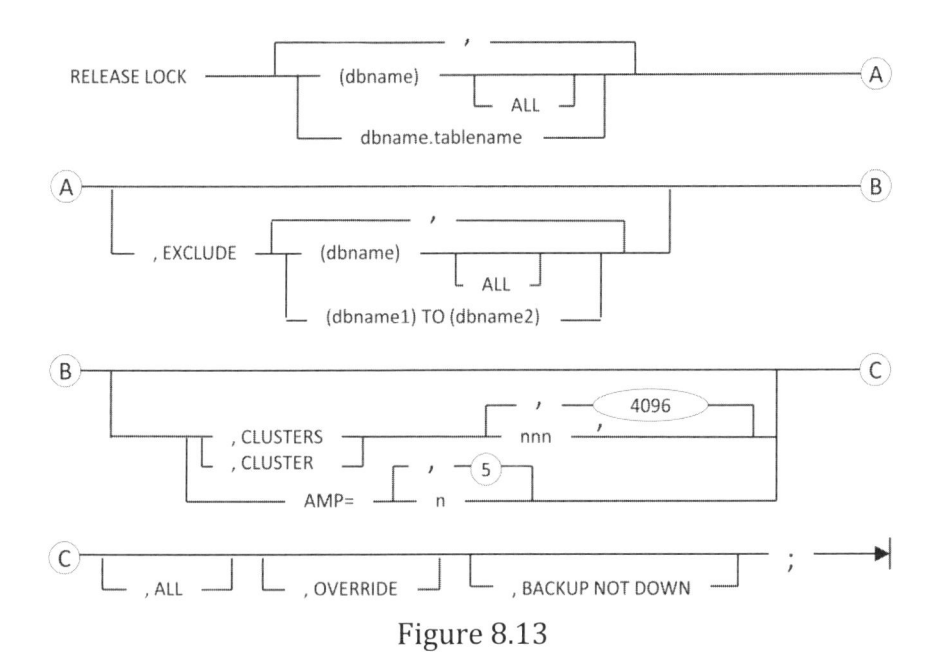

Revalidate References

When either a parent or child table is restored, the reference is marked inconsistent in the database dictionary definitions. As a result, the system does not allow UPDATE, INSERT, or DELETE statements on such tables.

The REVALIDATE REFERENCES FOR statement validates the inconsistencies, thereby allowing users to execute UPDATE, INSERT and DELETE statements on the tables. The functions performed by this statement include:

- Creates an error table
- Inserts into the error table rows that fail the referential constraint specified by the reference index
- Validates the inconsistent reference index on the target table

Teradata 12 Enterprise Architecture

If inconsistent restraints remain after you execute the statement, you can use the ALTER TABLE DROP INCONSISTENT REFERENCES statement to remove them. To use the REVALIDATE REFERENCES FOR statement, the username you have specified in the LOGON statement must have one of the following privileges:

- RESTORE privileges on the table you are re-validating
- Implicit privileges on the database or table

Note: The REVALIDATE REFERENCES statement does not validate soft RI (tables with NO CHECK option.).

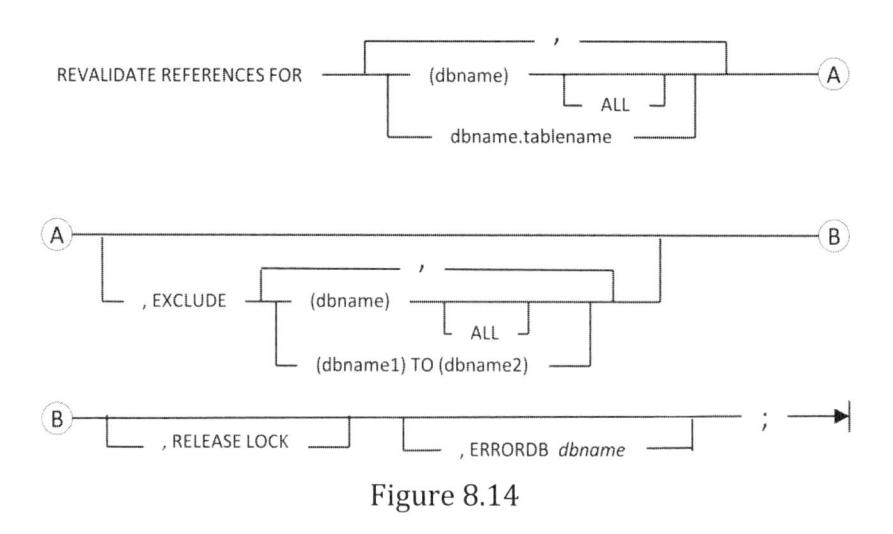

Figure 8.14

Recovery Control Data Dictionary Views

Several system views contain information about ARC utility events. You can use these views for recovery control.

This view...	Provides information about...
DBC.Association	objects (databases, users, tables, views, macros, indexes, stored procedures) that you imported from another Teradata Database system or created via the Archive/Recovery COPY statement
DBC.EventsX	archive/recovery activities, with a row (audit trail) for each archive and recovery event
DBC.Events_ConfigurationX	archive and recovery activities that did NOT affect all AMPs
DBC.Events_MediaX	archive and recovery activities that involved removable media

Figure 8.15

Association View

The Association view allows you to retrieve information about an object imported from another Teradata Database.

An existing object created with the ARC COPY command also appears in the Association view. If you later drop a copied object from its new destination, the information is deleted from the Association table and is no longer available.

Events View

The Events view tracks ARC activity. ARC inserts a new row in the Events system table each time another ARC activity begins. The Events view returns a row for each activity tracked.

The following table describes events the system creates depending on the type of object on which the activity was performed.

A row for this event type ...	Is created for each ...
Checkpoint Event Row	journal checkpointed.
Delete Event Row	journal deleted.
Dump Event Row	database or table dumped.
Restore Event Row	database or table restored.
Rollback Event Row	database or table rolled back.
Rollforward Event Row	database or table rolled forward.

Figure 8.16

Events_Configuration View

The Events_Configuration view contains rows for each archive activity that does not affect all AMPs in the database configuration. If the ARC command specifies all AMPs and there are one or more AMPs offline, a row is inserted in the system table for each offline AMPs. If the statement is for specific AMPs, a row is inserted for each specified and online AMPs.

Events_Media View

The Events_Media view provides information about ARC activities that used removable storage media. This information includes the volume serial numbers assigned to portable devices.

Archive Strategies

Daily Archive Routine

Perform the following procedure on a daily basis:

1. Submit a CHECKPOINT WITH SAVE statement for each journal table. This appends any changes stored in the active journal subtable to the saved journal table, and initiates a new active journal subtable.
2. Archive each current journal.
3. Delete the saved journal subtable from the saved journal.

Weekly Archive Routine

Teradata recommends that you submit an all-AMPs ARCHIVE of all data tables that change often, at least on a weekly basis. However, you may need to adjust how often you perform routine archiving based on the amount of data and based on how often your data changes.

Minimizing User Impact

Online archive

Archive a table or database when update transactions are still concurrently occurring by using the ONLINE option. Online archiving allows you to archive without using the after image journal option and without using the ARCHIVE statement with GROUP READ LOCK option.

The system creates and maintains a log for each table. It then captures all changes on the table in the log. The log of all changed rows is archived as a part of the archive process and will be restored and applied to undo the changes. These change logs are activated when

Teradata 12 Enterprise Architecture

the consistency point is established on the tables. The consistency point is set by getting table level read locks on all the tables specified to be in the same consistency point, starting change log on all those tables, and releasing all the locks.

Establishing the consistency points defines the state of the tables to which they will be restored. While waiting for the table read locks required to set the consistency point, new write transactions will wait behind those read lock requests. If it is important to reduce impact to the write transactions, then there are some important considerations for reducing the time to establish a consistency point. New write transactions can be expected to wait for at least as long as the longest running write transaction in the system that accesses one of the tables in the consistency point.

Determining Space Shortages

As mentioned in the previous chapter, the views DBC.TableSize and DBC.DiskSpace should be used to monitor space and usage consumption.

DBC.TableSize[X]

Vproc	AccountName	**CurrentPerm**
DatabaseName	TableName	**PeakPerm**

Figure 8.17

DBC.DiskSpace [V] [X]

Vproc	**MaxTemp**	**PeakSpool**
DatabaseName	**CurrentPerm**	**PeakTemp**
AccountName	**CurrentSpool**	**MaxProfileSpool**
MaxPerm	**CurrentTemp**	**MaxProfileTemp**
MaxSpool	**PeakPerm**	

Figure 8.18

SYSTEM PLANNING AND SPACE MANAGEMENT

An alternate way to compare current usage against the allocated space for the database/user is through the DBC.Databases or DBC.Users views.

DBC.Databases[V][X]

DatabaseName	**PermSpace**	LastAlterTimeStamp
CreatorName	**SpoolSpace**	DBKind
OwnerName	**TempSpace**	AccessCount
AccountName	CommentString	LastAccessTimeStamp
ProtectionType	CreateTimeStamp	
JournalFlag	LastAlterName	

Figure 8.19

DBC.Users[V]

UserName	StartupString	TimeZoneMinute
CreatorName	DefaultAccount	DefaultDateForm
PasswordLastModDate	DefaultDatabase	CreateTimeStamp
PasswordLastModTime	CommentString	LastAlterName
OwnerName	DefaultCollation	LastAlterTimeStamp
PermSpace	PasswordChgDate	DefaultCharType
SpoolSpace	LockedDate	RoleName
TempSpace	LockedTime	ProfileName
ProtectionType	LockedCount	AccessCount
JournalFlag	TimeZoneHour	LastAccessTimeStamp

Figure 8.20

PACKDISK

When Teradata Database runs out of free cylinders, you must run PACKDISK, an intensive overhead operation, to compact data and free up more cylinders.

To reduce the frequency of PACKDISK operations:

- When FastLoading tables to which rows will be subsequently added, set FSP to 5-20% to provide enough free space to add rows.
- For historical data, where you are adding and deleting data, provide enough free space to add rows. For example, you add up to 31 days before deleting on a table with six months history.
  - Add one month to six months: 1/7 = 14.3%
  - Safety - plan on 1.5 months, 1.5 / 7.5 = 20%.
  - Set Free Space Percent to 20%.
- For historical data and fragmented cylinders:
  - For large tables, either set FSP to 20 - 35%, or set MaxBlockSize to smaller size (16 KB, for example).
  - Translate free space to the number of data blocks. Plan on at least 6-12 blocks worth of free space.
- Specify the IMMEDIATE clause with the ALTER TABLE statement.

The table header contains the FSP for each table. If you change the default FSP, the system uses the new default the next time you modify the table. FSP has no effect on block size.

Running Other Utilities with PACKDISK

If you run PACKDISK frequently, use the following "tools," two of which are utilities, to determine the amount of free space:

- DBC.DiskSpace
- SHOWSPACE, a Ferret command, shows you the percent of free space per cylinder. If this figure is low, it will impact performance by performing "on the fly" cylpacks when the system needs contiguous space.
- SHOWFSP, a Ferret command like SHOWSPACE, is useful in discovering specific tables that need packing. SHOWFSP shows the number of cylinders that can be freed up for individual

tables by specifying a desired free space percent. SHOWFSP is useful in discovering which tables would free the most cylinders if PACKDISK were run on them. Certain tables exist that can free up a large percentage of cylinders.

Cylinder Splits

A FreeSpacePercent value of 0% indicates that no empty space is reserved on Teradata Database disk cylinders for future growth when a new table is loaded. That is, the current setting causes each data cylinder to be packed 100% full when a new table is loaded.

Unless data is deleted from the table prior to subsequent row inserts, this situation will guarantee that a cylinder split will be necessary the first time an additional row is to be inserted into the table (following the initial load). Cylinder splits consume system I/O overhead and result in poor utilization of data cylinders in most circumstances.

PACKDISK and Cylinder Splits

Running PACKDISK after setting the FreeSpacePercent will pack data to the percent specified (that is, 100 minus FreeSpacePercent).

Prior to a cylinder split, data occupies 100% of space available on a cylinder. After a cylinder split, half of the data is moved to a new cylinder. This results in twice the number of cylinders required to contain the same amount of data. In addition, the number of empty cylinders (needed for spool space) is depleted.

Running the PACKDISK command reverses the effect of cylinder splits and packs the cylinders full of data, leaving empty only the percentage of space indicated by the FreeSpacePercent parameter (unless you specify a different free space percent).

Shared Resources

Disk Space

To monitor the consumption of disk space, use the views DBC.DiskSpace and DBC.TableSize.

DiskSpace reports on a database while TableSize reports on the tables within a database. The following table compares the amounts returned by the CurrentPerm column of the DiskSpace and TableSize views.

SPACE	DBC.DISKSPACE	DBC.TABLESIZE
SUM(CurrentPerm)	Reports the space consumed by all the tables in the specified database or all databases. This amount should agree with the SUM(CurrentPerm) reported by TableSize.	Reports the total for all user tables in the specified database or all databases. The total is found by adding together the bytes consumed by each table. This amount should agree with the SUM(CurrentPerm) reported by DiskSpace.
MAX(CurrentPerm)	Returns results at the database level. MAX is the PERM defined for the database/user in the CREATE or MODIFY statement.	Returns the remainder of defined PERM space minus SUM space. This may or may not agree with MAX(CurrentPerm) returned by DiskSpace.

Figure 8.21

SYSTEM PLANNING AND SPACE MANAGEMENT

Resetting Peak Values

Each of the two views listed above are views of the non-hashed DBC.DatabaseSpace table. From time to time, you need to clear out the peak values accumulated in the DBC.DataBaseSpace table to restart the data collection process.

Teradata provides the DBC.ClearPeakDisk macro to reset the PeakPerm and PeakSpool values in the DBC.DataBaseSpace table. To review the definition of ClearPeakDisk, enter:

```
SHOW MACRO DBC.ClearPeakDisk;
```

Figure 8.22

Teradata Database returns the contents of the CREATE MACRO DDL:

```
REPLACE MACRO DBC.ClearPeakDisk
AS   ( UPDATE DataBaseSpace
        SET PeakPermSpace = 0,
            PeakSpoolSpace = 0,
            PeakTempSpace = 0 ALL;);
```

Figure 8.23

Before invoking the macro, save the peak values either in a separate collection-periods table or offline.

Teradata 12 Enterprise Architecture

AMP Worker Tasks

Use the ResUsage table ResUsageSawt when you want to monitor the utilization of the AWTs and determine if work is backing up because the AWTs are all being used.

CPU Usage Limits With Priority Scheduler

The Milestone Limit of CPU usage is defined in seconds or fractions of seconds.

If your Milestone Type is time-based, you can limit a Resource Partition to a specified percentage of CPU resource usage. This CPU limit has no effect on the scheduling strategy defined by other Priority Scheduler parameters. The relative weights of Allocation Groups and Resource Partitions are observed. The normal distribution of resources prevails within the specified amount of CPU usage.

Note: You can also limit the percentage of total CPU usage by sessions controlled by an Allocation Group.

FSG Cache

When the database software starts up and the system knows the number of AMPs and PEs, the system allocates a minimum amount of memory (64 MB per vproc needed for per-AMP and per-PE working memory for 32-bit systems or 96 MB per vproc for 64-bit systems).

The system calculates the maximum number of pages available for caching Teradata Database file system blocks (FSG Cache size) as the difference between initial free memory and this estimate.

For more efficient performance, it is critical that you reduce FSG Cache percentage to provide for 90 MB of memory per AMP on 32-bit systems or 135 MB for 64-bit systems instead of the 64 MB of memory

SYSTEM PLANNING AND SPACE MANAGEMENT

per AMP that is allocated in memory at startup for 32-bit systems or 96 MB of memory per AMP that is allocated in memory at startup for 64-bit systems.

Note: If you intend to run additional applications (with memory requirements unknown to Teradata Database software), reduce FSG Cache percentage to leave memory available for these applications.

BYNET

A possible problem is when an application on a large configuration generates many messages over the BYNET with concurrent row redistributions involving all nodes. The following are NOT a problem:

- Row duplications
- Merging of answer sets

To avoid the overhead of sending lots of smaller messages across the BYNET, buffers are used to batch up individual rows during the redistribution process. Both load utilities and queries involve such redistribution, but their approach to outbound buffering is different.
Row redistribution for query processing uses separate single buffers per AMP for each node in the system. This means that the amount of memory required for redistribution in a node grows as the system grows.

- Default query redistribution buffer size = 32 KB per target node
- Total memory for one sending AMP = 32 KB * number of nodes in system
- For eight AMPs per node, total memory required per node = 8 * 32 KB * number of nodes in system

The following example provides the calculations for a configuration of 8 nodes at eight AMPs per node. (The system only reserves 32 MB per AMP).

- Single node requirement (single user) = 32 KB * 8 = 256 KB
- Multi-user (for example, 20 concurrent users) = 20 * 256 KB = 5 MB (not a special problem)

The following example provides the calculations for a configuration of 96 nodes at 8 AMPs per node:

- Single node requirement (single user) = 32 KB * 96 = 3072 KB (3 MB)
- Multi-user (20 concurrent users) = 20 * 3072 KB = 64 MB (far exceeding 32 MB per AMP)

Symptoms of high-volume redistribution processing include:

- Excessive memory paging/swapping
- Possible I/O bottleneck on BYNET I/O
- Double AWT's used lowering concurrency

Memory-Consuming Features

Be aware that certain features may require more memory in order to show their optimal performance benefit. Of particular mention are:

- External Stored Procedures and table functions
- Join index, hash-join, stored procedures and 128 K datablocks
- Large objects (LOBs) and user-defined functions (UDFs)
- PPI and value-list compression

While each of the above features will function and even show performance gain in most instances without additional memory, the

SYSTEM PLANNING AND SPACE MANAGEMENT

gain may be countered by the impact of working with a fixed-sized memory.

In turn, you may experience more segment swaps and incur additional swap physical disk I/O. To counter this, you can lower the FSG cache percent to assure that 90 MB or 135 MB per AMP is allocated in OS memory for 32-bit or 64-bit systems respectively.

However, lowering the FSG cache percent may cause fewer cache hits on table data and instead cause a different type of additional physical disk I/O. In general, additional I/O on table data is not as severe a performance issue as swapping I/O, but it can still have a measurable impact on performance.

In a proactive mode prior to feature introduction, you can monitor the use of FSG cache memory to determine if you should add more memory to assure full performance.

To do this:

- Monitor your existing system during critical windows to understand the ratio of logical to physical I/Os.
- After the lowering of the FSG cache percent to provide more memory to the new feature, again monitor your existing system during critical windows to understand the ratio of logical to physical I/Os.
- If the amount of FSG cache misses increases by more than 20% *and* the system has become I/O-bound, then adding more memory, if possible, is recommended.

Ingesting Data - Planning for growth

To plan for the resources needed to accommodate growth, you must know how the current workload is affecting the system. To assess the

Teradata 12 Enterprise Architecture

effect of the current workload, you should collect and analyze information about resource utilization.

Collecting and analyzing current resource usage information is one component of data analysis but another valuable component is the collection of historical usage statistics. The accounting feature can be used to determine the activity on current workloads, which assists you in anticipating future needs.

Teradata Manager has a Table Growth Report which provides several view of permanent space usage on the system.

Practice Questions

Match the ARC operation with the proper data session requirement definition.

1. ___ All-AMPs archive	a. ARC calculates the nearest multiple of online AMPs for the operation and assigns tasks evenly among the involved AMPs
2. ___ Cluster	b. No more than one session per AMP
3. ___ Copy	c. Uses all the sessions specified by the sessions parameter
4. ___ Restore	
5. ___ Specific AMPs archive	

6. Which SQL statements cause full row images to be captured in the Transient Journal? (Choose 2)
    a. DELETE
    b. INSERT
    c. SELECT
    d. UPDATE

Teradata 12 Enterprise Architecture

7. Which of the following log tables are automatically purged by the system?
   a. DBC.ResUsage
   b. DBC.AccLogTbl
   c. DBC.SW_Event_Log
   d. All of the above
   e. None of the above

8. Which ASE variables can cause DBC.Acctg to grow too big? (Choose 2)
   a. &D
   b. &H
   c. &I
   d. &L
   e. &S
   f. &T

9. The HUT locks used by ARC remain active until a _____.
   a. CLEAR LOCKS statement
   b. client reset
   c. END LOCKS statement
   d. RELEASE LOCKS statement
   e. Teradata database reset

Chapter Notes

Utilize this space for notes, key points to remember, diagrams, areas of further study, etc.

Chapter 9 - Data Integration

Certification Objectives

- ✓ Given a scenario, determine the appropriate method for ingesting data.
- ✓ Describe the functions of the client software components in a Teradata environment.
- ✓ Given a scenario, identify the appropriate approach for data movement.
- ✓ Given a system restart scenario, identify the impact on data integration jobs.
- ✓ Define the purpose and benefits of Master Data Management in an enterprise architecture.
- ✓ Identify the benefits of data governance on a growing enterprise data warehouse environment.
- ✓ Identify the benefits of metadata capture on a growing enterprise data warehouse environment.

Before You Begin

You should be familiar with the following terms and concepts.

Terms	Key Concepts
Import	Bringing data into a Teradata system
Export	Transferring data to an external target
Data Movement	Transferring from staging tables to target tables
PPI	Partitioned Primary Indexes

FastLoad

Teradata FastLoad is a command-driven utility you can use to quickly load large amounts of data in an empty table on a Teradata Database.

You can load data from:

- Disk or tape files on a channel-attached client system
- Input files on a network-attached workstation
- Special input module (INMOD) routines you write to select, validate, and preprocess input data
- Any other device providing properly formatted source data

Teradata FastLoad uses multiple sessions to load data. However, it loads data into only one table on a Teradata Database per job. If you want to load data into more than one table in the Teradata Database, you must submit multiple Teradata FastLoad jobs—one for each table.

Full tape support is not available for any function in Teradata FastLoad for network attached client systems. If you want to import data from a tape, you will need to write a custom access module that interfaces with the tape device.

When you invoke Teradata FastLoad, the utility executes the Teradata FastLoad commands and Teradata SQL statements in your Teradata FastLoad job script. These direct Teradata FastLoad to:

- log you on to the Teradata Database for a specified number of sessions, using your username, password, and tdpid/acctid information.
- load the input data into the Teradata FastLoad table on the Teradata Database.
- log you off from the Teradata Database.

If the load operation was successful, return the following information about the Teradata FastLoad operation and then terminate:

- Total number of records read, skipped, and sent to the Teradata Database
- Number of errors posted to the Teradata FastLoad error tables
- Number of inserts applied
- Number of duplicate rows

Teradata FastLoad processes a series of Teradata Fastload commands and Teradata SQL statements you enter either interactively or in batch mode.

You use the Teradata FastLoad commands for session control and data handling of the data transfers. The Teradata SQL statements create, maintain, and drop tables on the Teradata Database.

During a load operation, Teradata FastLoad inserts the data from each record of your data source into one row of the target table. The target table must be empty and have no defined secondary indexes.

Teradata FastLoad does not load duplicate rows from your data source to the Teradata Database. (A duplicate row is one in which every field contains the exact same data as the fields of an existing row.) This is true even for MULTISET tables. If you want to load duplicate rows in a MULTISET table, use MultiLoad.

On network-attached workstations, Teradata FastLoad uses the TCP/IP network protocol for all data transfer operations.

On channel-attached systems, Teradata FastLoad transfers data as either:

- A multi-volume data set or file

- A number of single-volume data sets or files in separate Teradata FastLoad jobs

You can restart serial Teradata FastLoad operations by loading the next tape in a series instead of beginning with the first tape in a set.

In either case, Teradata FastLoad:

- Uses multiple Teradata sessions, at one session per AMP, to transfer data
- Transfers multiple rows of data within a single message

Until you complete the Teradata FastLoad job and have loaded the data into the Teradata FastLoad table:

- There is no journaling or fallback data
- You cannot define the secondary indexes

Restarting FastLoad

A paused Teradata FastLoad job is one that was halted, before completing, during the loading or end loading phase of the Teradata Fastload operation. The paused condition can be intentional, or the result of a system failure or error condition.

You can pause a Teradata FastLoad job intentionally by using the LOGOFF or QUIT command before the END LOADING command in your Teradata FastLoad job script, as when running a multi-file Teradata FastLoad job.

Unintentional conditions that can pause a Teradata FastLoad job include:

- Client system or Teradata FastLoad failures
- Unrecoverable error conditions

DATA INTEGRATION

- Database or table overfills
- Teradata Database failures
- AP reset conditions

When a Teradata FastLoad job is in the paused state, the Teradata FastLoad target table and the two error tables on the Teradata Database are locked.

Restart Procedures

The procedure that you use and the Teradata FastLoad response to restarting a paused Teradata FastLoad job depends on the phase that the Teradata FastLoad job was in when it was paused.

You can restart a job that was paused during loading, either from the beginning, or from the most recent checkpoint if the BEGIN LOADING command specified the checkpoint option.

Or, you can restart a job that was paused during end loading from wherever it was interrupted. This is because the Teradata Database uses internal checkpointing during this phase. You generally do not need to do anything in this case because processing after the END LOADING command is executed on the Teradata Database does not depend on Teradata FastLoad.

To restart the job if the Teradata FastLoad job was paused during the loading phase

Remove the CREATE TABLE statement and any DROP TABLE and DELETE statements from the Teradata FastLoad job script. You do not want your restarted job to drop the partially loaded Teradata FastLoad table or delete the entries in the two error tables.

Invoke Teradata FastLoad to start the job. The Teradata FastLoad utility:

Teradata 12 Enterprise Architecture

- Establishes new sessions using your LOGON command.
- Reads the restart log to determine the restart point.
- In response to the BEGIN LOADING command, indicates that the job is being restarted

Note: If the Teradata FastLoad job was paused during the loading phase and uses an INMOD routine, the INMOD routine must be able to handle restarts and checkpoints when restarted in the loading phase. Following a restart, Teradata FastLoad passes a status code of 2 or 4 to an INMOD routine that is participating in a load operation. The routine must adjust the record to be read to the position of the last checkpoint and, upon subsequent calls, send records to Teradata FastLoad.

To restart the job if the Teradata FastLoad job was paused during the end loading phase:

- Use the same LOGON command described in the preceding procedure.
- Submit BEGIN LOADING and END LOADING commands, as in the following example:

```
LOGON dbc/sjn,music ;
BEGIN LOADING Fast_Table
ERRORFILES Error_1, Error_2 ;
END LOADING ;
```

Figure 9.1

Note: If you use your Teradata FastLoad job script to assemble these commands, make sure you delete the CREATE TABLE and any DROP TABLE and DELETE statements before restarting the job

MultiLoad

MultiLoad is a command-driven utility for fast, high-volume maintenance on multiple tables and views of a Teradata Database. A single MultiLoad job performs a number of different import and delete tasks on database tables and views:

- Each MultiLoad import task can do multiple data insert, update, and delete functions on up to five different tables or views.
- Each MultiLoad delete task can remove large numbers of rows from a single table.

Use MultiLoad to import data from:

- Access modules
- Any device providing properly formatted source data
- Disk or tape files (using a custom Access Module) on a channel-attached client system
- Input files on a network-attached workstation
- Special input module (INMOD) programs you write to select, validate, and preprocess input data

The table or view in the database receiving the data can be any existing table or view for which you have access privileges for the maintenance tasks you want to do.

Restarting a Paused MultiLoad Job

A paused MultiLoad job is one that was halted, before completing, during the acquisition phase of the MultiLoad operation. The paused condition can be intentional, or the result of a system failure or error condition.

You can pause a MultiLoad job intentionally by using a PAUSE ACQUISITION command between the BEGIN MLOAD command and the END MLOAD command in the MultiLoad job script.

Unintentional conditions that can pause a MultiLoad job include:

- A down AMP recovery
- A job abort or client system failure
- A MultiLoad job script error
- A Teradata Database restart
- A Teradata Database system reconfiguration
- An application processor reset condition
- An unrecoverable I/O error

After Using the PAUSE ACQUISITION Command

To restart a MultiLoad job that was paused by a PAUSE ACQUISITION command in the MultiLoad job script:

- Remove the PAUSE ACQUISITION command from the MultiLoad job script.
- Invoke MultiLoad to restart the job. The MultiLoad utility:
- Reestablishes sessions with the Teradata Database
- Reads the restart log table to determine the restart point
- Resumes processing the MultiLoad job script

After a MultiLoad Job Script Error

When MultiLoad encounters an error in your job script, it generates a diagnostic error message and stops with a nonzero return code. At this point, you can modify the script to correct the error and resubmit the MultiLoad job. The utility resumes processing at the statement following the last one that completed successfully.

When correcting script errors, you can make changes at or after the indicated error. MultiLoad does not repeat the commands that executed successfully, but the job will fail, with additional error messages, if the utility detects changes before such errors.

After an Unrecoverable I/O Error

The MultiLoad utility automatically attempts a restart operation after encountering an unrecoverable I/O error while accessing a fallback type table.

Status messages on screen 7 of the database operator's console reflect the progress of the restart operation, and some I/O error conditions can force an AMP to become a nonparticipant in the MultiLoad job. In this case, the MultiLoad job is stopped with error messages. Additional error messages indicate errors that may occur during the restart operation.

After a Down AMP is Recovered

When a down AMP with a fallback type MultiLoad worktable is recovered, status messages on screen 7 of the database operator's console may indicate that special procedures might be required to recover the table.

After a Teradata Database Restart

If the Teradata Database restarts while a MultiLoad job is running, MultiLoad automatically resumes processing after the normal recovery operation. You do not have to intervene for a normal Teradata Database restart/recovery operation.

If, however, the work tables or error tables are missing, MultiLoad aborts the restart attempt with an error message.

After a Teradata Database System Reconfiguration

If you run the Reconfiguration program while a MultiLoad job is active, the associated target tables, work tables, and possibly the error tables, are not redistributed. The MultiLoad restart log table is redistributed.

After a Job Abort or Client System Failure

Restarting a MultiLoad job that was either aborted or stopped after a client system failure or restart depends on whether the MultiLoad job stopped during the application phase.

If the job was stopped before or after the application phase, then you can restart the MultiLoad job as is, with no changes to the job script. MultiLoad uses the entries in the restart log table to determine its stopping point and resumes processing there.

The BEGIN MLOAD command is the first step in a multiple-step job. If you re-execute commands that modify tables or databases involved in the MultiLoad job, you may corrupt them.

DATA INTEGRATION

After an Application Processor Reset Condition

When your MultiLoad job is interrupted by a resetting application processor on the Teradata Database, the restart alternatives depend on the environment in which the utility is running:

On the *resetting* application processor. In this case, your MultiLoad job is halted and must be manually restarted.

On a *non-resetting* application processor. In this case, your MultiLoad job may or may not be halted, depending on whether it has sessions connected through the resetting AP. If your MultiLoad job has sessions connected through the resetting AP, the utility automatically:

- Logs off all sessions.
- Logs them back on.
- Rolls back to the most recent checkpoint.
- Resumes processing.

If the MultiLoad job does not have sessions connected through the resetting AP, the utility is not affected by the AP reset condition.

FastExport

FastExport is a command-driven utility that uses multiple sessions to quickly transfer large amounts of data from tables and views of the Teradata Database to a client-based application. You can export data from any table or view to which you have the SELECT access privilege.

The destination for the exported data can be:

- A file on your channel-attached or network-attached client system

- An Output Modification (OUTMOD) routine you write to select, validate, and preprocess the exported data

When you invoke FastExport, the utility executes the FastExport commands and Teradata SQL statements in your FastExport job script. These direct FastExport to:

- Log you on to the Teradata Database for a specified number of sessions, using your username, password, and tdpid/acctid information
- Retrieve the specified data from the Teradata Database, in accordance with your format and selection specifications
- Export the data to the specified file or OUTMOD routine on your client system
- Log you off the Teradata Database

Restarting FastExport

A paused FastExport job is one that terminates abnormally, without dropping the restart log table from the Teradata Database. The paused condition can be intentional, or the result of a system failure or error condition.

Unintentional conditions that can pause a FastExport job include:

- A FastExport job script error
- A hardware failure or software error condition
- An application processor (AP) reset condition

FastExport automatically restarts some paused jobs. You must manually restart others. The following subsections describe the manual restart procedure and the factors that affect FastExport restart operations under the different pause conditions.

To manually restart a paused FastExport job, resubmit the entire FastExport job script, using the same restart log table specification.

The FastExport utility:

- Reestablishes sessions with the Teradata Database
- Reads the restart log table to determine the restart point
- Resumes processing your FastExport job script

After a Job Script Error

When FastExport encounters an error in a job script, it generates a diagnostic error message and stops with a nonzero return code. At this point, you can modify the script to correct the error and resubmit the FastExport job. The utility resumes processing at the statement following the last one that completed successfully.

When correcting script errors, you can make changes at or after the indicated error. FastExport does not repeat the commands that executed successfully, but the job will fail, with additional error messages, if the utility detects changes before the indicated error.

After Hardware Failures or Software Error Conditions

FastExport restarts automatically after system recovery from the following types of hardware failures and software error conditions:

- CLIv2 error on your client system
- Down AMP
- Network failure
- Nonrecoverable I/O error
- Teradata Database restart

Teradata 12 Enterprise Architecture

If the failure occurred while FastExport was processing a job script with a *single* select request, then the utility resumes processing after system recovery by resubmitting the one select request.

If the failure occurred while FastExport was processing a job script with *multiple* select requests, then the utility resumes processing after system recovery by resubmitting the last select request that was submitted before the failure occurred.

After an AP Reset Condition

When a FastExport job is interrupted by a resetting AP on the Teradata Database, the restart response depends on the environment in which the utility is running:

- On the resetting AP
- On a non-resetting AP
- On a channel-attached client system

If an AP reset condition occurs and FastExport is running on a *resetting* AP, then the FastExport job is halted and must be manually restarted.

If an AP reset condition occurs and FastExport is running on a *non-resetting* AP, then the FastExport job may or may not be halted, depending on whether it has sessions connected through the resetting AP:

If the FastExport job has sessions connected through the resetting AP, the utility automatically:

- Logs off all sessions
- Logs them back on
- Rolls back to the most recent checkpoint
- Resumes processing

DATA INTEGRATION

If the FastExport job *does not* have sessions connected through the resetting AP, the utility is not affected by the AP reset condition.

The increased session loading caused by the reconnection of other sessions through the resetting AP may degrade the system response time.

If an AP reset condition occurs and FastExport is running on a channel-attached client system with AP reset containment enabled, then the FastExport job is halted, but does not need to be manually restarted. FastExport automatically:

- Logs off all sessions
- Logs them back on
- Rolls back to the most recent checkpoint
- Resumes processing

TPump

TPump is a data loading utility that helps you maintain (update, delete, insert, and atomic upsert) the data in your Teradata Database. TPump allows you to achieve near-real time data in your data warehouse.

TPump uses standard Teradata SQL to achieve moderate to high data loading rates to the Teradata Database. Multiple sessions and multistatement requests are typically used to increase throughput.

TPump provides an alternative to Teradata MultiLoad for the low volume batch maintenance of large Teradata databases. Instead of updating Teradata Databases overnight, or in batches throughout the day, TPump updates information in real time, acquiring data from the client system with low processor utilization. It does this through a continuous feed of data into the data warehouse, rather than through

Teradata 12 Enterprise Architecture

traditional batch updates. Continuous updates result in more accurate, timely data.

Unlike most load utilities, TPump uses row hash locks rather than table level locks. This allows you to run queries while TPump is running. This also means that TPump can be stopped instantaneously. TPump provides a dynamic throttling feature that enables it to run "all out" during batch windows, but within limits when it may impact other business uses of the Teradata Database.

Operators can specify the number of statements run per minute, or may alter throttling minute-by-minute, if necessary.

TPump's main attributes are:

- Efficient, time-saving operation – jobs can continue running in spite of database restarts, dirty data, and network slowdowns. Jobs restart without intervention.
- Flexible data management – accepts an infinite variety of data forms from an infinite number of data sources, including direct feeds from other databases. TPump is also able to transform that data on the fly before sending it to Teradata. SQL statements and conditional logic are usable within the utilities, making it unnecessary to write wrapper jobs around the utilities.
- Simple, hassle-free setup – does not require staging of data, intermediary files, or special hardware.

Recovering an Aborted TPump Job

An aborted TPump job is one that has been terminated early for any number of reasons (out of database space, accidental cancellation by mainframe operators, UNIX kernel panic, error limit in the TPump job exceeded, and so on) and all TPump database objects, the restart log table, the error table, and DML macros are intact.

An aborted TPump job may be restarted using the same job script that was used in the original job, and TPump will perform the recovery of the job.

Recovering from Script Errors

When TPump encounters an error in the input script, a diagnostic message is generated and the operation is stopped with a non-zero return code. You can then modify the script, correct the faulty code, and resubmit the job. Operations begin with the statement following the last one that was successfully completed.

BTEQ

BTEQ is an abbreviation of Basic Teradata Query. It is a general-purpose, command-based program that allows users on a workstation to communicate with one or more Teradata Database systems, and to format reports for both print and screen output. Using BTEQ you can submit SQL queries to the Teradata Database. BTEQ formats the results and returns them to the screen, a file, or to a designated printer.

A BTEQ session provides a quick and easy way to access a Teradata Database. In a BTEQ session, you can do the following:

- Enter Teradata SQL statements to view, add, modify, and delete data.
- Enter BTEQ commands.
- Enter operating system commands.
- Create and use Teradata stored procedures.

BTEQ operates in both batch and interactive modes:

- In interactive mode, you start a BTEQ session, and submit commands to the database as needed.
- In batch mode, you prepare scripts or macros, and then submit them to BTEQ for processing.

To use BTEQ to load rows into the database, you use the normal SQL INSERT command.

When you logon to BTEQ, the default is your SQL will go through a single session.

BTEQ can log on to Teradata sessions in sets, so that a number of sessions can run in parallel within a given set. This is especially helpful when you need to process a high volume of repetitive tasks whose order does not matter, such as loading a large number of rows onto a database. In this case, having a number of parallel sessions with each handling some of the requests can substantially speed up operations.

Though BTEQ can support a maximum of up to 200 sessions, the actual maximum depends on the configuration of your system and your terminal or workstation. The maximum for your system could be less than 200, and as few as 16 for PC workstations.

You specify the number of sessions in a set by entering the SESSIONS command prior to the LOGON command. The default number of sessions is 1, as stated above.

Through the use of the .IMPORT command, you can specify a data file to be used as input.

DATA INTEGRATION

Transactions and BTEQ

BTEQ does not recognize BT/ET transactions. BTEQ handles Request Parcels, which may contain 1 or more SQL statements. If certain errors occur, and RETRY is ON (the default), BTEQ will resend the failing request parcel. <u>BTEQ only has RETRY logic, not RESTART logic.</u>

You can create multistatement requests by proper semicolon placement in your BTEQ script, or you can put the SQL statements in a macro and have BTEQ execute the macro.

You can speed up BTEQ by specifying QUIET ON. If you use the QUIET command with the REPEAT or = command, BTEQ determines the reporting of time statistics by the number of sessions being run. With multiple sessions, BTEQ only reports the summary times for each cycle (start time, finish time, and total time). During a single session, BTEQ reports summary and processing times of queries executed in each cycle.

Typically, the QUIET and REPEAT commands are used together in multi-session data-load operations.

Teradata Parallel Transporter

The following are the principal features of TPT:

- **Single Script Language**
  This simplifies the creation of load/unload operations.
- **Complex 'Multi-Step' Load Scenarios**
  A TPT script can contain multiple job steps, each of which may be performing a load or unload function.
- **Increased Throughput**

Teradata 12 Enterprise Architecture

TPT permits multiple instances of each operator in a script, thereby eliminating the single input stream of the traditional utilities.

- **Direct API**
  The Application Program Interface (API) allows customers and vendors to write programs to directly load or unload Teradata tables using C or C++.
- **Reduced File Storage**
  TPT eliminates the need for intermediate file storage by holding data in data buffers (called 'streams').

TPT integrates the traditional utilities (FastlLoad, MultiLoad, TPump, and FastExport) into one platform using a single scripting language that uses 'operators'. To load a table, you now invoke a 'load' operator instead of running FastLoad. To update a table, you invoke an 'update' operator instead of running MultiLoad, and so on. Each operator can, of course, use multiple user sessions for additional parallelism.

Additional TPT Features

Teradata Parallel Transporter replaces the former Teradata Warehouse Builder. It uses the same script language so migration from TWB to TPT is seamless.

Here are some of the features of TPT:

- Concurrent Load from Multiple Sources
  - TPT can simultaneously load data from multiple and dissimilar sources in a single job.
  - It can execute multiple instances of an operator.
  - It can export, transform, and load one or more tables in a single job.
  - It can perform in-line filtering and transformation of data.

- Improved Performance through Parallelism and Scalability
    - TPT automatically distributes input and output data into data streams.
    - Data is streamed between operators without being written to disk.
    - Each data stream can be shared with multiple instances of the operators.
- Checkpoint Restart
    - TPT can automatically resume load jobs from the last checkpoint if the job aborts.
- Directory Scan
    - Permits multiple files in a client directory to be simultaneously processed as source data.
- Improved Throughput
    - Overcome input file I/O and CPU bottlenecks with multiple operator instances, as opposed to single-threaded applications such as MultiLoad or FastLoad.

Figure 9.2 illustrates the Teradata PT architecture. The three tiers represent source, load, and target environments, which can either reside on different servers or on the same server.

Teradata 12 Enterprise Architecture

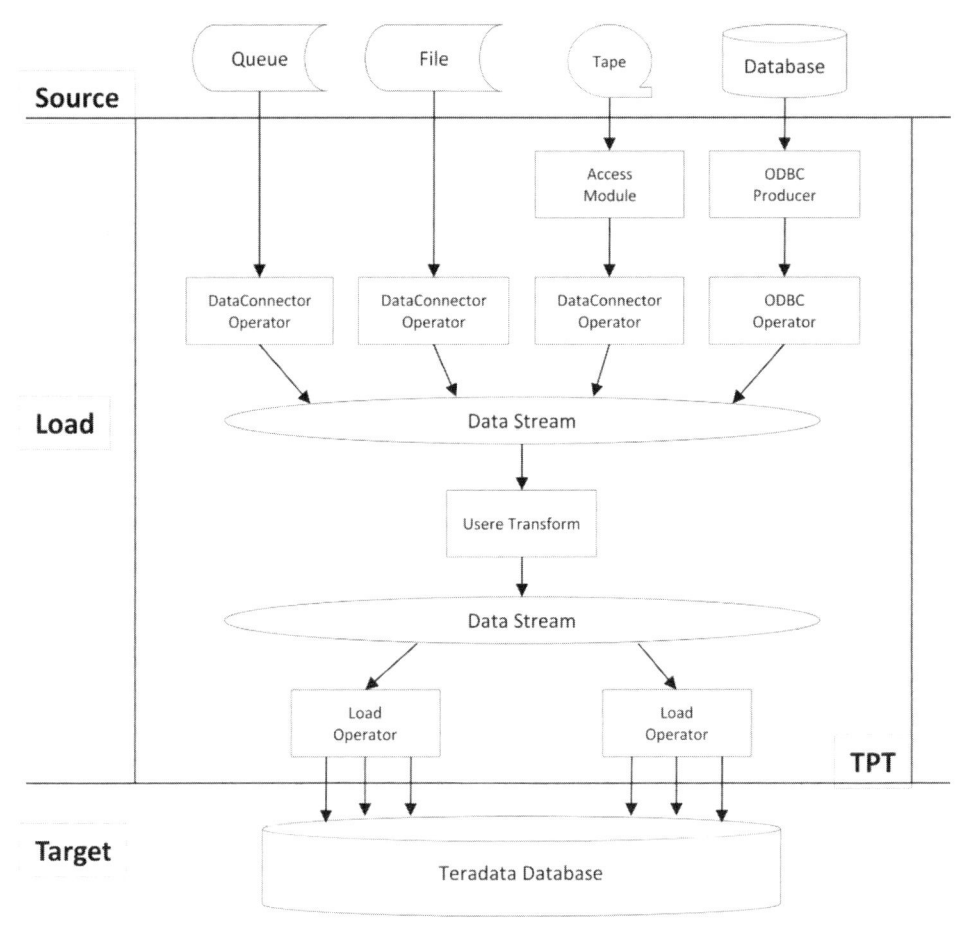

Figure 9.2

TPT achieves pipeline parallelism by connecting operator instances through data streams.

Figure 9.3 shows the major components of a TPT job.

COMPONENT	FUNCTION
Input Sources	These can be databases (both relational and non-relational) or database servers, data storage devices (i.e. tape or DVD readers), file objects, such as images, pictures, voice & text.

Teradata 12 Certification Study Guide

DATA INTEGRATION

COMPONENT	FUNCTION
Producer Operators	These extract data from a source and write it to a data stream. They 'produce' a data stream.
Data Stream	A data buffer in memory used to temporarily hold data. A data stream can accept data from multiple producer instances, and can distribute the data to multiple consumer operator instances.
Consumer Operators	These accept data from a data stream. They 'consume' the data and write it to the output target.
Output Target	These can be databases (both relational and non-relational) or database servers, data storage devices. For a load operator, the target must be a Teradata database.

Figure 9.3

Figure 9.4 illustrates the differences between TPT and the stand-alone utilities.

Operator	Standalone Equivalent	Purpose
DataConnector operator	Data Connector (PIOM)	Read data from and write data to flat files
DataConnector operator with WebSphere MQ Access Module	Data Connector (PIOM)	Read data from IBM WebSphere MQ
DataConnector operator with Named Pipes Access Module	Data Connector (PIOM)	Read data from a named pipe
DDL operator	BTEQ	Execute DDL, DCL, and self-

Teradata 12 Enterprise Architecture

Operator	Standalone Equivalent	Purpose
		contained DML SQL statements
Export operator	FastExport	High-volume export of data from Teradata Database
FastExport OUTMOD Adapter operator	FastExport OUTMOD Routine	Preprocess exported data with a FastExport OUTMOD routine before writing the data to a file
FastLoad INMOD Adapter operator	FastLoad INMOD Routine	Read and preprocess data from a FastLoad INMOD data source
Load Operator	Fastload	High-volume load of an empty table
MultiLoad INMOD Adapter operator	MultiLoad INMOD Routine	Read and preprocess data from a MultiLoad INMOD data source
ODBC operator	OLE DB Access Module	Export data from any non-Teradata database that has an ODBC driver
OS Command operator	Client host operating system	Execute host operating system commands
SQL Inserter operator	BTEQ	Insert data into a Teradata table using SQL protocol
SQL Selector operator	BTEQ	Select data from a Teradata table using SQL protocol
Stream operator	TPump	Continuous loading of Teradata tables using SQL protocol
Update operator	MultiLoad	Update, insert, and delete rows

Figure 9.4

DATA INTEGRATION

In addition to producer and consumer operators, TPT also has filter operators and standalone operators.

Figure 9.5 summarizes the operators and their characteristics.

OPERATOR TYPE	FUNCTION
Producer Operators They *Produce* a Data Stream	Get data from the Teradata database or an external data source. Write the data to a data stream. Typically make the data available to other operators.
Consumer Operators They *Consume* a Data Stream	Typically receive data from other operators. Read data from a data stream. Load data into a Teradata database or external data store.
Filter Operators They *Consume* and *Produce* Data Streams	Perform data selection, data validation, data cleansing, and data condensing. Filter operators function as both consumers and producers since they consume an input stream, handle the data, and then produce an output data stream.
Standalone Operators No Data Stream action	Used for submitting DDL commands. Also used for doing Delete Tasks (functioning as an update operator). Do not depend on input data from any sources other than the job script. Do not send or receive data from other operators – no data streams.

Figure 9.5

CHECKPOINT AND RESTART

Export operator

The Export operator behaves differently from other Teradata PT operators in that it does not support a user-defined restart log table. Instead, it takes a checkpoint only when all data is sent to the data stream. If a restart occurs, the operator either must send all of the data or none of the data depending on whether the checkpoint has taken place.

DDL operator

The DDL operator restarts at the beginning of the group of SQL statements whose execution is interrupted by an abnormal termination. If the interrupted group has only one SQL statement, the DDL operator restarts at that statement.

Because SQL statements are sent to Teradata Database by group in the order in which they are specified in the Teradata PT APPLY statement, the DDL operator can take a checkpoint after each group is executed. A group can contain one or more SQL statements. A checkpoint, in the case of the DDL operator, marks the last group of DDL/DML SQL statements to execute successfully.

If the last request was successful prior a restart, the operator can resume at the next request in line. If the last request failed prior to a restart, then the operator resumes at the failed request.

Load operator

Teradata PT can automatically resume load jobs from the last checkpoint if the job aborts.

Update operator

The Update operator cannot be rolled back. Once changes are applied to target tables in the application phase, a job can only move forward. Since a target table cannot be returned to its original state, it is advisable to archive tables prior to running Update operations against them.

Stream operator

Checkpoint options control how often a row is written to the checkpoint file for the purposes of restarting a job. Unless otherwise specified, a checkpoint is taken at the start of and at the end of the input data. Since this process does not provide granular restartability in the case of longer running jobs, checkpoint intervals can be user-specified in terms of minutes or seconds.

Insert/Select

Empty Table INSERT/SELECT Requests and Performance
An INSERT/SELECT optimizes performance when the target table is empty. If the target table has no data, INSERT/SELECT operates on an efficient block-by-block basis that bypasses transient journaling.

Using multiple input tables, you can build a single table by combining data via a multistatement INSERT/SELECT statement.

All multistatement INSERT/SELECT statements output to the same spool table. The output is sorted and inserted into an empty table.

INSERT/SELECT Into an Empty SET Table

INSERT/SELECT into an empty SET table from a source known not to have duplicate rows avoids duplicate checking of the target table during insertion. This occurs even during direct insertion from another SET table.

This should offer significant performance improvement in cases where there is a NUPI that is relatively non-unique or has few values that are very non-unique.

INSERT/SELECT with FastLoad

Use the optimized INSERT/SELECT to manipulate FastLoaded data:

1. FastLoad into a staging table.
2. INSERT/SELECT into the final table, manipulating the data as required.

FastLoad and INSERT/SELECT are faster than using an INMOD to manage data on the host. The host is a single bottleneck as opposed to parallel AMPs that populate temporary tables for reports or intermediate results.

Multiple source tables may populate the same target table. If the target table is empty before a request begins, all INSERT/SELECT statements in that request run in the optimized mode.

INSERT/SELECT with Join Index

The fastest way of processing inserts into a table with a join index is as follows:

1. Use FastLoad to load the rows into an empty table with no indexes or join indexes defined.
2. Do an INSERT/SELECT from the freshly loaded table into the target table with the join index.

DATA INTEGRATION

If the target table has multiple join indexes defined, the Optimizer may choose to use reusable spool during join index maintenance, if applicable.

Processing for these steps is performed a block at a time and should provide the best throughput.

SQL Merge

Merges a source row set into a target table based on whether any target rows satisfy a specified matching condition with the source row.

IF the source and target rows ...	THEN the merge operation is an ...
satisfy the matching condition	update based on the specified WHEN MATCHED THEN UPDATE clause.
do not satisfy the matching condition	insert based on the specified WHEN NOT MATCHED THEN INSERT clause.

Figure 9.6

Teradata Database supports bulk SQL error handling for MERGE and INSERT/SELECT statements. This permits bulk SQL inserts and updates to be done without the target table restrictions that apply to Teradata Database load utilities.

If logging is not specified, the system does no error handling. If an error occurs, an ANSI request aborts and rolls back, and a Teradata transaction aborts and rolls back.

Teradata 12 Enterprise Architecture

LOGGING OPTIONS	
LOGGING [ALL] ERRORS	Log all data errors, reference index errors, and USI errors. If you do not specify a limit, the system defaults to a 10 error limit.
LOGGING ERRORS WITH NO LIMIT	There is no limit to the number of errors that can be logged in the error table associated with the target data table for this MERGE operation, other than the system-determined limit of 16,000,000 errors is reached.
LOGGING ERRORS WITH LIMIT OF *error-limit*	The value you specify for *error_limit* can be anything in the range of 1 to 16,000,000, inclusive. If this limit is exceeded, the system aborts the transaction in Teradata session mode or the request in ANSI session mode, and rolls back all changes made to the target table, but does not roll back the logged error table rows.

Figure 9.7

If the reorganization of partitions of a PPI would cause too many rows to be moved from their current partition to a different partition, use a CREATE TABLE request to create a new table with the partitioning you want, then use an INSERT/SELECT or MERGE request with error logging to move the rows from the source table into the newly created target table with the desired partitioning.

NUPI

Keep in mind that target tables may be SET or MULTISET. Inserts and Updates to populated NUPI SET tables require the system to do duplicate row checking.

Unique indexes (UPI, USI) require duplicate index checking.

Partitioned DML

PPI allows the data rows of a table to be:
- Hash partitioned to the AMPs by the hash of the PI columns
- Partitioned on some set of columns on each AMP
- Ordered by the hash of the PI columns within that partition

PPI introduces syntax that you can use to create a table or non-compressed join index with a PPI and to support the index. The table may be a base, global temporary, or volatile table.

One or more partitioning expressions can be defined for a PI. The syntax supports altering a PPI along with changes, for example, to the output of various support statements. You can use two functions, RANGE_N and CASE_N, to simplify the specification of a partitioning expression.

Performance Impact

PPI improves performance as follows:

- Uses partition elimination (static, delayed, or dynamic) to improve the efficiency of range searches when, for example, the searches are range partitioned.
- Provides an access path to the rows in the base table while still providing efficient join strategies.

Moreover, if the same partition is consistently targeted, the part of the table updated may be able to fit largely in cache, significantly boosting performance.

Performance Considerations

Performance tests indicate that the use of PPI can cause dramatic performance improvements both in queries and in table maintenance.

Teradata 12 Enterprise Architecture

For example, NUSI maintenance for insert and delete requests can be done a block at a time rather than a row at a time. Insert and delete requests done this way show a reduction in I/O per transaction. The reduction in I/O in turn reduces the CPU path need to process the I/Os. Be aware of the following:

- While a table with a properly defined PPI will allow overall improvement in query performance, certain individual workloads involving the table, such as primary index selects, where the partition column criteria is not provided in the WHERE clause, may become slower.
- There are potential cost increases for certain operations, such as empty table INSERT/SELECTs.
- You must carefully implement the partitioning environment to gain maximum benefit.
- Benefits that are the result of using PPI will vary based on:
    - The number of partitions defined
    - The number of partitions that can be eliminated given the query workloads, and
    - Whether or not you follow an update strategy that takes advantage of partitioning.

Multilevel Partitioned Primary Index

Multilevel partitioning allows each partition to be sub-partitioned. Each level must define at least two partitions. The number of levels of partitioning cannot exceed 15. The limit is 65,535 partitions for a combined partitioning expression. The number of levels of partitioning may be further restricted by other limits such as, for example, the maximum size of the table header or data dictionary entry sizes.

An MLPPI can be used to improve query performance via partition elimination at each of the levels or a combination of levels. An MLPPI provides an access path to the rows in the base table. As with other indexes, the Optimizer determines if the index is usable for a query and, if usable, whether its use provides the best cost plan for executing the query. No modification of the query is required.

Recursive Views

You cannot update, in the most general use of the word, a base table through a recursive view. In other words, you cannot reference a recursive view using any of the following SQL DML statements:

- DELETE
- INSERT
- MERGE
- UPDATE

If you attempt to update a view using any of these statements, the system returns an error to the requestor. Because of this, there are no privileges associated with update operations on a recursive view.

In addition, you cannot reference a recursive view

- UDF
- Table
- WITH clause
- WITH RECURSIVE clause from a stored procedure definition.

Note: You can specify both aggregate and arithmetic operators in the seed query of a view definition expression, but *not* in its recursive query.

Metadata Management

Teradata Meta Data Services (MDS) provides an infrastructure for managing Teradata Warehouse metadata and for creating tools to interchange metadata with external operational systems, Extraction Transformation and Load (ETL) tools, Business Intelligence tools, Database Modeling tools, and any other metadata sources.

Components of Teradata MDS include:

- A repository database where metadata is stored in Teradata tables
- Two predefined Application Information Metamodels (AIMs)
- Tools and utilities to:
    - Define entirely new AIMs
    - Extend existing AIMs
    - Build metadata interchange bridges
- Administrative and support tools and features for managing metadata.

The MDS repository is a collection of tables, views and macros stored in a Teradata Database. These tables are used to store metadata. The macros and views are used internally by MDS.

Note: The Teradata ODBC Driver is used for database access.

The MDS software performs services to persist and retrieve metadata from the repository database and controls access to the repository and its objects. Access to the repository is controlled by database security permissions. Access to objects within the repository is controlled by MDS security permissions.

How metadata is stored in the repository is defined by Application Information Metamodels (AIMs). An AIM consists of:

- Classes, which are types of metadata objects
- Properties, which are data fields associates with a particular class
- Relationships, which are associations between two classes

The two AIMs supplied with Teradata MDS are:

- The Teradata Database Information Metamodel (DIM) is a predefined AIM for storing the Teradata Data Dictionary information from Teradata databases and associated business data.
- The Client Load Metamodel (CLM) is a predefined AIM for storing the information obtained from Teradata client FastLoad, MultiLoad and TPump utility scripts and output files.

These AIMs can be extended or entirely new AIMs can be created to store other metadata in the MDS repository.

Teradata MDS provides a number of different Administrative and Support tools and utilities to create, modify and manage metadata in the MDS repository. This section provides a brief description of these tools and utilities.

MetaManager

MetaManager is a Windows based Graphical User Interface (GUI) program for performing administrative tasks.

MetaSurf

Use MetaSurf 's HTML files and Active Server Pages (ASP) scripts to set up a powerful Web-based application for viewing, navigating and analyzing Business and Technical metadata stored in the MDS repository.

Teradata 12 Enterprise Architecture

MetaBrowse

MetaBrowse is a Windows based GUI program for performing such tasks as:

- Browsing and searching the repository
- Creating new AIMs
- Extending existing AIMs by creating new classes, properties and relationships
- Editing or manually adding data in the repository
- Deleting objects from the repository
- Starting the MetaXML or MetaClient Utility

Metacreate

The **metacreate** program creates the initial MDS repository.

Metaviews

The metaviews program installs a set of MDS views into the DBC database. If installed, the metaload program will use the views to access the DBC tables when loading the data dictionary information into the repository. Although not required, it is strongly recommended that the MDS views be installed for all Teradata systems to be tracked in the MDS repository. If the Automatic DIM Update feature is enabled on a system, the MDS views must be installed on the system.

Metamigrate

The **metamigrate** program migrates an existing repository to a newer MDS repository version.

Metaload

The **metaload** program is a command line alternative to and the program MetaManager uses for loading, unloading or resynchronizing databases. The **metaload** program loads the Teradata metadata into the MDS repository Database Information Metamodel (DIM). Beginning with MDS 12.0, the **metaload** program is Unicode-enabled. It will attempt to make a UTF16 session character set connection to Teradata databases.

If the program can establish a UTF16 connection, the program does not require that the MDS views be installed into the DBC database with the **metaviews** program.

If the program cannot establish a UTF16 connection, it will run in a mode that requires that the MDS views be installed into the DBC database with the **metaviews** program.

MetaClient

The **metaclient** program loads CLM information into the repository. It can be run by any MDS user from either the command line, through MetaManager, or MetaBrowse.

Metadelete

The **metadelete** program drops all MDS repository tables, views, and macros in the MDS repository database, effectively deleting the MDS repository.

MetaXML

The **metaxml** program imports data from an XML file into the repository or export metamodel definitions to an XML file.

Teradata 12 Enterprise Architecture

Special Features

In addition to the administrative support tools and utilities discussed above, Teradata MDS also provides some special features that allow for highly customized metadata solutions.

Application Programming Interfaces (APIs)

Using the MDS supplied APIs, programmers can create, modify and delete the metadata objects and the application information metamodels in the MDS Repository. They can also import and export metadata in the repository. MDS provides the following APIs:

- C++
- Java
- Microsoft Component Object Model (COM)
- Web Services
- XML

Note: The Web Services API is being deprecated with the 12.0 release of Teradata Meta Data Services. The API is based on the Microsoft MSSoap 3.0 component. Microsoft has deprecated this component in favor of using their .Net technology.

DATA INTEGRATION

Practice Questions

1. Which utilities support multiple sessions?
    a. BTEQ
    b. FastExport
    c. FastLoad
    d. MultiLoad
    e. TPump
    f. All of the above
    g. None of the above

2. Which utilities have restart logic? (Choose 4)
    a. BTEQ
    b. FastExport
    c. FastLoad
    d. MultiLoad
    e. TPump
    f. All of the above
    g. None of the above

3. Which utilities support INMOD routines? (Choose 3)
    a. BTEQ
    b. FastExport
    c. FastLoad
    d. MultiLoad
    e. TPump
    f. All of the above
    g. None of the above

Teradata 12 Enterprise Architecture

4. Which utilities can load duplicate rows into a Multiset table? (Choose 3)
   a. BTEQ
   b. FastExport
   c. FastLoad
   d. MultiLoad
   e. TPump
   f. All of the above
   g. None of the above

5. Which utilities can be used to delete rows from a table? (Choose 3)
   a. BTEQ
   b. FastExport
   c. FastLoad
   d. MultiLoad
   e. TPump
   f. All of the above
   g. None of the above

6. Which utilities can be used to export data? (Choose 2)
   a. BTEQ
   b. FastExport
   c. FastLoad
   d. MultiLoad
   e. TPump
   f. All of the above
   g. None of the above

7. Which of the following can be used with recursive views?
    a. DELETE
    b. INSERT
    c. MERGE
    d. SELECT
    e. Stored procedures
    f. Table functions
    g. UDF
    h. UPDATE

Chapter Notes

Utilize this space for notes, key points to remember, diagrams, areas of further study, etc.

Chapter 10 - Data Migration

Certification Objectives

- ✓ Identify what needs to be considered when developing a data mart solution.
- ✓ Describe the functions of exporting data from a Teradata environment.
- ✓ Determine strategies that are available to migrate data from an EDW to another system.

Before You Begin

You should be familiar with the following terms and concepts.

Terms	Key Concepts
NPARC	Named Pipes ARChive
Pipes	Bidirectional interprocess communication mechanisms
Replication	Copying table contents from one system to another
X views	User-restricted dictionary views
Data Governance	Ensures that data can be trusted
Metadata	Technical information about data
Master Data	Business data that is shared between groups

Data Marts

A data mart is generally a relatively small application- or function-specific subset of the data warehouse database created to optimize application performance for a narrowly defined user population.

Data marts are often categorized into three different types, as shown in Figure 10.1.

```
                    Operational Data Source
                   /                        \
                  /                          \
         Independent                    Data Warehouse
         Data Mart                      ( Logical
                                          Data
                                          Mart )
                                       /        \
                                      /          \
                              Dependent        Dependent
                              Data Mart        Data Mart
```

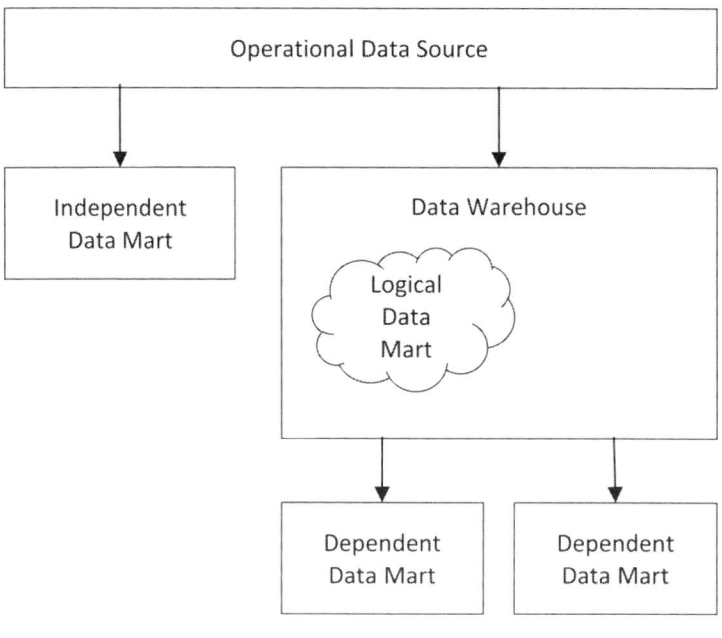

Figure 10.1

Independent data marts

Independent data marts are isolated entities, entirely separate from the enterprise data warehouse. Their data derives from independent sources and they should be viewed as data pirates in the context of the enterprise data warehouse because their independent inputs, which are entirely separate from the enterprise data warehouse, have a high likelihood of producing data that does not match that of the warehouse. These independent data marts are sometimes referred to as *data basements*, and Teradata strongly discourages their use.

Dependent data marts

Dependent data marts are derived from the enterprise data warehouse. Depending on how a dependent data mart is configured, it might or might not be useful.

The recommended process uses only data that is derived from the enterprise data warehouse data store and also permits its users to have full access to the enterprise data store when the need to investigate more enterprise-wide issues arises.

Logical data marts

Perhaps the ideal approach to incorporating the data mart concept into your data warehouse is to construct one or more logical, or virtual, data marts. By using a system of carefully constructed views on the detail data of the warehouse, you can design multiple user- or department-specific virtual data marts that provide the same sort of highly tailored information a physical data mart would without the need for massive data loads, cleansing, and other necessary transformations. Care needs to be taken when developing these types of data marts. Poorly constructed logical data marts can have performance issues.

Strategies

Data migration can take many forms. These strategies will be discussed below.

BTEQ

Import

An import file is an input file that you use primarily for writing new data to the Teradata Database. BTEQ transfers the import file data to the Teradata Database in response to the USING modifier in a Teradata SQL request.

Export

An export file is an output file that you use primarily for storing data read from the Teradata Database in response to a subsequent SQL request.

Recordmode or Indicdata Mode

By default, BTEQ initializes in Field mode to support interactive operations. Field mode is defined when both the RECORDMODE and INDICDATA command options are set to OFF. There is no corresponding FIELD command to specify the Field mode.

You can use Record or Indicator mode in interactive operations, when you need to test scripts or macros that send responses to an export file. This lets you see the data that would be diverted to the export file on your terminal screen.

Normally, you would specify either Record mode or Indicator mode in batch operations when:

DATA MIGRATION

- Using the BTEQ EXPORT command to direct output data from the Teradata Database to an export file either for reloading later or for transfer to another system.
- Using the BTEQ IMPORT command to direct input data from a client system file to the Teradata Database.

Use the following BTEQ RECORDMODE or INDICDATA commands to specify Record or Indicator mode. If the return data will have null values, use the INDICDATA command; if not, use the RECORDMODE command.

```
     .SET RECORDMODE ON
or
     .SET INDICDATA ON
```

Recordmode

When returning data in Record mode, BTEQ does not format it. Instead, BTEQ presents each row in the format specified in the Teradata SQL SELECT statement using the representation that is appropriate for the client system. BTEQ usually presents each selected row as a hexadecimal dump, ignoring FORMAT and TITLE command specifications. Null values, data types and data lengths are implicit, and you can use Teradata SQL data conversion to change the format of the data.

Indicdata

When the INDICDATA command option is set to ON, data is returned in Indicator mode. In Indicator mode, BTEQ does not format data. Instead, each selected row is presented in the format specified in the Teradata SQL SELECT statement.

Each row of data returned by the Teradata Database in Indicator mode begins with the indicator variables for the data values in that row. One indicator bit corresponds to each data item, indicating whether or not a value represents a null as follows:

- 0 – Indicates that the value contained in a data item is not null.
- 1 – If the field is nullable, indicates that the data item contains a null value.

The DataInfo parcel, which immediately precedes the first response row returned by the Teradata Database, contains information on the total number of columns returned by a request, and the data type and length of each column.

TERADATA NAMED PIPES ACCESS MODULE.

Teradata Named Pipes Access Module provides an interprocess communication link between a writer process, such as Teradata FastExport, and a reader process, such as Teradata FastLoad.

Pipes are bidirectional interprocess communication mechanisms on UNIX, Linux, Windows 2000/XP/2003 systems. They provide input and output file structures accessed by different applications and processes on a first-in-first-out (FIFO) basis.

Using pipes, instead of disk or tape files, provides a substantial performance improvement for data transfer operations between two complementary data extract and load utilities, such as FastExport, FastLoad, and TPump. However, standard pipe mechanisms do not support checkpoint and restart functions because FIFO file structures are not cached, leaving them no way to revert to an earlier position after a system failure or restart. Teradata Named Pipes Access Module caches pipe output data stream in a fallback data file that supports checkpoint and restart functions and provides quick, easy recovery from the following:

- Restarts on the destination database

DATA MIGRATION

- Crashes on the system running the load utility

Note: Teradata Named Pipes Access Module does not support checkpoint or restart operations on the source database.

The writer process can be a client extraction utility, such as FastExport, or any other application, data source, or device that can provide data in a format supported by the reader process.

The reader process can be a client load utility, such as Teradata FastLoad, Teradata MultiLoad, or Teradata TPump.

On UNIX systems the writer process must run on the same system as the reader process. UNIX pipes cannot span a network.

Because Windows named pipes can span networks, the reader and writer processes can reside on different network-connected Windows systems.

TPT

The Named Pipes Access Module can be used transparently with any Teradata Parallel Transporter (Teradata PT) consumer operator through the DataConnector operator.

ARC

Keep in mind that Archive and Recovery data can be restored to the same or different system.

Dual System Architecture

Dual system architecture, also known as Dual-Active Solutions, is provided by Teradata Replication Services.

Teradata Replication Services allows users to capture changes made to a specific set of tables in one database and apply those changes to corresponding tables in another database in near real-time. Replication can serve several purposes in database information management:

- Replication can provide a backup of specified table data in the event of problems with your source database.
- If your site has Teradata Dual-Active Solutions, and one system becomes unavailable, the remaining system can automatically take over database operations. The data on the systems will have been automatically synchronized via replication. There are various database replication tools and methodologies available for use with Teradata Dual-Active Solutions. GoldenGate is one such tool.
- When implemented between Teradata Database and databases from other vendors, you can migrate data from one system to the other, making data accessible across the different environments. This capability can support data acquisition, and Active Data Warehousing.

Teradata Replication Services are made up of Teradata Database and GoldenGate. Figure 10.2 illustrates the various ways Replication Solutions can be used.

DATA MIGRATION

```
┌─────────────────────────────────┐  ┌─────────────────────────────────┐
│  Teradata Dual Active Solutions │  │    Active Data Warehousing      │
│   ┌─────────────────┐           │  │   ┌─────────────────┐           │
│   │    Teradata     │           │  │   │  Non-Teradata   │           │
│   │    Alternate    │           │  │   │     System      │           │
│   │     System      │           │  │   │                 │           │
│   └────────▲────────┘           │  │   └────────▲────────┘           │
│            │                    │  │            │                    │
│            ▼                    │  │            ▼                    │
│   ┌─────────────────┐           │  │   ┌─────────────────┐           │
│   │    Teradata     │           │  │   │    Teradata     │           │
│   │   Production    │           │  │   │   Production    │           │
│   │     System      │           │  │   │     System      │           │
│   └─────────────────┘           │  │   └─────────────────┘           │
└─────────────────────────────────┘  └─────────────────────────────────┘

┌─────────────────────────────────┐  ┌─────────────────────────────────┐
│        Data Acquisition         │  │            Testing              │
│   ┌─────────────────┐           │  │   ┌─────────────────┐           │
│   │  Non-Teradata   │           │  │   │    Teradata     │           │
│   │     System      │           │  │   │   Production    │           │
│   │                 │           │  │   │     System      │           │
│   └────────┬────────┘           │  │   └────────┬────────┘           │
│            │                    │  │            │                    │
│            ▼                    │  │            ▼                    │
│   ┌─────────────────┐           │  │   ┌─────────────────┐           │
│   │    Teradata     │           │  │   │    Teradata     │           │
│   │   Production    │           │  │   │  Non-Production │           │
│   │     System      │           │  │   │     System      │           │
│   └─────────────────┘           │  │   └─────────────────┘           │
└─────────────────────────────────┘  └─────────────────────────────────┘
```

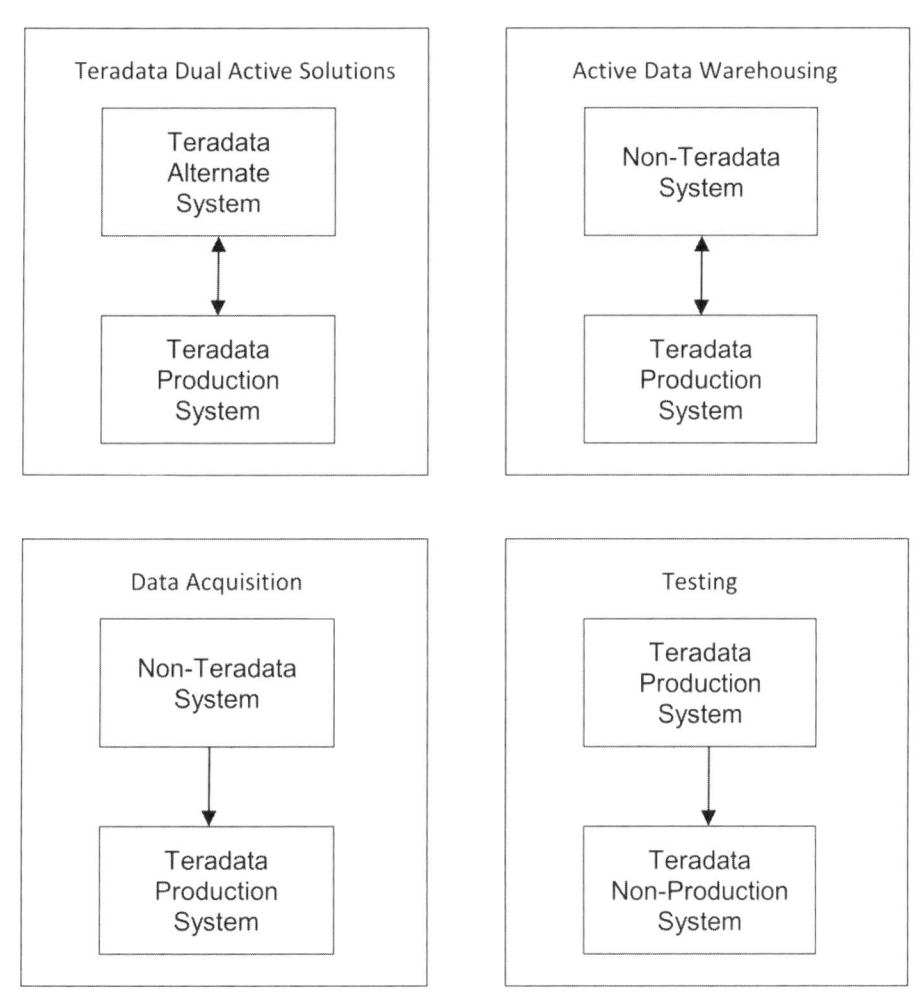

Figure 10.2

A Dual-Active solution is a set of components or technologies that allow a secondary instance of Teradata Database to act as a backup for a primary instance of Teradata Database. Such a solution addresses a number of business continuity needs:

- Allows business operations to continue if a planned or unplanned outage occurs.

Teradata 12 Enterprise Architecture

- Provides quick restoration of access to system resources.
- Enables businesses to enjoy consistent levels of service from their systems. Replication support is a key capability of a Dual-Active solution. When implemented as part of Teradata Dual-Active Solutions, Teradata Replication Services captures and synchronizes data between two instances of a database, where one is a production system and the other is a backup. As a result, the backup system can take over if the production system fails and maintain data availability and integrity.

Figure 10.3 illustrates the architecture of a Dual-Active system.

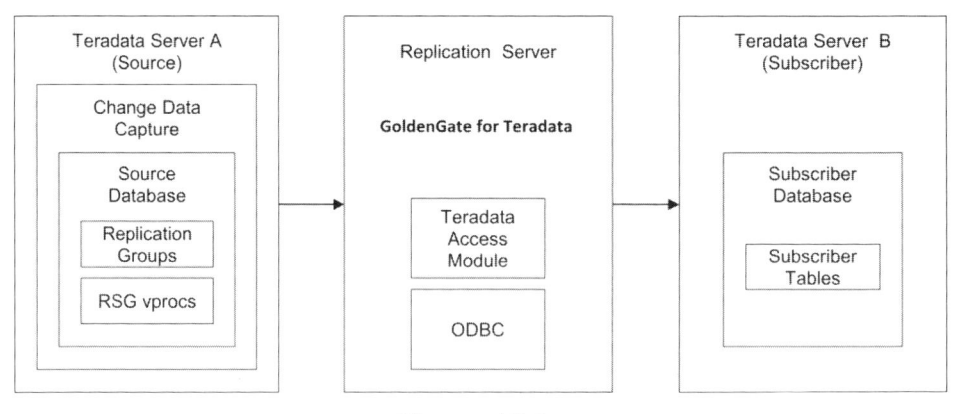

Figure 10.3

Teradata Replication Services can capture data from other types of databases and apply it to a Teradata Database. This data acquisition capability is not a replacement for a high-volume ETL (extract, transform, load) capability that requires significant transformation capabilities, but is designed to be used where:

- Real-time capture and apply is required
- There is a need to eliminate batch windows
- The volume of data that changes regularly is relatively moderate

- The customer wants to pull data from a non-Teradata database, minimizing the overhead to the source system

Note that Teradata Replication Services *does not* replace bulk data loading utilities, such as FastLoad and MultiLoad.

Costs

Keep in mind that the costs involved with data migration include, but are not limited to, the following:

1. Disk Space
    - Is the same "fact" being stored in more than one location?
    - Which copy is the "authoritative"?
    - Is Fallback in use?
    - Can data be exported/imported with an AMP down?
    - What is the cost of "downtime" (salaries, SLAs, etc.)?
2. CPU Cycles
    - Are the batch windows large enough to handle the load?
3. Hardware
    - Will offloading data from a system prolong its usefulness?
4. Software
    - Will new software be required (e.g. replication services)?
5. Network Connectivity
    - Are the users and data in the same building?
    - Is there more than one path to the data?
6. Floor Space
    - Is there sufficient room in the data center for additional hardware?
7. Air Conditioning

- Can the current system handle a major increase in BTUs?
8. Power
    - Can the current UPS handle any additional hardware?

Security

Chapter 5 discussed using software controls to limit access to data, securing transmitted data using encryption, and monitoring user actions to detect security threats and violations.

However, the most basic level of security is to limit access by unauthorized persons to the physical components of the Teradata Database system. These components include processor nodes, disk storage units, and the Administration Workstation (AWS).

Controlling access to physical components involves the following elements:

- Protect the system against deliberate damage by locating it in a secure room
- Control access to external devices used to connect to the system, such as remote terminals

At sites where security is a concern, even a minimal security policy should include the following procedure:

1. Restrict access to the computer room to authorized personnel only. Either escort or deny unauthorized personnel access.
2. Maintain a log of all escorted visitors to the computer room.
3. When it is not possible to escort unauthorized personnel to the computer room, take the following precautions:

    - Log off any administrator users in the computer room.
    - Physically power down the entire computer system.

DATA MIGRATION

4. When long-term access is required for personnel not involved in normal operations, screen them as if they were joining your operations staff.
5. Review the computer room access list and keep it current. Delete names of personnel who no longer require access.
6. Instruct the operations staff to challenge any strangers encountered in the computer room.
7. Store media that contains sensitive data in a controlled area such as the computer room.
8. Remove all sensitive data from all media before removing it from the controlled area or releasing it to unsecured personnel.
9. When the system restarts, it produces a dump file. A database named CRASHDUMPS stores the dump file. The system user DBC owns the CRASHDUMPS database. The system initialization scripts explicitly grant user SYSTEMFE SELECT access to dump data. It is important that you carefully guard the password to user SYSTEMFE, because a dump is the image of physical memory at the time the dump occurred and is therefore highly sensitive data.
10. Restrict access to the operating system to only system administrators with special privileges. Establish operating system and network security controls to secure Teradata Database running on the Teradata server platform. Restrict users without special privileges from accessing the LAN through the operating system to prevent inadvertent corruption of Teradata Database data files.

Privacy

The use of good database design, Access Rights and views, all contribute to maintaining data privacy mandated by external regulations. Examples of these regulations include Sarbanes-Oxley, Basel I, Basel II, HIPAA, and a number data privacy regulations.

Restricted Views

System view names followed by an X appended to the viewname indicate a user-restricted view. This means that the contents shown from the view apply only to the user submitting the query that acts upon a viewname.

In some cases, separate viewnames are defined for restricted and non-restricted views; for example, UserRoleRights and AllRoleRights. DiskSpaceX, TableSizeX, and SessionInfoX are the names of restricted views that show only information for objects owned or are accessible by the submitting user; data from DiskSpace, TableSize, and SessionInfo is information about all users in the system.

Returns from Non-Restricted Views

An unqualified select on a non-restricted view returns all rows from the underlying tables, which can overflow user spool space. Also, unless you explicitly revoke access to it, the view lets any user access all the information.

Returns from Restricted Views

X views have the same columns as non-X views. One difference, however, is that the definition includes a WHERE clause which limits access on the underlying tables to only those rows associated with the requesting user. The user can only view objects he or she owns, is associated with, has been granted privileges on, or is assigned a role which has privileges. For example, if UserA submits:

SELECT * FROM DBC.ProfileInfoX ;

Figure 10.4

DATA MIGRATION

The response is the name and parameter settings only for the profile assigned to UserA. This makes the response meaningful, limits its row count, and protects user privacy.

Restricted views typically run three different tests before returning information from Data Dictionary tables to a user. Each test focuses on the user and his or her current privileges.

If the current role of the user is not NULL or ALL, then the system checks for privileges granted to the current role and its nested roles before returning information from the restricted views. If the current role of the user is ALL, then the system checks privileges granted to all the roles to which he or she is directly granted and to all their nested roles. Consequently, it may take longer to receive a response when selecting from a qualified restricted view.

Restricting PUBLIC Access to Views

By default, the SELECT privilege is granted to PUBLIC (and is therefore available to all users) on most views in both the restricted and non-restricted versions.

Some views are applicable only to users who have a need to see specialized information, such as a database administrator, security administrator, or Teradata field service representative. Access to these views should be limited to only applicable users. For example, you should grant privileges to the DBC.DBQLRules view only to appropriate users or roles.

You can revoke from PUBLIC to remove one or more privileges so that those privileges are no longer available via PUBLIC to all users. Also, you can use GRANT and REVOKE to give or take away one or more privileges on any view for a particular user or role.

Renaming Views

Some sites rename the unrestricted views to something different, and then give the unrestricted viewname to the restricted view.

```
RENAME SessionInfo AS DBA_VIEW_123;
RENAME SessionInfoX AS SessionInfo;
```

Figure 10.5

Data Governance

Data governance encompasses the people, processes, and information technology required to create a consistent and proper handling of an organization's data across the business enterprise. Goals may be defined at all levels of the enterprise and doing so may aid in acceptance of processes by those who will use them. Some goals include:

- Acknowledge and hold all gains
- Decreasing the risk of regulatory fines
- Designating accountability for information quality
- Enable better planning by supervisory staff
- Establish process performance baselines to enable improvement efforts
- Improving data security
- Increasing consistency and confidence in decision making
- Maximizing the income generation potential of data
- Minimizing or eliminating re-work
- Optimize staff effectiveness

These goals are realized by the implementation of data governance initiatives using Change Control Management techniques.

Data governance initiatives improve data quality by assigning a team responsible for data's accuracy, accessibility, consistency, and completeness, among other metrics. This team usually consists of executive leadership, project management, line-of-business managers, and data stewards. The team usually employs some form of methodology for tracking and improving enterprise data, and tools for data mapping, profiling, cleansing, and monitoring data.

Data governance initiatives may be aimed at achieving a number of objectives including offering better visibility to internal and external customers (such as supply chain management), compliance with regulatory law, improving operations after rapid company growth or corporate mergers, or to aid the efficiency of enterprise knowledge workers by reducing confusion and error and increasing their scope of knowledge. Many data governance initiatives are also inspired by past attempts to fix information quality at the departmental level, leading to incongruent and redundant data quality processes. Most large companies have many applications and databases that can't easily share information. Therefore, knowledge workers within large organizations often don't have access to the information they need to best do their jobs. When they do have access to the data, the data quality may be poor. By setting up a data governance practice or Corporate Data Authority, these problems can be mitigated.

Implementation of a Data Governance initiative may vary in scope as well as origin. Sometimes, an executive mandate will arise to initiate an enterprise wide effort, sometimes the mandate will be to create a pilot project or projects, limited in scope and objectives, aimed at either resolving existing issues or demonstrating value. Sometimes an initiative will originate lower down in the organization's hierarchy, and will be deployed in a limited scope to demonstrate value to potential sponsors higher up in the organization.

A data governance committee or board is cross-functional. It's populated with a mix of technical data experts and business people whose management effectiveness depends on complete, clean, and consistent data. In addition, its technical people represent multiple data management practices, including data warehousing, data quality, MDM, metadata management, database administration, enterprise data architecture, and so on. For all these people, governing data is a part-time responsibility that complements their "day jobs." The data governance committee provides common ground where data stakeholders can collaborate about how to share and improve data. And it establishes change management processes for proposing, reviewing, and implementing changes to data, systems that manage it, and business processes that handle it. In short, data governance unites IT and the business through people and processes to effect data improvements.

Master Data Management (MDM)

Most companies rely on "master data" that is shared across operational and analytic systems. This data includes information about customers, suppliers, accounts, or organizational units and is used to classify and define transactional data. The challenge is keeping master data consistent, complete, and controlled across the enterprise.

Misaligned and inaccurate master data can cause costly data redundancies and misleading analytics. Processes based on such an environment tend to be complex, slow, and error-prone, limiting an organization's ability to answer questions such as:

- Can I get a consolidated view of a business entity across all channels and departments?
- How do I ensure data consistency?
- How many databases contain customer, product and vendor data?
- How many divisions within the company use the same data?

DATA MIGRATION

The answer to these and other related issues is master data management (MDM), a set of processes that creates and maintains an accurate, consistent view of reference data that the entire organization can access for decision making. By standardizing business entity definitions, improving data quality, and aggregating and distributing data across the organization, MDM:

- aids supplier consolidation
- enables revenue enhancement
- enhances compliance/risk management
- improves enterprise agility
- increases organizational speed
- leads to a consistent, holistic view of the entire enterprise
- simplifies new processes
- supports real-time decision making

Metadata is technical information about data (such as data types and field names), whereas **Master Data** is information that represents different views of the business (such as business entities or product lines). For example, companies with multiple implementations of the same ERP application have an issue with master data management, because *master data* is managed separately in each implementation. Yet, in such cases, the *metadata* across every instance of the application is the same.

With the recent acquisition of Aprimo, Teradata can now offer an MDM solution, Aprimo® Master Data Manager. Aprimo offers a data management solution that synchronizes disparate values and creates a tightly controlled, workflow-driven data stewardship environment. Now business users can safely step up to reference data responsibilities, freeing IT staff to focus more on development and technical support. As a result, maintaining a single view of critical business data becomes an enforced and measurable process—instead of a last-minute scramble.

Change Control Management

It is the responsibility of the Data Governance committee to oversee all change control, which generally include the following steps:

1. Record/classify - The client initiates change by making a formal request for something to be changed. The change control team then records and categorizes that request. This categorization would include estimates of importance, impact, and complexity.

2. Assess - The impact assessor or assessors then make their risk analysis typically by answering a set of questions concerning risk, both to the business and to the process, and follow this by making a judgment on who should carry out the change. If the change requires more than one type of assessment, the head of the change control team will consolidate these. Everyone with a stake in the change then must meet to determine whether there is a business or technical justification for the change. The change is then sent to the delivery team for planning.

3. Plan - Management will assign the change to a specific delivery team, usually one with the specific role of carrying out this particular type of change. The team's first job is to plan the change in detail as well as construct a regression plan in case the change needs to be backed out.

4. Build/test - If all stakeholders agree with the plan, the delivery team will build the solution, which will then be tested. They will then seek approval and request a time and date to carry out the implementation phase.

5. Implement - All stakeholders must agree to a time, date and cost of implementation. Following implementation, it is usual to carry out a post-implementation review which would take place at another stakeholder meeting.

6. Close/gain acceptance - When the client agrees that the change was implemented correctly, the change can be closed.

Teradata 12 Enterprise Architecture

Practice Questions

1. Which data mart is defined in your semantic layer?
    a. Dependent
    b. Independent
    c. Logical

2. Checkpoint and restart on the source database _____ supported by NPARC.
    a. is
    b. is not

3. Technical information about data is called _____.
    a. Master Data
    b. Metadata
    c. Data Governance

4. Knowledge of the people, processes, and information technology required to create a consistent and proper handling of an organization's data across the business enterprise is called _____.
    a. Master Data Management
    b. Metadata Management
    c. Data Governance

5. Which data mart is sometimes referred to as a *data basement*?
    a. Dependent
    b. Independent
    c. Logical

Chapter Notes
Utilize this space for notes, key points to remember, diagrams, areas of further study, etc.

Chapter 11 - Measuring Performance

Certification Objectives

- ✓ Given a performance tuning requirement scenario, determine which Teradata system resources should be used to assist in analyzing and improving the situation.
- ✓ Given a scenario, determine the effects of database optimization techniques (including techniques on tables or indexes).
- ✓ Identify the characteristics of a good physical data model.
- ✓ Identify the application performance impact of database design when implementing Referential Integrity (RI and soft RI).
- ✓ Given a scenario, determine which alternative is the best choice: in-database analytics, external processing, ROLAP technology, or External Cube technology. (Write at least 1 item for each of in-db analytics, ROLAP, and External Cube. External processing.)

Before You Begin

You should be familiar with the following terms and concepts.

Terms	Key Concepts
SLA/SLG	Service Level Agreement/Service Level Goals
DBQL	Database Query Log
PMON	Performance Monitor
Sync Scans	Concurrent queries against the same table
ResUsage/AMPUsage	Resource Usage Data
Explain	Major performance measurement tool
Join Plans	Fastest to slowest
Analytical Processing	Aggregate, Grouping, Window functions

SLA Statistics

System saturation and bottleneck identification are interrelated. When Teradata Database is saturated, the bottleneck is usually some key resource, such as a CPU or IO. Use the information obtained from performance monitoring, resource usage, query capture and process tracking tools to find the cause of repeated bottlenecks.

If a resource has been a bottleneck consistently during peak utilization periods and you have determined that your database design, data modeling, and query structures are efficient, consider expanding your Teradata Database configuration to improve performance. There are several kinds of system performance data that should be collected, including:

- Acctng/AMPUsage
- BYNET traffic
- AMP Worker Tasks
- CPU
- Data space, which includes spool, perm, and temporary space
- DBQL data
- Canary Queries
- Heartbeat response times
- Host network traffic (i.e. channel or TCP-IP networks).
- I/O subsystem
- Locking Logger (dumplocklog) data
- Schmon
- Memory
- Resource usage data
- User counts (that is, concurrent active and logged on sessions)

Expansion involves adding any combination of disk arrays, memory, vprocs, or nodes (with BYNETs), and then running the Parallel Upgrade Tool (PUT) and Configuration and Reconfiguration utilities.

MEASURING PERFORMANCE

The Reconfiguration utility can provide an estimate of the duration of outage based on parameters you supply interactively.

STATISTICS

Use the Optimizer form of COLLECT STATISTICS to collect statistics on the following:

- Unique Index (primary or secondary)
    - Single or multiple column
    - Partitioned or nonpartitioned

    Note: Collect partition statistics on all partitioned tables using system derived column PARTITION and the column name of the partitioned column. This helps the optimizer do more accurate costing with partitioned tables which helps produce more optimal plans.

- Non-unique Index
    - Primary or secondary
    - Single or multiple column
    - Partitioned or nonpartitioned
    - With or without COMPRESS fields
- Non-indexed column or set of columns
    - With or without COMPRESS fields
- Join index (JI)
- Hash index (HI)

In order for the Optimizer to make the best use of indexes, set up a schedule to regularly collect/refresh statistics.

Index Choices

The following list of factors illustrates how highly multi-determined the selection of Teradata Database indexes is.

- Nonspecific Factors
    - Degree of normalization of the database
    - How the Optimizer might use the index
    - Table type indexed
        - Major entity
        - Minor entity
        - Subentity
- Primary index partitioning type
    - Nonpartitioned
    - Partitioned
        - Single-level
        - Multilevel
- Space utilization factors
    - How much space does the index occupy?
    - Type of data protection specified
- Demographic factors
    - Cardinality of the table
    - Number of distinct column values
    - Maximum rows per value
    - Columns most frequently used to access table rows
    - Are rows most commonly accessed by values or by a join?
    - Degree of skew of column values
- Application factors
  In which application environment are rows most commonly accessed?
    - Decision support
    - OLTP
    - Event queues
    - Tactical queries

MEASURING PERFORMANCE

- - Ad hoc queries
    - Range queries
    - Batch reporting
    - Batch maintenance
- Transaction factors
    - How are transactions written?
    - How are transactions parceled?
    - What levels and types of locking does a transaction require?
    - How long does the transaction hold locks?
- DML Factors
    - Number of DELETE operations and when they occur
    - Number of INSERT operations and when they occur
    - Number of UPDATE operations and when they occur

Access Method	Relative Efficiency	# AMPs Accessed	# Rows Accessed
UPI	Very efficient	1	1
UPPI	Very efficient	1	1
NUPI NUPPI	Efficient when selectivity is high and skew is low and if limited to one internal partition by partition elimination. Otherwise, performance degrades as a function of the number of internal partitions that must be accessed.	1	Multiple
USI	Very efficient	2	1
NUSI	Efficient when the number of rows accessed is less than	• One if NUSI defined on same	Multiple

263

Access Method	Relative Efficiency	# AMPs Accessed	# Rows Accessed
	the number of data blocks in the table.	column set as NUPPI • All otherwise	
JI accessed by its primary index	Very efficient	1	Multiple
JI not accessed by its primary index	Very efficient	All	All (FTS)
JI with NUPPI	Efficient when selectivity is high and skew is low and if limited to one internal partition by partition elimination. Otherwise, performance degrades as a function of the number of internal partitions that must be accessed.	1	Multiple
HI	Very efficient	Depends on the primary index	Multiple
FTS	Efficient because the system touches each row and data block only once.	All	All

Figure 11.1

REFERENCE INDEXES

A Reference Index is an internal structure that the system creates whenever a referential integrity constraint is defined between tables using a PRIMARY KEY or UNIQUE constraint on the parent table in the relationship and a REFERENCES constraint on a foreign key in the child table.

The index row contains a count of the number of references in the child, or foreign key, table to the PRIMARY KEY or UNIQUE constraint in the parent table.

A maximum of 64 referential constraints can be defined for a table. Similarly, a maximum of 64 tables can reference a single table. Therefore, there is a maximum of 128 Reference Indexes that can be stored in the table header per table.

However, the Reference Index subtable for a table stores only the Reference Indexes that define its relationship with its child tables, so only 64 Reference Indexes are stored in the subtable per base table.

Apart from capacity planning issues, Reference Indexes have no user visibility.

Soft RI

To maximize the usefulness of join elimination, you can specify RI constraints that Teradata Database does not enforce. You must guarantee that these constraints are valid for tables. The Optimizer can use the constraints without incurring the penalty of database-enforced RI.

CREATE TABLE and ALTER TABLE statements allow you to ADD and DROP both column and table-level constraints for enforcing RI. You can use the WITH NO CHECK OPTION clause to specify statements with soft RI.

When you use the WITH NO CHECK OPTION clause, the system does not enforce RI constraints. This implies that a row having a non-null value for a referencing column can exist in a table even if an equal value does not exist in a referenced column. Error messages, that would otherwise be provided when RI constraints are violated, do not appear when you specify soft RI.

Note: Soft RI relies heavily upon your knowledge of the data. If the data does not actually satisfy the soft RI constraint that you provide and the Optimizer relies on the soft RI constraint, then queries can produce incorrect results.

Standard RI and Batch RI

In standard RI, whether you are doing row-at-time updates or set-processing INSERT/ SELECT requests, each child row will be separately matched to a row in the parent table, one row at a time. A separate select against the parent table is performed for each child row. Depending on your demographics, parent rows may be selected more than once.

With batch RI, all of the rows within a single statement, even if this is just one row, will be spooled and sorted, and will have their references checked in a single operation, as a join to the parent table. Depending on the number of rows in the INSERT/SELECT request, batch RI could be considerably faster, compared to checking each parent-child relationship individually.

If you plan to do row-at-time updates, there will be very little difference between standard RI and batch RI. But if you plan to load primarily using INSERT/SELECT requests, batch RI is recommended.

DBQL

The Database Query Log (DBQL) is an optional feature that you can employ to log query processing activity for later analysis. Query counts and response times can be charted and SQL text and processing steps can be compared to fine-tune your applications for optimum performance. It should be noted that this is the primary query tuning facility available in Teradata.

DBQL collects information based on rules you specify and flushes the DBQL cache as defined by the DBQLFlushRate field in the DBSControl record every (the default is 10 minutes) and writes to the DBQL dictionary tables (which are a series of predefined tables also referred to as logs). This information includes historical records of queries and their duration, performance data, and target activity.

DBQL is controlled by the Teradata SQL statements BEGIN QUERY LOGGING and END QUERY LOGGING. Only a user with EXECUTE privilege on DBC.DBQLAccessMacro can invoke the statements.

You cannot issue a BEGIN/END QUERY LOGGING statement while running in ANSI session mode. In Teradata session mode, you cannot issue a BEGIN/END QUERY LOGGING statement within a BT/ET transaction. Instead, use these statements outside a BT/ET transaction or, for ANSI session mode, log off and set the transaction mode to Teradata session mode.

PMON

Teradata Performance Monitor uses the Teradata Database Performance Monitor to collect near real-time system configuration, Resource usage, and Session information from the Teradata Database. It then formats and shows this information as requested.

Teradata 12 Enterprise Architecture

Teradata Performance Monitor shows this performance data on four sets of screens, one for each of the following types of data:

- General health information (configuration and summary)

    This data is displayed on the main screen and is refreshed automatically at a user defined interval. This data can also be displayed as a chart of summary values over time by clicking **Chart**.

- Resource information (nodes and vprocs)

    This data is collected and displayed only when the user requests it. Graphs showing a user selected data point for each node (or vproc) may be displayed by double-clicking the required data point.

- Session Information (statistics and lock information)

    This data is collected and displayed only when the user requests it. The session summary screen shows all the sessions currently logged onto the system and allows the user to filter these sessions and to sort them in various ways. It also shows which sessions are currently blocked.

    Detail session information, for a specific session may be seen by double-clicking on that session. Graphs showing a user selected data point for each Session may be displayed by double-clicking the required data point. Graphs showing data point A by data point B may be displayed by clicking on one data point and dragging it to the other.

    Detail lock information may be displayed by double-clicking on any session that is shown to be blocking, or blocked by, another session.

Display session skew information and SQL text and Explain steps.

- Historical session information

  A list of historical session files is displayed. By choosing from this list, the user may analyze a problem after the fact. The data itself is displayed on the regular Session Information screens.

ResUsage

Resource usage data is stored in Teradata Database tables and views in the DBC database. Macros installed with Teradata Database generate reports that display the data.

You can also write your own queries or macros on resource usage data. As with other database data, you can access resource usage data using SQL.

You need to decide what resource usage data you want to collect and the level of detail you want it to cover.

Once you set up your resource usage data collection the way you want, the only maintenance required is to purge old data regularly.

Figure 11.2 illustrates the flow of ResUsage data.

Teradata 12 Enterprise Architecture

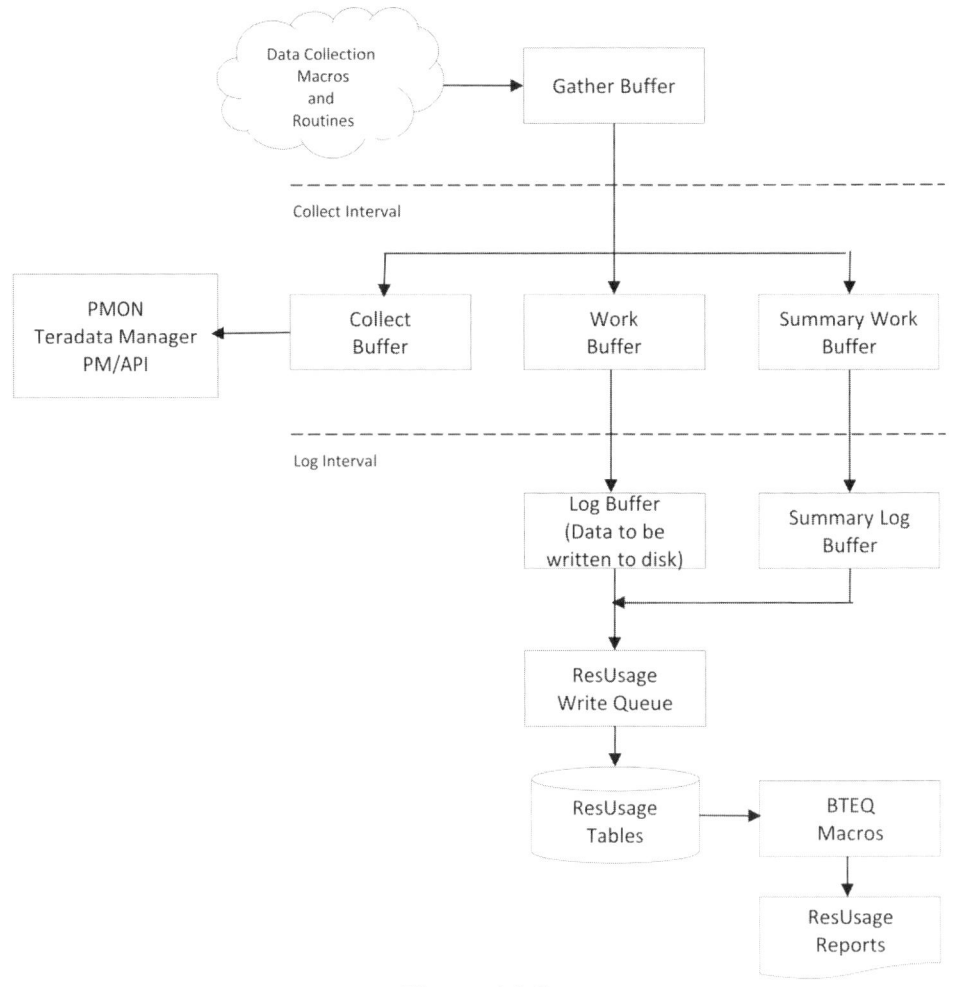

Figure 11.2

Specifying ResUsage Tables and Logging Rates

The default collection and logging settings provide a good start for basic system monitoring. The default results in the ResUsageSpma (SPMA) table being logged every 10 minutes (600 seconds).

The applications that use the collect buffer generally require more frequent data updates; therefore, the collection rate is typically adjusted to 60 seconds. PMON and other collect buffer based applications: Teradata Manager or PM/API, do not require the logging rate to be changed or any of the tables to be enabled for logging in order to access the RSS data they use.

The ResUsageSpma table provides a high level summary of how the system is operating and contains summarized or key elements from most of the other tables. If you want to record detailed statistics covered by any of the ResUsage tables, then you should enable them for logging, along with specifying the largest logging period that will meet your needs. You should not log data that you do not have a planned need for since this does incur additional database system overhead and uses up additional database space.

Naturally, the more tables you enable for logging and the shorter the logging period used, the more overhead the system will use.

You can use the Teradata Multitool, ctl, or xctl to enable or disable the ResUsage tables.

Full Table Scans

Full table scans are the least efficient way to acquire data on Teradata but they are still efficient since each data block and row are only touched once. If multiple queries are reading from the same table, the system may be able to do a sync scan.

The following FSG Cache parameters affect the system's ability to do sync scans.

DBSCacheThr

The value in DBSCacheThr specifies the percentage of FSG Cache to use for calculating the cache threshold when DBSCacheCtrl is set to TRUE.

Depending on the size of File System Segments (FSG) Cache and the size of the tables in the databases, the value in this field can make a big difference to how much useful data the system actually caches. Using cache saves on physical disk I/Os, which implies that caching the smaller and more frequently-accessed tables (usually reference tables) is recommended. You can use the DBSCacheThr value to encourage these smaller tables to stay in memory longer.

If a full-file scan is performed on a spool or permanent table, and the subtable size per AMP is greater than or equal to the Cache Threshold, scanning tasks request that data blocks be discarded immediately upon release. This full-file scan can be overridden by other, simultaneously occurring operations on the same subtable that are not full-file scans. Otherwise, data blocks are cached in memory when released.

Use DBSCacheThr to prevent a large, sequentially read or written table from pushing other data out of the cache. Since the system probably will not access table data blocks again until they have aged out of memory, it does little good to cache them, and may cause more heavily accessed blocks to age out prematurely.

Large history tables are not the primary tables to cache. In the case of multiple users that access the same table at the same time, the system can do a synchronized scan (sync scan) on the table.

SyncScanCacheThr

The value in SyncScanCacheThr indicates how much memory the system can use to keep scans for large tables in synchronization scan (sync scan) mode. Sync scan can occur when two or more queries perform a full table scan on the same large table that exceeds DBSCacheThr. Multiple tables can also be in sync scan mode at the same time.

A scan of a permanent table qualifies for synchronized full-file scan if the subtable is larger than the Teradata Database cache threshold value calculated by the optimizer. If so, the scan starting position is synchronized with the current position of an existing scan in order to use the same I/Os.

AmpUsage

The DBC.AMPUsage view provides information about the usage of each AMP for each user and account. It also tracks the activities of any console utilities. By user, account, or console utility session, DBC.AMPUsage stores information about:

- CPU time consumed
- Number of logical read/write (I/O) operations generated

AMPUsage reports logical I/Os explicitly requested by the database software, even if the requested segment is in cache and no physical I/O is performed.

The DBC.AMPUsage view displays CPU usage information differently than the way such information is displayed in resource usage data.

Figure 11.3 summarizes the difference.

Teradata 12 Enterprise Architecture

This facility...	Provides...
ResUsage	metrics on the whole system, without making distinctions by individual user or account ID.
DBC.AMPUsage view	AMP usage by individual user or account ID. Good account string definition is important for this view Some CPU used for the system cannot be accounted for in AMPUsage. Therefore, ResUsage CPU metrics will always be larger than AMPUsage metrics. Typically, AMPUsage captures about 70-90% of ResUsage CPU time.

Figure 11.3

Explain

Use of the EXPLAIN modifier, or Visual Explain, will show the retrieval paths chosen by the Parser.

Modifying the structure of the tables will change performance. As an example:

- Changing a UPI/NUSI to a NUPI/USI
- Creating/dropping SIs
- Collecting/refreshing statistics
- Creating/dropping Join Indexes
- Creating/dropping Partitioned Primary Indexes
- Creating/dropping Hash Indexes
- Using/eliminating temporary (Global/Volatile) tables

Use Query Capture Facility (QCF) to put the Explain output into a Query Capture Database (QCD). Data in the QCD is used by

- Index Wizard

- Statistics Wizard
- TSET
- Visual Explain

Joins

Depending on the indexes defined for the tables involved and whether statistics are available for the indexes, the Optimizer processes a join using one of the following join algorithms:

- Correlated Join
- Exclusion Join (merge and product)
- Hash Join
- Inclusion Join (merge and product)
- Merge Join
- Minus All Join
- Nested Join (local and remote)
- Product Join
- RowID Join
- Self-Join

All JOIN columns should have statistics collected on them.

Columns, whether indexed or not, appearing in a WHERE clause should have statistics collected on them as well.

The Optimizer is not affected by the order of tests in a WHERE clause. As an example, A = 10 AND B = 300, AND C = 'XYZ' is the same as B = 300 AND A = 10 AND C = 'XYZ, which is the same as C = 'XYZ' AND A = 10 AND B = 300, which is the same as . . .

Teradata 12 Enterprise Architecture

The important thing is whether statistics on the columns are available. Without statistics, the Parser is very conservative. With statistics, it is far more aggressive.

Though the WHERE clause limits the number of rows appearing in Spool, the number of columns being projected, and their data type size, determine the width of Spool rows.

Analytical Processing Choices

Grouping

In addition to the standard GROUP BY, Teradata also provides:

- GROUP BY CUBE
- GROUP BY ROLLUP
- GROUP BY GROUPING SETS

The following is a CUBE coding example.

```
SELECT Product_id AS PID
      , sale_date
      , SUM(daily_sales) AS Sales
FROM  sales_table
GROUP BY CUBE (pid, sale_date)
ORDER BY pid, sale_date
;
```

Figure 11.4

Here's a ROLLUP coding example.

```
SELECT Product_id AS PID
       , sale_date
       , SUM(daily_sales) AS Sales
FROM sales_table
GROUP BY ROLLUP (pid, sale_date)
ORDER BY pid, sale_date
;
```

Figure 11.5

The following GROUPING SETS query returns the same result as the previous CUBE example.

```
SELECT Product_id AS PID
       , sale_date
       , SUM(daily_sales) AS Sales
FROM sales_table
 GROUP BY GROUPING SETS  (pid, ( ) )
, GROUPING SETS (sale_date, ( ) )
ORDER BY pid, sale_date
;
```

Figure 11.6

TERADATA ON-LINE ANALYTICAL PROCESSING FUNCTIONS

The OLAP functions are the cousins of the aggregate functions, but are very different in their use. Like traditional aggregates, OLAP functions operate on groups of rows and permit qualification and filtering of the group result. Unlike aggregates, OLAP functions also return the individual row detail data and not just the final aggregated value.

Teradata 12 Enterprise Architecture

Figure 11.7 contains the OLAP aggregates and their functions:

WINDOW AGGREGATE FUNCTION	DESCRIPTION
AVG	Returns the arithmetic average of all values in the specified expression for each row in the group.
CORR	Returns the Pearson product moment correlation coefficient of its arguments for all non-null data point pairs.
COUNT	Returns a column value that is the total number of qualified rows in a group.
COVAR_POP	Returns the population covariance of its arguments for all non-null data point pairs.
COVAR_SAMP	Returns the sample covariance of its arguments for all non-null data point pairs.
MAX	Returns a column value that is the maximum value for *value_expression* for a group.
MIN	Returns a column value that is the minimum value for *value_expression* for a group.
PERCENT_RANK	Returns the relative rank of rows for a *value_expression*.
RANK	Returns an ordered ranking of rows
REGR_AVGX	Returns the mean of the *independent_variable_expression* for all non-null data pairs of the dependent and independent variable arguments.
REGR_AVGY	Returns the mean of the *dependent_variable_expression* for all non-null data pairs of the dependent and independent variable arguments.
REGR_COUNT	Returns the count of all non-null data pairs of the dependent and independent variable arguments.

WINDOW AGGREGATE FUNCTION	DESCRIPTION
REGR_INTERCEPT	Returns the intercept of the univariate linear regression line through all non-null data pairs of the dependent and independent variable arguments.
REGR_R2	Returns the coefficient of determination for all non-null data pairs of the dependent and independent variable arguments.
REGR_SLOPE	Returns the slope of the univariate linear regression line through all non-null data pairs of the dependent and independent variable arguments.
REGR_SXX	Returns the sum of the squares of the *independent_variable_expression* for all non-null data pairs of the dependent and independent variable arguments.
REGR_SXY	Returns the sum of the products of the *independent_variable_expression* and the *dependent_variable_expression* for all non-null data pairs of the dependent and independent variable arguments.
REGR_SYY	Returns the sum of the squares of the *dependent_variable_expression* for all non-null data pairs of the dependent and independent variable arguments.
ROW_NUMBER	Returns the sequential row number, where the first row is number one, of the row within its window partition according to the window ordering of the window.
STDDEV_POP	Returns the population standard deviation for the non-null data points in *value_expression*.
STDDEV_SAMP	Returns the sample standard deviation for the non-null data points in *value_expression*.

Teradata 12 Enterprise Architecture

WINDOW AGGREGATE FUNCTION	DESCRIPTION
SUM	Returns a column value that is the arithmetic sum for a specified expression for a group.
VAR_POP	Returns the population variance for the data points in *value_expression*.
VAR_SAMP	Returns the sample variance for the data points in *value_expression*.

Figure 11.7

TERADATA EXTENSIONS

DEPRECATED TERADATA EXTENSIONS	DESCRIPTION	EQUIVALENT ANSI SQL-2003 WINDOW FUNCTIONS
CSUM	Cumulative sum of a referenced value, for a range or dimension.	SUM
MAVG	Computation of a moving average of a referenced value, based on a specified window.	AVG
MDIFF	Computation of a moving difference between two referenced data values, based on a specified window.	Composable from SUM
MLINREG	Computation of a moving linear regression between two referenced data values, based on a specified window.	Composable from SUM and COUNT
MSUM	Computation of a moving	SUM

MEASURING PERFORMANCE

DEPRECATED TERADATA EXTENSIONS	DESCRIPTION	EQUIVALENT ANSI SQL-2003 WINDOW FUNCTIONS
	sum of a referenced value, based on a specified window.	
RANK	Ranking based on high order or low order of a referenced data value, based on a specified value.	RANK

Figure 11.8

OVER (...) WINDOW DEFINITIONS

PARTITION BY col1 [, ... , coln]	Defines the "GROUP" or "Window" of rows over which the aggregate function operates. If there is no PARTITION BY clause, then the entire result set, delivered by the FROM clause, constitutes a single group or partition.	
ORDER BY value_expression [ASC	DESC]	The ordering of rows within the Group, not the final result.	
ROWS	The starting point for the aggregation group within the partition. The aggregation group end is the current row. The aggregation group of a row R is a set of rows, defined relative to R in the ordering of the rows within the partition. If there is no ROWS or ROWS BETWEEN clause, the default aggregation group is ROWS BETWEEN UNBOUNDED PRECEDING AND UNBOUNDED FOLLOWING.	
	UNBOUNDED PRECEDING	Include all group rows preceding the current row.

281

Teradata 12 Enterprise Architecture

	Value PRECEDING	Include the specified number of rows before the current row.
	CURRENT ROW	Report only on the current row.
ROWS BETWEEN	\multicolumn{2}{l	}{The aggregation group start and end, which defines a set of rows relative to the current row in the ordering of the rows within the partition. The row specified by the group start must precede the row specified by the group end. If there is no ROWS or ROWS BETWEEN clause, the default aggregation group is ROWS BETWEEN UNBOUNDED PRECEDING AND UNBOUNDED FOLLOWING.}
	UNBOUNDED PRECEDING AND	UNBOUNDED FOLLOWING
		value PRECEDING
		CURRENT ROW
		value FOLLOWING
	value PRECEDING AND	UNBOUNDED FOLLOWING
		value PRECEDING
		CURRENT ROW
		value FOLLOWING
	CURRENT ROW AND	UNBOUNDED FOLLOWING
		CURRENT ROW
		value FOLLOWING
	value FOLLOWING AND	UNBOUNDED FOLLOWING
		value FOLLOWING

Figure 11.9

Figure 11.10 contains some of the OLAP commands and their functions:

MEASURING PERFORMANCE

ANSI OLAP functions:

Command	Functionality
SUM/OVER	Cumulative sum of a referenced value, for a range or dimension.
SUM / OVER (Moving Sum)	Computation of a moving sum of a referenced value, based on a specified window.
RANK / OVER	Ranking based on high order or low order of a referenced data value, based on a specified value.
RANK / OVER (QUANTILE)	Categorize a referenced data value, based on a number of partitions.
ROW_NUMBER / OVER	Assigns a unique number to each row to which it is applied, either each row in the partition or each row returned by the query. In the ordered sequence of rows specified in the order by clause, the rows begin with the number one.

Figure 11.10

As an example, the deprecated CSUM function can be replaced with the following ANSI code:

```
SELECT Product_ID
      ,Sale_Date
      ,Daily_Sales
,SUM(Daily_Sales)
   OVER ( ORDER BY Sale_Date  ROWS UNBOUNDED PRECEDING)
   AS  Like_CSum
FROM  Sales_table
WHERE Product_ID BETWEEN 1000 and 2000 ;

Product_ID   Sale_Date   Daily_Sales    Like_CSum
-----------  ---------   -----------   -----------
      1000   07/09/28       45850.40      45850.40
      2000   07/09/28       42787.88      88638.28
      1000   07/09/29       64500.22     153138.50
      2000   07/09/29       46090.00     199228.50
      2000   07/09/30       44850.03     244078.53
      1000   07/09/30       36000.07     280078.60
      2000   07/10/01       58850.29     338928.89
      1000   07/10/01       45700.43     384629.32
      2000   07/10/02       35599.93     420229.25
      1000   07/10/02       33700.50     453929.75
      2000   07/10/03       41900.18     495829.93
      1000   07/10/03       66200.00     562029.93
      2000   07/10/04       32878.50     594908.43
      1000   07/10/04       54575.10     649483.53
```

Figure 11.11

In the previous example, all rows participate as a single group.

If you perform frequent ROLAP analyses of your data and performance is not what you expect to see, consider off-loading the data to a dependent data mart designed around the multidimensional model that many OLAP proponents advocate. You should not denormalize the entire database just to support a few OLAP applications.

MEASURING PERFORMANCE

PERFORMANCE MEASUREMENT SUMMARY

Here are some additional thoughts on performance measurement.

Response Time

- Baseline Testing
    - Response time samples
    - Execution plans
    - DBQL Query Logs
- Canary Queries
    - General heartbeat response time samples
    - Used to measure tactical query response
- System Upgrades
    - Response times before/after
    - DBQL Query Logs

Changes In Query Run Times

- DBQL
    - Turn on for all users

Resource Utilization

- AMPUsage
    - CPU and I/O for every account
- ResUsage
    - Summarize SPMA to one row per node

Data Growth

- Row counts
- Perm space
- Save a daily collection of database, table and spool space

Teradata 12 Enterprise Architecture

Changes In Data Access

- Access log
    - Save a summary row of accesses per table per day
    - Object in use count

Changes In Number Of Active Sessions

- LogOnOff
- Object use count
- DBQL
- SPS

Workload Management

- DBQL
- AWT
- SPS
- TDWM Tables

Practice Questions

Match the following definitions with their correct syntax.

1. ___ Batch Referential Integrity	a. REFERENCES
2. ___ Soft Referential Integrity	b. REFERENCES WITH CHECK OPTION
3. ___ Standard Referential Integrity	c. REFERENCES WITH NO CHECK OPTION

4. What is the maximum number of referential constraints that can be defined for a table?
    a. 8
    b. 16
    c. 32
    d. 64

5. PMON and Teradata Manager take their ResUsage data from _____.
    a. Collect Buffer
    b. Log Buffer
    c. Summary Log Buffer
    d. Summary Work Buffer
    e. Work Buffer

Teradata 12 Enterprise Architecture

6. Which ResUsage table provides system-wide node information?
   a. ResUsageSawt
   b. ResUsageScpu
   c. ResUsageShst
   d. ResUsageSldv
   e. ResUsageSpdsk
   f. ResUsageSpma
   g. ResUsageSps
   h. ResUsageSvdsk

7. Which of the following statements are true about DBQL BEGIN/END QUERY LOGGING statements?
   a. They cannot be executed while in ANSI mode
   b. They cannot be executed within BT/ET transactions
   c. They require EXEC privilege on DBC.DBQLAccessMacro
   d. All of the above
   e. None of the above

Chapter Notes

Utilize this space for notes, key points to remember, diagrams, areas of further study, etc.

Teradata 12 Enterprise Architecture

Chapter 12 - Improving Performance

Certification Objectives

- ✓ Given a scenario where a query is running slowly, determine improvement options.
- ✓ Given a scenario, determine the tools within the Teradata Analyst Pack that are applicable for planning system expansion and workload optimization.
- ✓ Given a scenario, determine the application profile characteristics that affect table design and the use of the different types of advanced indexes.
- ✓ Given a scenario, determine the trade-offs between an ETL or ELT design.
- ✓ Given a scenario where multiple business subjects areas and their supporting applications are being integrated in the data warehouse, determine where surrogate keys would be a choice.
- ✓ Given a scenario, determine when summary data is necessary.

Before You Begin

You should be familiar with the following terms and concepts.

Terms	Key Concepts
Analyst Pack	The suite of software tools
I/O efficiency	Cylinder read feature
Data Dictionary	The system tables, views, and macros
Object use counts	Determine which objects the system heavily accesses
ampload and awtmon utilities	Monitor available AWTs or AMP message queue
Surrogate keys	System-generated Primary Keys

Teradata Index Wizard

There is a suite of software tools called the Teradata Analyst Pack. The Teradata Analyst Pack is targeted at query or workload-based analysis and focuses on the execution performance at the individual query level.

Teradata Analyst tools include:

- Teradata Index Wizard
- Teradata Statistics Wizard
- Teradata System Emulation Tool
- Teradata Visual Explain

We will begin our review with Teradata Index Wizard.

Teradata Index Wizard consists of a database server component and a front-end client application. The index analysis engine is inside the Teradata parser and works closely with the parallel optimizer to enumerate, simulate, and evaluate index selection candidates. The client front end is a graphical Microsoft Windows interface, providing step-by-step instructions for workload definition and index analysis, and reports for both workload and index analysis. This is shown in the following illustration.

IMPROVING PERFORMANCE

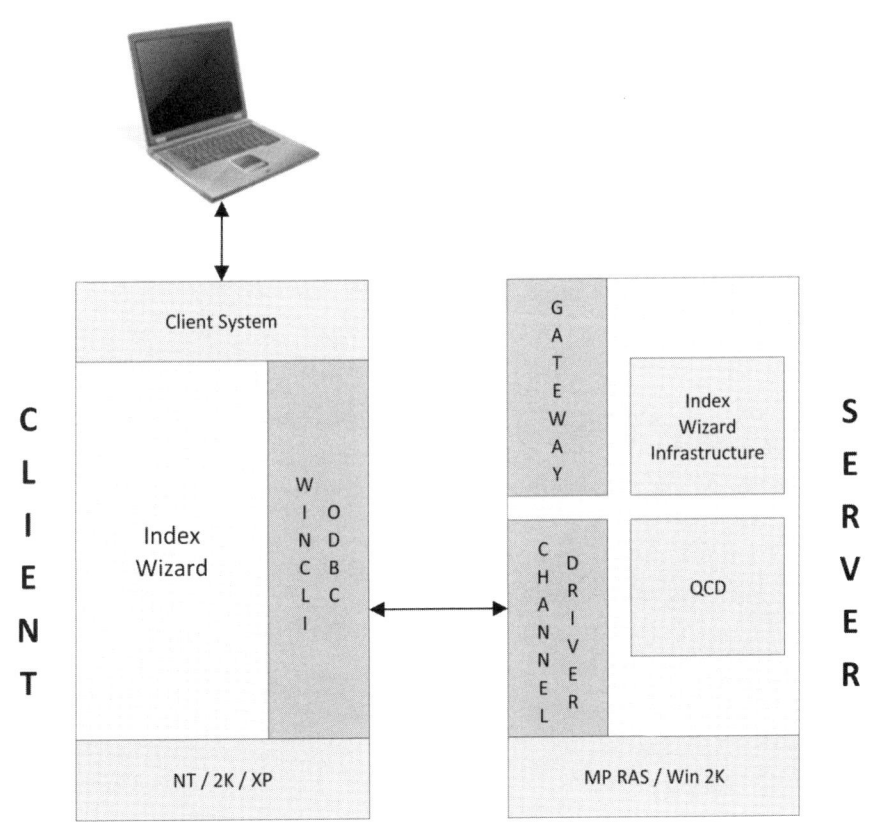

Figure 12.1

A basic feature is a Graphical User Interface (GUI) supported on Microsoft Windows platforms.

It interfaces with the Teradata Database Query Log (DBQL) facility to define workloads from a collection of SQL statements captured in the query log.

It works with other client tools including Teradata Statistics Wizard, Teradata System Emulation Tool, and Teradata Visual Explain.

Teradata 12 Enterprise Architecture

You can import workloads onto a test system for analysis, saving production system resources.

You can use it to validate recommendations on the production system before actually creating the new set of indexes.

Basic Index Wizard Steps

The following steps describe what you do:
1. Define a workload.

   A workload is a set of SQL statements created or defined using the workload Definition dialog box. Index Wizard creates several workload reports after a workload is defined.

   - Using Database Query Log (DBQL)
   - Using statement text
   - From QCD statements
   - Importing workload
   - From an existing workload

2. Workload is analyzed.

   After the workload is defined, it is analyzed and a new set of indexes is recommended. Index Wizard may also recommend that indexes be added or dropped to enhance system performance.

   There are four types of analysis:

   - Index analysis
   - Partition analysis
   - Restarting an analysis
   - What-if analysis

3. Indexes are recommended.

IMPROVING PERFORMANCE

Index Wizard creates several reports about workloads and indexes. Some reports are created when a workload is defined. Others are created when a workload is analyzed.

4. Index recommendations are validated (optional).

   Index Wizard validates index recommendations on a production system without actually updating the production table index. This feature is optional, but highly recommended because it ensures the index recommendation will help database performance before actually adding the indexes.

   The execution plans obtained with the recommendation can be compared with the original query plans (those without the index recommendations) using Teradata Visual Explain's Compare feature. Index Wizard interfaces with Teradata Visual Explain in providing a query-by-query compare.

5. Index recommendations are applied to the production system.

   After an index recommendation is validated, Index Wizard allows you to apply (execute) the index to the production system. You can execute an index immediately or schedule the execution to occur at a different time and day.

The reports that are available are Workload Reports and Analysis Reports.

This Workload Report...	Shows...
Existing Indexes Report	a general view of the information about the table including index type, unique flags, and index names.
Update Frequency Report	the percentage statements within a table that are UPDATE

Teradata 12 Enterprise Architecture

This Workload Report . . .	Shows . . .
	statements.
Table Usage Analysis Report	information on how often the table is accessed within the workload.
Table Scan Report	general information about the usage of a table including table cardinality, AMP usage, and geography information in the workload.
Workload Analysis Report	the cost estimate of a workload and the relative execution cost of a workload compared to the entire workload, statement text, frequency, and column types.
Object Global Use Count Report	object use count information to help identify objects most often accessed.

Figure 12.2

This Analysis Report . . .	Shows . . .
Index Recommendation Report	the recommended secondary index for each table if one is recommended.
Query Cost Analysis Report	the query cost of specific types of statements (SELECT, INSERT, DELETE) without the original recommended index and with the proposed recommended index.
Disk Space Analysis Report	the space estimate to store the recommended indexes
Summary Report	details about the secondary index counts and recommendation counts made in a specific analysis

IMPROVING PERFORMANCE

This Analysis Report...	Shows...
	for all tables in the workload.
Index Maintenance Cost Report	the estimated cost of maintaining recommended indexes for a particular recommendation ID on a workload.

Figure 12.3

Index validation is the process of checking to see if the recommended indexes actually improve system performance. Validation does not involve the actual execution of the recommendations, but permits the Teradata Optimizer to use the recommended indexes in the plan generation. If the recommendations are created with a COLLECT STATISTICS option, Index Wizard collects statistics on a sample size and saves them in the QCD. The sampled statistics are used during index validation.

The validation process occurs in a simulated session mode. The index and the required statistics (as indicated by the recommendations) are simulated for the plan generation. Index recommendations are validated on the set of statements that were analyzed. The statements are submitted to the Teradata Database in a "no execute" mode. During validation, the query plans are saved into the specified QCD.

Validation can be done in any of the following ways:

Analysis performed on...	Validation performed on...
Production System	Production System
Test System	Production System
Production System	Test System (not recommended)
Test System	Test System (not recommended)

Figure 12.4

Teradata 12 Enterprise Architecture

Once validation is complete, Index Wizard has an execute recommendation feature that allows you to execute index recommendations immediately or schedule them for a later time.

Teradata Statistics Wizard

Statistics Wizard can be used to automate the process of collecting statistics for a particular workload or selecting arbitrary indexes or columns for collection/re-collection purposes. Additionally, you can validate the proposed statistics on a production system which enables you to verify the performance of the proposed statistics before applying the recommendations.

Statistics Wizard enables the database administrator (DBA) to:

- Defer executing the collection and dropping of statistics and schedule for a later time.
- Display and modify the interval statistics for a column or index.
- Make recommendations, based on a specific workload.
- Make recommendations, based on table demographics and general heuristics.
- Select an arbitrary database or selection of tables, indexes, or columns for analysis, collection, or re-collection of statistics.
- Specify a workload to be analyzed for recommendations specific to improving the performance of the queries in a workload.

As changes are made within a database, Statistics Wizard identifies those changes and recommends which tables should have statistics collected, based on age of data and table growth, and which columns/indexes would benefit from having statistics defined and collected for a specific workload. The DBA is then given the opportunity to accept or reject the recommendations.

IMPROVING PERFORMANCE

The steps for Best Practices are:

- Identify the set of SQL statements that must be analyzed for performance improvements.
- Define the identified set of SQL statements. This will be known as a workload.
- Run the statistics analysis.
- Validate the statistics.
- Apply or schedule the execution of the recommendations in a sequential fashion looking for performance improvements since collecting stats is very CPU intensive.

Like the Index Wizard, the first step is to define a workload. This can be done in the following ways.

- From an Existing Workload
- From DBQL Statements
- From QCD Statements
- Importing a Workload
- Using Statement Text

The reports available are:

This Report...	Shows...
Statistics Recommendations Report	information about the recommended set of statistics for the tables in the workload.
Update Cost Analysis Report	the percentage of statements within the workload that are UPDATE statements.
Table Usage Report	information about how often the table is accessed within the workload.
Table Scan Report	general information about the usage of a table including table

Teradata 12 Enterprise Architecture

This Report...	Shows...
	cardinality, AMP usage, and geography information in the workload.
Workload Analysis Report	the cost estimate of the workload, relative execution cost compared to the entire workload, statement text, frequency, and column types.

Figure 12.5

COLLECTED STATISTICS can help the Optimizer make better decisions using actual row counts and data distribution information.
Collect Statistics on:

- All indexes for Join Index table
- All non-unique secondary indexes with ALL option
- All partitioned tables
- All VOSI (Value ordered NUSI)
- Non-index join columns
- Non-unique indexes
- Small tables

Teradata Visual Explain

Teradata VE adds another dimension to the EXPLAIN modifier by depicting the execution plans of complex SQL statements visually and simply. The graphical view of the statement is displayed as discrete steps showing the flow of data during execution.

By making the comparison of optimized queries easier, Teradata VE helps application developers, Database Administrators, and database support personnel fine-tune SQL statements to ensure Teradata Database accesses data in the most effective manner.

The first step is to create a Query Capture Database (QCD).

Once that is accomplished, the next step is to begin capturing queries into the QCD.

A powerful feature of VE allows you to compare different versions of SQL statements.

Once you have two, or more, queries loaded into the QCD, you can select which plans to compare. VE will also display the selected plans side-by-side. It will also display a Summary for each plan. The Summary for a displayed plan will appear when you click on the plan. VE will also produce a series of reports for the chosen plans. The reports are as follows:

- Complete Information Report
- Estimated Cost Report
- Index Condition Report
- Indexes Used Report
- Join Condition Report
- Join Order Report
- Operands Report
- Operation Report
- Residual Condition Report
- Source Attributes Report
- Step Information Report
- Target Attributes Report
- Teradata Database Configuration Report

One or more execution plans can be saved to a file (*.vec*). Saving an execution plan creates what is referred to as an *offline* plan. Optionally, the corresponding visual plan, Explain text, statement text, or tool tips can be saved.

Teradata 12 Enterprise Architecture

Teradata System Emulation Tool (TSET)

Teradata SET imitates a target (production) system on a test system. System-level environmental data is captured from the target system, placed into workstation files, and then imported into relational tables in a test system. The Teradata Query Optimizer processes information from these tables, together with appropriate column and index statistics, to generate query plans on the test system as though the operation occurred in the production environment.

Figure 12.6 illustrates the relationship between Teradata SET, target systems, and test systems.

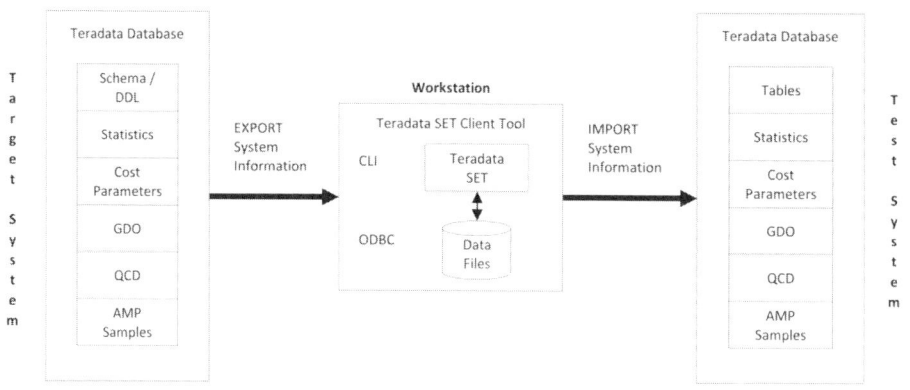

Figure 12.6

Imported data is used to:

- Generate query plans that emulate those created on the target system under a given set of conditions. A small test system can be used to generate query plans that emulate a much larger target system.
- Perform *what-if* modeling.
- Recreate the Optimizer performance characteristics of the target system. The Optimizer generates query execution plans based on many factors, such as available system resources,

Teradata 12 Certification Study Guide

IMPROVING PERFORMANCE

indexes, primary and secondary keys, and available statistics. All of these factors impact how the Optimizer creates the most effective execution plan.
- Test, diagnose, and solve Optimizer-related performance questions that might occur in the target system.

Teradata SET also works with Teradata Visual Explain to emulate how a target system performs under specific conditions and workloads.

Teradata SET also synchronizes all of the elements of a target environment. For example, all the configuration settings, databases, data models, and data dependencies maintain the correct relationships when exported and imported. In addition, database objects are duplicated on the test system. Tables, views, macros, triggers, join indexes, and stored procedures function just like they do on the target system. Use Teradata SET to thoroughly debug and optimize queries in a safe, but equivalent, emulated environment prior to introducing them into the production system.

Set access rights prior to performing export operations. When exporting by query, the right to execute the SHOW QUALIFIED SQL statement and configuration data (Random AMP Sample (RAS), statistics, object definitions) is required if only those objects returned from this statement can be exported.

The following table lists the access rights required to export each type of information:

Exported Information	Required Rights
Cost parameters	INSERT, SELECT, and DELETE on *SystemFE.Opt_Cost_Table* and *SystemFE.Opt_DBSCtl_Table*.
Cost profiles	SELECT on the DBC.CostProfiles_v and DBC.CostProfileValues_v views.

Teradata 12 Enterprise Architecture

Exported Information	Required Rights
Demographics	SELECT on the data demographics table and corresponding views of the table, and sufficient rights to execute the COLLECT DEMOGRAPHICS statement. SELECT on QCD views. EXECUTE on QCD macros.
Execution plans	For an existing plan: - SELECT on the QCD tables or on the QCD - EXECUTE on QCD macros For a new plan, sufficient rights to execute the DUMP EXPLAIN statement for the given query. For a new plan with demographics: - Sufficient rights to execute the INSERT EXPLAIN statement for the given query - EXECUTE on the QCD macros.
Machine configuration	MONRESOURCE on the database.
Object definitions	For join indexes, macros, tables, triggers, stored procedures, and User-Defined Types (UDTs), sufficient rights to execute the corresponding SHOW statement for the database objects. To export object definitions for view, SELECT on the view in order to perform the SHOW QUALIFIED statement. To export by database, SELECT on DBC.Columns and DBC.Tables to export

IMPROVING PERFORMANCE

Exported Information	Required Rights
	referenced UDTs.
QCD data	SELECT on QCD tables and views. EXECUTE on QCD macros.
RAS	SELECT on the tables selected for export. INSERT, SELECT, and DELETE on *SystemFE.Opt_RAS_Table*.
Statistics	All rights required to execute the HELP STATISTICS statement on the table or join index referenced. SELECT on the DBC.IndexStats, DBC.ColumnStats, and DBC.MultiColumnStats views.
Workloads	SELECT on QCD tables and views. EXECUTE on QCD macros.

Figure 12.7

Set access rights prior to performing import operations. The following table lists the access rights required to import each type of information.

Imported Information	Required Rights
Cost parameters	INSERT on *SystemFE.Opt_Cost_Table* and *SystemFE.Opt_DBSCtl_Table*.
Cost profiles	EXECUTE on the DBC.CreateNewCostProfile and DBC.InsertConstantValue macros.
Demographics	INSERT, SELECT, and UPDATE on the data demographics table and corresponding table views.

305

Teradata 12 Enterprise Architecture

Imported Information	Required Rights
	EXECUTE for demographics macros.
Execution plans	INSERT, SELECT, and UPDATE on QCD tables and views.
Object definitions	CREATE on the user or database into which the information is imported. (Use to create database objects such as join indexes and stored procedures.) CREATE PROCEDURE WITH GRANT OPTION for the database in which stored procedures are created. UDTTYPE on the SYSUDTLIB database, to create a UDT. UDTUSAGE, to include a UDT with a CREATE TABLE statement.
QCD data	INSERT, SELECT, and UPDATE on QCD tables. SELECT on QCD views.
RAS	INSERT on *SystemFE.Opt_RAS_Table*.
Statistics	All rights required to execute the COLLECT STATISTICS statement for the table or join index referenced.
Workloads	INSERT, SELECT, and UPDATE on QCD tables. SELECT on QCD views.

Figure 12.8

The next table lists the access rights required in order to restore the default test system environment (also known as *undo-import* or *cleanup* operations).

IMPROVING PERFORMANCE

Undo_Import Information	Required Rights
Cost parameters	DELETE on *SystemFE.Opt_Cost_Table* and *SystemFE.Opt_DBSCtl_Table* or on SystemFE.
Cost profiles	EXECUTE on the DBC.DeleteCostProfile macro.
Demographics	DELETE on the data demographics table and corresponding views of the table. EXECUTE on demographics macros and QCD macros.
Execution plans	DELETE on the QCD tables or on the QCD. EXECUTE on QCD macros.
Object definitions	Sufficient DROP rights on the parent database or DELETE on the database object.
QCD data	DELETE on QCD tables and views. EXECUTE on QCD macros.
RAS	DELETE on *SystemFE.Opt_RAS_Table* or on the SystemFE =database.
Statistics	All rights required to execute the DROP STATISTICS statement for the table or join index referenced.
Workloads	DELETE on QCD tables and views. EXECUTE on QCD macros.

Figure 12.9

The Export feature of SET can be customized to ensure that the test system imitates the features of the target system being analyzed. The following topics explain how to capture information from a target system.

Teradata 12 Enterprise Architecture

Export by Query

This export method uses DML statements to identify database objects to export. The export-by-query operation uses the SHOW QUALIFIED statement; therefore, use only DML statements as input. In other words, do not use Data Definition Language (DDL) statements.

The SHOW QUALIFIED returns the CREATE VIEW text and the CREATE TABLE text of any tables referenced by the view. The same holds true for macros.

Export by Database

Use the export-by-database method to select database objects for individual export and to define the information to export.

Export by Workload

Use this export method to choose a QCD database and multiple workloads for export and to define the details for the specific emulation information to capture.

Teradata SET allows multiple versions of the emulation information to be saved in order to test different scenarios. While offline, the following tasks can be performed to modify the information and create multiple scenarios:

- Open and edit emulation information.
- Change import options.
- Select objects for import.
- Edit import information.

An import cannot be performed without a connection to a Teradata Database.

IMPROVING PERFORMANCE

Note: SET also has many administrative functions to facilitate the export and import of data.

System Resources

There are several tools and features you can use to manage resources.

IF you want to ...	THEN use ...
customize the delegation of resources among the various workload processes	Teradata Dynamic Workload Manager and Priority Scheduler.
determine which objects the system heavily accesses	system object use counts and access logging.
dynamically manage resource utilization, throughput, and workloads	Teradata Dynamic Workload Manager and Priority Scheduler.
find unused objects and delete them from the database	system object use counts.
manage and maximize I/O efficiency	query tuning and DBQL logs
manage and maximize CPU efficiency	DBQL logs
see the number of available AMP worker tasks (AWTs) or the number of messages waiting on a particular AMP	the ampload utility, the awtmon utility or ResUsageSawt

Figure 12.10

309

TRACKING SYSTEM OBJECT USAGE

Database object use counts provide a simple way to identify how frequently user queries access or use specific database objects. You can analyze system performance by noting objects that are heavily used and adjust accordingly. Or, you can improve resource availability by deleting objects the system rarely accesses to reclaim disk space.

You can determine the number of times user queries access or use the following objects:

Columns	Stored Procedures	UDFs
Databases	Tables	Users
Indexes	Triggers	Views
Macros		

Figure 12.11

Note: Object use count information is not counted for EXPLAIN, INSERT EXPLAIN or DUMP EXPLAIN request modifier.

How Counts Are Collected

When you enable count collection, the system collects use counts from the Optimizer execution plan.

Then it stores counts into cache buffers and writes them to Data Dictionary tables. The ObjectUseCountCollectRate field in the DBS Control record controls when the system writes the counts to the Data Dictionary. The field sets the number of minutes you want the system to wait before it writes the cached counts to the Data Dictionary columns AccessCount and LastAccessTimeStamp. (The default value of 0 means that collection is disabled.)

The following table lists the Data Dictionary views that report the count data.

IMPROVING PERFORMANCE

This view...	Provides AccessCount and LastAccess TimeStamp for...
ColumnsX	selected columns.
DatabasesX	selected databases.
IndicesX	hash indexes or join indexes
TablesX	selected tables, views, macros, stored procedures, triggers, and functions.
Users	users that the requesting user owns or has MODIFY or DROP privileges on.

Figure 12.12

Note: Storing object counts in the Data Dictionary runs independently of DBQL.

Enabling Count Collection

The object use count data held in cache writes to disk when one of the following happens:

- The value ObjectUseCountCollectRate in DBS Control is reached
- The cache fills up

IF ObjectUseCountCollectRate is...	THEN...
a negative value	a warning message is displayed.
0	the system does not collect object use counts. This is the default.
an integer *n* between 1 and 32767	the system collects object use counts. The Data Dictionary fields AccessCount and LastAccessTimeStamp are updated

IF ObjectUseCountCollectRate is . . .	THEN . . .
	every *n* minutes.

The recommended minimum value is 10 minutes. Any rate below 10 minutes may impact performance of systems with heavy workloads. |
| a value higher than 32767 | a warning message is displayed. |

Figure 12.13

To examine object use counts, use the views listed in the table above.

Note: The system reports the counts but you are responsible for deleting and cleaning up unused objects.

Caution: Do not enable count collection if you are performing a dump or restore on the Data Dictionary. Object use count collection is automatically disabled if dictionary locks are held longer than the rate set for ObjectUseCountCollectRate.

Note that a restart causes the information in the cache to be lost and the counts in the Data Dictionary will not be updated with that information.

Usage Recommendations

When collecting object use counts, remember the following:

- Do not enable collection when a dictionary DUMP or RESTORE is in progress.

- The system does not collect counts if it cannot get all dictionary locks (buffer) for the defined collection rate. For example, a dictionary DUMP or RESTORE prevents the system from flushing

IMPROVING PERFORMANCE

the cache to the appropriate dictionary fields for a defined collection rate.

- However in the case where an individual dictionary lock for a particular lock is not granted for a defined collection rate, counts are still cached but the dictionary field is not updated and a warning message is written to the DBC.SW_Event_Log table.

- The recommended value of ObjectUseCountCollectRate is 10 minutes or more. Setting ObjectUseCountCollectRate less than 10 minutes impacts system performance.

- Collecting object use counts, like access logging, is resource-intensive. Enable this feature only if necessary, and set the collection rate as needed.

- Move results to a historical database so you can trend changes over time since there is no timeframe in the tables

Resetting the Use Count Fields
To clear the use counts, manually update the AccessCount field to zero and the LastAccessTimeStamp field in the Data Dictionary to zero or use the macros described below.

Note: You must have the EXECUTE privilege on the macros in order to use them.

This macro ...	resets LastAccessTimeStamp and AccessCount of objects in ...
ClearAllDatabaseUseCount	the system.
ClearDatabaseUseCount	a specified database.
ClearTVMUseCount	a specified table, view, macro (or other objects in the TVM table).

Figure 12.14

Teradata 12 Enterprise Architecture

To create these macros, use the DIP utility to run the DIPVIEW script if the script has not already been run.

Running the System Initializer (SYSINIT) utility or the upgrade script is required to grant user DBC the "UPDATE" privilege on the AccessCount and LastAccessTimeStamp columns of the Dbase, TVM, TVFields, and Indexes tables.

Note: All SQL statements used by the ClearAllDatabaseUseCount and ClearDatabaseUseCount macros place write locks on the database objects involved.

Dictionary Objects

The tables and views in database DBC are reserved for use by the system. The macros may be used by authorized users. The dictionary tables contain current definitions, control information, and general information about the following:

Access Rights	Accounts	Authorization
Character Sets	Columns	Constraints
Databases	Disk space	End Users
Events	External Stored Procedures	Indexes
Journal Tables	Logs	Macros
Profiles	Resource Usage	Roles
Rules	Sessions	Session Attributes
Statistics	Stored Procedures	Tables
Translations	Triggers	User-Defined Functions
User-defined Methods	User-defined Types	Views

Figure 12.15

ELT vs. ETL

Extract, Load, Transform (ELT) provides significant performance benefits over the typical Extract, Transform, Load (ETL) process. The idea is to get the raw data into the Teradata system as quickly as possible, and then use the power of parallel processing to transform the data as it moves from the staging table(s) to the target table.

Use the optimized INSERT/SELECT to manipulate FastLoaded data:

1. FastLoad into a staging table(s).
2. INSERT/SELECT into the final table, manipulating the data as required.

Multiple source tables may populate the same target table. If the target table is empty before a request begins, all INSERT/SELECT statements in that request run in the optimized mode. This eliminates Transient Journaling each row.

Compression

Basically, compression enables more rows to be stored per physical block, which results in less overall blocks to store the data. In turn, this means less work is required during a query operation. Disk I/O is further reduced because the compressed values are more likely to be memory resident and don't require disk access. Compression is great for full table scan operations, and any extra CPU utilization for these efforts is negligible in today's Teradata systems.

The best candidates for compression are fixed-width columns with a small number of frequently occurring values. Even though these column characteristics are for the very best candidates, you may choose to compress other columns just to save space. This is perfectly legitimate.

Here are some general rules and facts about compression:

- Nulls are automatically compressed when the COMPRESS clause is assigned.
- Only fixed width columns can be compressed at present.
- There is also an 8192 byte/character limit for the entire list of compressed items.
- Up to 255 values can be compressed per column, including NULL values.
- You can't compress primary index columns.
- You can't compress referencing foreign key columns.
- You can't compress volatile or derived table columns.

Surrogate Keys

A surrogate key is an artificial, <u>non-composite</u>, key used to identify individual entities when there is no natural key or when the situation demands a non-composite key, but no natural non-composite key exists. In a logical model they are typically identified as PK, SA.

Surrogate keys do not identify individual entities in a meaningful way. They are simply an arbitrary method to distinguish among them. Surrogate keys can be created through the use of Identity Columns.

Changing Indexes

Secondary, join, and hash indexes can be created and dropped whenever performance can be improved by the action. Dropping an index is fairly fast since all the system has to do is to put the index blocks on the free block list. Creating an index entails a great deal of processing, so the run time benefit should outweigh the setup costs.

Primary indexes should be defined on columns that rarely, if ever, change. Changing the value of a primary index almost certainly means that affected rows must be redistributed to different AMPs, which results in excessive I/O traffic on the BYNET and disk subsystems. The guideline is to minimize system-wide performance degradations caused by frequently changed primary index values.

Depending on the columns making up the primary index, hash synonyms might occur. Hash synonyms, which usually occur when the primary index is composed of only small integer columns, always degrade query performance.
Keep the following points in mind:

- Define the primary index for a table on as few columns as possible.
- Hashing efficiency increases as the number of primary index columns decreases.
- Retrievals on columns that do not match the *entire* primary index do not use the primary index to retrieve the matching rows.

For PPI tables, the following should be considered:

- The key guideline for determining the optimum granularity for the partitions of a PPI is the nature of the workloads that most commonly access the PPI table.
- The higher the number of partitions you define for a PPI, the more likely an appropriate range query against the table will perform more quickly, if the partition granularity is such that the Optimizer can eliminate all but one partition.
- Avoid specifying too fine a partition granularity. If query workloads never access data at a granularity of less than one month, there is no benefit to be gained by defining partitions with a granularity of less than one month.

- Unnecessarily fine partition granularity is likely to increase the maintenance load for a PPI table, which can lead to overall system performance degradation. Even though too fine a partition granularity itself does not introduce performance degradations, the underlying maintenance on such a table can indirectly degrade performance.

Queries and Joins

WHERE clause analysis

Obviously, all JOIN columns should have statistics collected on them. Columns, whether indexed or not, appearing in a WHERE clause should have statistics collected on them as well.

Join and Hash Indexes

Because neither hash indexes nor join indexes can be accessed directly, you cannot specify access logging for either type of object. If you need to perform access logging, specify it for the relevant base tables.

ON and WHERE Clause

In order to get the results you expect when doing a join, specify the Inner Join conditions in the ON clause, and the Outer Join conditions in the WHERE clause.

Changing Data Types to Enhance Performance

If possible, design your tables and queries so that joined fields are from the same domain (of the same data type), and if numeric, of the same size. If the joined fields are of different data types (and different sizes, if numeric), changing the type definition of one of the tables should improve join performance.

Product Joins

Product joins are generally more expensive than the other join plans. The system can choose to do a Product join if it is less expensive than other choices. Product joins are caused by inequality and ORed join conditions.

Note: Internal compares become very costly when there are more rows than AMP memory can hold at one time.

Statistics

Keep in mind that access paths and join plans can change when the characteristics of the data change (e.g. Reconfig, Inserts, Updates).

Stale statistics may cause the Parser to generate non-optimal execution plans. In Teradata 12 a random amp sample is used to compare collected stats to the sample to see if collected statistics are stale and the sample instead of the collected stats are used.
Remember, keep your statistics up-to-date.

Summary Data

Aggregate Join Indexes

Aggregate join indexes permit you to define a persistent summary table without violating the normalization of the database schema. It is a database object created using the CREATE JOIN INDEX statement, but specifying one or more columns that are derived from SUM or COUNT aggregate operations. A GROUP BY clause may also be used.

Teradata 12 Enterprise Architecture

This allows a join index to pre-compute an aggregate value that would otherwise potentially require a table scan and sort operation.

Aggregate join indexes can be especially helpful for queries that roll up values for dimensions other that the primary key dimension, which would otherwise require redistribution.

Aggregate join indexes are dynamic summary tables, not snapshots. Update anomalies are eliminated because the system handles all updates to the join index, thereby ensuring the integrity of your database.

You can create aggregate join indexes as either single-table or as multitable join indexes.

Global Temporary Tables

You can create a global temporary table definition and then populate a materialized instance of it with aggregated result sets. This, of course, requires table scans and processing overhead every time.

Global temporary tables are private to the session that materializes them. Unless provisions are made to write their content to a persistent base table before a session ends, their data is not saved.

This solution is an alternative for applications that do not require persistent storage of summary results as provided by aggregate join indexes.

Volatile Tables

You can create a volatile table with aggregate expressions defined on some or all its columns. The drawbacks and benefits of global temporary tables apply equally to volatile tables.

Denormalized Base Tables

You can create a denormalized base table and populate it with an aggregated result set. Denormalization always reduces the generality of the database as well as introducing various update anomalies. Because there is no mechanism for keeping such a table synchronized with its base table(s), it can become quickly outdated.

Teradata 12 Enterprise Architecture

Practice Questions

1. Which of the following are part of the Teradata Analyst Pack? (Choose 4)
    a. Index Wizard
    b. PMON
    c. Statistics Wizard
    d. Target Level Emulation
    e. Teradata Manager
    f. TSET
    g. Visual Explain

Match the following definitions to the proper tool or feature.

2.	____ Customize the delegation of resources among the various workload processes	a.	ampload/awtmon
3.	____ Determine which objects the system heavily accesses	b.	Cylinder read
4.	____ Dynamically manage resource utilization, throughput, and workloads	c.	Priority Scheduler
5.	____ Find unused objects and delete them from the database	d.	System object use counts
6.	____ Manage and maximize I/O Efficiency	e.	Dynamic Workload Manager
7.	____ Manage system resources priorities of jobs		

8. ____ See the number of available AMP Worker tasks (awts) or the number of messages waiting on a particular AMP	

Chapter Notes

Utilize this space for notes, key points to remember, diagrams, areas of further study, etc.

Chapter 13 - Maintaining Performance

Certification Objectives

- ✓ Given a scenario, determine solutions to best manage tactical workloads to meet SLAs.
- ✓ Describe the implications of designing and managing an ad-hoc environment.
- ✓ Given a scenario, determine optimization techniques that should be used to manage a high-volume tactical workload.

Before You Begin

You should be familiar with the following terms and concepts.

Terms	Key Concepts
3NF Data Model	Support for Tactical and Ad Hoc workloads
Locking	Blocking and concurrent access
Deadlocks	a.k.a. Deadly Embrace
AWTs	AMP Worker Tasks

Ad hoc Environment

Ad hoc is a Latin phrase meaning "for this." More generally, the expression refers to performing an act for specific or immediate needs, or improvisation. When used to modify the word "query," it might be taken to mean "unplanned," and that is sometimes the case, particularly for simple queries used to provide reports.

However, in the data warehousing world, the phrase *ad hoc query* generally refers to a query composed at the keyboard for immediate performance (as opposed to a permanent query stored in a macro, stored procedure, or embedded SQL application that is performed over and over again without alteration). The goal of this type of ad hoc query is not the reporting of data, but the discovery of information. Such a query frequently undergoes careful, extended planning before being performed for the first time and then is often revised and refined interactively until the desired response is returned.

Discovery is the critical focus of data warehousing, not simple reporting. The value of data warehousing comes from being able to ask unplanned questions on detail data.

Two general situations typically drive ad hoc queries:

- detailed analysis of why some complicated event that had a negative impact on the enterprise occurred
- exploratory analysis to discover business opportunities

The enterprise needs a 3NF logical model to address the precise needs of *any* analytical methodology, whether it be a complicated ad hoc SQL query, an OLAP analysis, exploratory work using data mining, or something entirely different.

Tactical and Workload Consistency

Tactical queries are focused on operational decision making rather than enterprise discovery or bookkeeping activities. They typically have the following characteristics:

- Direct access
- Have expected response times on the order of 20 seconds or less.
- Highly tuned
- Relatively simple syntax

Teradata provides facilities such as the Priority Scheduler to fully integrate workload mixes of both tactical and strategic queries across the enterprise, enabling executives and frontline decision makers alike to access the same single version of the truth concurrently.

Lock Conflicts and Blocked Jobs

Transaction locks are used to control processing concurrency. The type of lock (exclusive, write, read, or access) imposed by a transaction on an entity (database, table, or rowhash) determines whether subsequent transactions can access the same entity.

A request is queued when a lock it needs cannot be granted because a conflicting lock is being held on the target entity. Unless NO WAIT is specified, there is no time limit for a transaction to wait for a lock to be granted. Such lock conflicts can hamper performance. For example, several jobs could be blocked behind a long-running insert into a popular table. This might be eliminated through the use of INSERT/SELECT processing.

To resolve lock conflicts, you need to identify what entity is blocked and which job is causing the block. Then you may want to abort the session that is least important and later reschedule the long job to run in off hours.

Deadlocks

A deadlock can occur when two transactions each need the other to release a lock before continuing, with the result that neither can proceed. This occurrence is rare because Teradata Database uses a pseudo table locking mechanism at the AMP level, but it is possible. You should always acquire the most restrictive locks at the start of a transaction. Upgrading locks during a transaction is very deadlock prone.

Whenever the system detects a deadlock, it rolls back the most recently initiated (newest, or youngest) transaction of the two in the deadlock.

You can control the time it takes for a deadlock to detect and handle a deadlock automatically by shortening the cycle time of the Deadlock Detection mechanism. You can modify this value in the tunable *DeadLockTimeOut* field of the DBS Control Record. Keep in mind that the global deadlock detector does *not* detect HUT deadlocks.

Controlling Session Elements

Figure 13.1 summarizes the most commonly used tools to control session elements.

IF you want to . . .	THEN use one or more of the following . . .
control logon access	• User identifiers (name, password, account identifier(s), user group(s), profile) • Host group IDs, to authorize logons from specific client platforms with GRANT/REVOKE LOGON ... *host_groupid* • Teradata Dynamic Workload Manager

MAINTAINING PERFORMANCE

IF you want to ...	THEN use one or more of the following ...
	(DWM), to control access to objects as well as active sessions by user, account, PG, and users within PG

control object access	- User spool space, to limit response sizes
	- User, role, and/or object access privileges with GRANT/REVOKE
	- Implement operations so that users access portions of data through views, macros, and stored procedures
	- Teradata DWM, to:
	   - Control access to database objects
	   - Limit parameters (such as response rows) based on query type
	   - Limit the number of active queries by user, account, Performance Group (PG), and users within a PG

manage access to resources	- Priority Scheduler Administrator (PSA) to schedule priority of account access to resources such as CPU and memory - Teradata DWM, based on concurrent sessions, query type, account priority, quantity of response rows, and/or workload flow
justify an upgrade or expansion of your Teradata system	- Baseline profiling comparisons - Resource Check Tools - ResUsage reports

Figure 13.1

Concurrent Load Jobs

As discussed in Chapter 7, the setting of two control fields, *MaxLoadTasks* and *MaxLoadAWT*, affect how many utilities can run concurrently.

The *MaxLoadTasks* field specifies the combined number of FastLoad, MultiLoad, and FastExport tasks (jobs), and their TPT counterparts, that are allowed to run concurrently on Teradata Database.

Throttle rules for load utility concurrency set by Teradata Dynamic Workload Manager override the *MaxLoadTasks* setting.

MaxLoadAWT specifies how many AMP Worker Tasks can be used by load utilities.

If *MaxLoadAWT* is greater than zero, new FastLoad and MultiLoad jobs are rejected when the *MaxLoadAWT* limit is reached, regardless of the *MaxLoadTasks* setting. Therefore, FastLoad and MultiLoad jobs may be rejected before *MaxLoadTasks* limit is reached.

Practice Questions

Match the characteristic to the proper query type.

1. ___ OLAP analysis	a. Ad hoc queries
2. ___ Performed repetatively	b. Tactical queries
3. ___ Short response times	
4. ___ Simple, highly tuned syntax	
5. ___ Used for detailed event analysis	
6. ___ Used for exploratory analysis	
7. ___ Used for operational decision making	

Chapter Notes

Utilize this space for notes, key points to remember, diagrams, areas of further study, etc.

APPENDIX

Answers to the Chapter Review Questions

Chapter 2	Chapter 3	Chapter 4	Chapter 5	
1. a	1. c	1. a-3	1. b, c	8. e
2. b, d	2. a	b-2	2. b, c	9. d
3. b, e	3. e	c-4	3. b	10. a
4. c	4. d	d-1	4. a	11. b
5. b	5. f	2. b	5. a	12. c
6. a	6. b	3. b, e	6. b, c	13. a, b, c
7. b		4. a, g	7. a – O	
8. c		5. c	b – R	
			c – R	
			d – O	

Chapter 6	Chapter 7	Chapter 8	Chapter 9	Chapter 10
1. c	1. a	1. b	1. f	1. c
2. a	2. c	2. a	2. b, c, d, e	2. b
3. f	3. d	3. c	3. b, c, d	3. b
4. d	4. e	4. c	4. a, d, e	4. c
5. b	5. d	5. a	5. a, d, e	5. b
6. e	6. a, c, e	6. a, d	6. a, b	
7. d	7. b	7. e	7. d	
8. d	8. b	8. c, f		
9. d		9. d		
10. b				
11. d				
12. e				

Teradata 12 Enterprise Architecture

Chapter 11	Chapter 12	Chapter 13
1. b	1. a, c, f, g	1. a
2. c	2. e	2. b
3. a	3. d	3. b
4. d	4. e	4. b
5. a	5. d	5. a
6. f	6. b	6. a
7. d	7. c	7. b
	8. a	

INDEX

3

3NF, 37, 38, 325, 326

A

Access Monitoring, 80
Access Rights, 49, 62, 247, 314
Account Strings, 54
AmpUsage, 273
Analytical Processing Choices, 276
Application Deployment, 119
ARC, 94, 149, 150, 151, 152, 156, 160, 161, 162, 167, 171, 172, 175, 176, 189, 190, 241
Architecture, i, 5, 11, 97
Archive Strategies, 177

B

Before You Begin, 11, 29, 37, 49, 91, 119, 143, 193, 235, 259, 291, 325
BTEQ, 22, 34, 93, 113, 132, 151, 172, 209, 210, 211, 215, 216, 231, 232, 238, 239
BYNET, ii

C

Certification, 1, 6, 7, 8, 9
Certification Objectives, 11, 29, 37, 49, 91, 119, 143, 193, 235, 259, 291, 325
Certified Professional, i, 1, 3, 6, 9
Cliques, 16, 26
COMPRESS, 316
Compression, 315
Connectivity Options, 32
CRASHDUMP, 148

D

Data Marts, 236
Databases, 20, 50, 54, 69, 108, 179, 207, 310, 314
DBQL, 80, 81, 93, 106, 146, 147, 259, 260, 267, 285, 286, 288, 293, 294, 299, 309, 311
Dictionary Tables, 145
Disk I/O, 315
DML, 93, 108, 208, 215, 218, 223, 225, 263, 308
Dual Systems, 13

E

Encryption, 68, 69, 70
Exam, i, 1, 5, 6, 7, 8
Explain, 122, 259, 269, 274, 275, 292, 293, 295, 300, 301, 303, 322

F

Fallback, 24, 26, 143, 157, 158, 169, 245
FastExport, 108, 122, 123, 124, 140, 151, 172, 203, 204, 205, 206, 207, 212, 216, 231, 232, 240, 241, 330
FastLoad, 16, 22, 26, 94, 108, 122, 123, 124, 140, 151, 172, 194, 195, 196, 197, 198, 212, 213, 216, 220, 227, 231, 232, 240, 241, 245, 315, 330
Full Table Scans, 271

G

Governance, 235, 250, 251, 254, 256

Teradata 12 Enterprise Architecture

H

Hot-standby Node, 17, 26

I

Index, 11, 37, 43, 122, 126, 128, 129, 143, 169, 220, 224, 261, 262, 265, 274, 292, 294, 295, 296, 297, 298, 299, 300, 301, 322
Integration, 193

J

Joins, 37, 275, 318, 319

L

LDAP, 59, 60, 61, 81
LDM, 37, 38, 44
Logging Rates, 270
Logons, 50, 69

M

MDM, 252, 253
Metadata, 226, 235, 253, 256
Migration, 235
MultiLoad, 16, 22, 26, 108, 122, 123, 124, 140, 172, 195, 199, 200, 201, 202, 203, 207, 212, 213, 216, 227, 231, 232, 241, 245, 330

N

Nodes, 12, 16, 69
NUPI, 25, 220, 222, 263, 274

O

Operating System, 12, 29, 32

P

PACKDISK, 179, 180, 181
Partitioned, 143, 166, 193, 223, 224, 261, 262, 274
Passwords, 53
PDE DUMP, 148
PDM, 37, 38, 44
Performance Groups, 56, 99, 102
Personally Identifiable Information, 74, 75
PII, 74, 75, 76, 77, 78, 79
PMON, 259, 267, 271, 287, 322
Practice Questions, 26, 35, 45, 86, 115, 140, 189, 231, 256, 287, 322, 331
primary index, 316
Priority Scheduler, 94, 96, 97, 98, 99, 104, 105, 106, 113, 115, 139, 147, 184, 309, 322, 327, 329
Profiles, 49, 56, 161, 314

R

Recursive, 225
Resource Partitions, 97, 99, 101, 104, 116, 184
ResUsage, 145, 146, 184, 190, 259, 269, 270, 271, 274, 285, 287, 288, 329
Roles, 22, 49, 66, 161, 314

S

Schmon Utility, 105
Security, 22, 49, 50, 79, 80, 246
Semantic Layer, 37, 43
Shared Resources, 182
SLA, 259, 260
Space Allocation, 11, 17, 135
Space Management, 143
SQL Merge, 221
Statistics, 113, 122, 260, 275, 292, 293, 298, 299, 300, 305, 306, 307, 314, 319, 322
Stored Procedures, 56, 70, 71, 108, 186, 310, 314
System Planning, 143

T

Tables, 22, 108, 116, 270, 286, 303, 304, 310, 314, 320, 321
TCPP, 1, 7, 9
TDWM, 93, 97, 146, 286
Technology, iv
Teradata, i, ii, iv
Teradata Administrator, ii
Teradata Manager, 106, 112, 113, 115, 122, 138, 146, 147, 188, 271, 287, 322
Teradata Parallel Transporter, 122, 172, 211, 212, 241
Teradata Query Director, 110
Teradata Query Scheduler, 108, 109
Teradata Workload Analyzer, 106
Test Environments, 120
TPT, 122, 123, 211, 212, 213, 214, 215, 217, 241, 330
TPump, 22, 122, 207, 208, 209, 212, 216, 227, 231, 232, 240, 241

Transient Journal, 119, 125, 131, 134, 140, 144, 145, 189, 315
TTU, 29, 30

U

Users, 50, 55, 79, 179, 310, 311, 314
Utilities, 4, 5

V

Views, 43, 49, 56, 82, 83, 108, 135, 175, 225, 248, 249, 250, 310, 314
Volatility, 42

W

Workload Management, 91, 286